BASIC WORD ORDER: FUNCTIONAL PRINCIPLES

CROOM HELM LINGUISTICS SERIES

Basic Word Order
Functional Principles

RUSSELL S. TOMLIN

NOTTINGHAM UNIVERSITY LIBRARY

CROOM HELM
London • Sydney • Wolfeboro, New Hampshire

© 1986 Russell S. Tomlin
Croom Helm Ltd, Provident House, Burrell Row,
Beckenham, Kent BR3 1AT

Croom Helm Australia Pty Ltd, Suite 4, 6th Floor,
64-76 Kippax Street, Surry Hills, NSW 2010, Australia

British Library Cataloguing in Publication Data

Tomlin. Russell S.
    Basic word order: functional principles.
    1. Grammar. Comparative and general –
    Word order
    I. Title
    415   P295
    ISBN 0-7099-2499-2

Croom Helm, 27 South Main Street,
Wolfeboro, New Hampshire 03894-2069, USA

Library of Congress Cataloging-in-Publication Data

Tomlin, Russell S.
    Basic word order.

    Revision of author's thesis—university of Michigan,
1979, originally presented under this title: an
explanation of the distribution of basic constituent
orders.
    Bibliography: p.
    1. Grammar, comparative and general—word order.
I. Title.
P295.T65   1986   415   86-6409
ISBN 0-7099-2499-2

312412

Printed and bound in Great Britain by Mackays of Chatham Ltd, Kent

EDITORIAL STATEMENT

CROOM HELM LINGUISTICS SERIES

Chief Editor
Professor John Hawkins, University of Southern California

Consultant Editors
Professor Joseph Aoun, University of Southern California
Professor Bernard Comrie, University of Southern California
Dr Richard Hudson, University College London
Professor James Hurford, University of Edinburgh
Professor Douglas Pulleyblank, University of Southern California

The Croom Helm Linguistics Series does not specialise in any one area of language study, nor does it limit itself to any one theoretical approach. Synchronic and diachronic descriptive studies, either syntactic, semantic, phonological or morphological, are welcomed, as are more theoretical 'model-building' studies, and studies in socio-linguistics or psycholinguistics. The criterion for a work's acceptance is the quality of its contribution to the relevant field. All texts published must advance our understanding of the nature of language in areas of substantial interest to major sectors of the linguistic research community. Traditional scholarly standards, such as clarity of presentation, factual and logical soundness of argumentation, and a thorough and reasoned orientation to other relevant work, are also required. Within these indispensable limitations we welcome the submission of creative and original contributions to the study of language.

The editors and publisher wish to draw this series to the attention of scholars, who are invited to submit manuscripts or book-proposals to:
Professor John Hawkins, Department of Linguistics, University of Southern California, Los Angeles, CA 90089-1693, USA: *or to* Jonathan Price, Linguistics Editor, Croom Helm Publishers, Provident House, Burrell Row, Beckenham, Kent BR3 1AT, UK.

To
R. Lance Factor
Knox College
Galesburg, Illinois

CONTENTS

Contents

PREFACE

This volume represents a modest revision of my 1979 PhD
dissertation, An Explanation of the Distribution of Basic
Constituent Orders (Department of Linguistics, University of
Michigan). At that time it was my belief that typological
research, as interesting as it was, needed improvement in two
areas. First, it needed to increase its methodological rigor
where possible; and, second, it needed to frame explanations
in functional rather than structural terms, recognizing the
possibility that functional principles might interact to
produce observed typological distributions.

   In this revision these same issues are raised again. I
have tried to contribute to methodological rigor by taking
seriously the sampling problems described so well by Bell
(1978). In determining the relative frequencies of basic
word order types, I have taken great care to produce a truly
representative sample of the world's languages,
representative of both genetic classifications and areal
distribution. In motivating the three principles, I have
tried very much to maximize genetic and areal diversity in
the languages described.

   And, I have tried to contribute to the functional issues
by motivating well the three functional principles on which
the explanation hinges and showing that the relative
frequencies of the six basic constituent order types is
explained well through the interaction of these principles. I
have also tried to link these general principles to
principles of human cognition, for it is my feeling that the
general characteristics of language and languages as objects
of investigation are derived ultimately from human and
individual-specific constraints on memory, attention, and
human information processing. While this link cannot be
conclusively demonstrated at this time, it does, I believe,
represent an important way to conceptualize typological
explanation.

   The volume is composed of two parts. The first part
deals with the problem of establishing the relative
frequencies of the six basic constituent order types and

explaining why the frequencies pattern as they do. The second part of the volume presents the data on which rests the statistical arguments of the second chapter. The first appendix contains information on the basic word order, genetic affiliation, and areal location of 1063 of the world's languages, along with the full references consulted in assembling the database. It is my hope that some will find this useful beyond the problem addressed in this volume.

I would like to thank all of the individuals who provided data, criticism, or suggestions for this effort. They include: Matthew Dryer, T. Givón, Scott DeLancey, Rick Bayless, Richard Rhodes, John Lawler, Ann Borkin, Peter Hook, Fred Lupke, John Grima, Deborah Keller-Cohen, Penelope Eckert, Kensaku Yoshida, Liberty Sihombing, and Linda Jones. None is responsible for any errors or omissions, those remain uniquely my own

I would also like to thank Katrina Andretta, Diane Prokop and Sharri Galick for their patient assistance in preparing the final typescript.

Chapter 1

INTRODUCTION

If one reads through older grammatical descriptions of
languages, especially grammars written in the late nineteenth
and early twentieth centuries, one often finds only a very
brief section devoted to syntax, which deals almost
exclusively with word order. In a similar vein, the new
second language learner often is intrigued as much by word
order differences in the new language as by any other feature
except, perhaps, phonology. Word order, thus, represents the
most overtly noticeable feature of cross-linguistic syntax,
yet at the same time it remains a tantalizing problem, both
to describe the pertinent facts of word order variability and
to provide some explanation for the great diversity one can
see cross-linguistically.

In broad outline, the modern history of systematic
linguistic study of word order reveals two primary waves of
interest, each stimulated by an earlier seminal work. In
1844, Henri Weil published a volume titled *De l'Ordre des
Mots dans les Langues Anciennes Comparée aux Langues Modernes*
(translated by C. Super in 1877). This book addressed a
basic diachronic and typological problem: why modern European
languages, including Romance languages, Germanic languages,
and modern Greek, exhibit so little flexibility in word order
when their historical predecessors exhibited such great
flexibility. Weil framed his analysis in terms of the
interaction of two independent grammatical levels: the
objective, syntactic order and the subjective "march of
ideas" (pragmatic order).

Weil's contribution was a principal stimulus to the work
of Wilhelm Mathesius, whose efforts, along with many others,
resulted in the development of a theory of word order
variability, functional sentence perspective, within the
Prague school of linguistics (cf. Daneš 1974, for a
pertinent and detailed review).

More than a century after Weil's contribution, the
second primary wave of research into word order issues was
stimulated by the seminal paper on word order universals by

1

Introduction

Joseph Greenberg (1963). Greenberg observed that the
actually occurring word order variability across languages
comprised only a limited inventory of the mathematically
possible orderings of constituents. His implicational
universals represented an initial explanation for those
limitations. Subsequent work by members of the Stanford
Language Universals Project and others pursued the
cross-linguistic issues raised by Greenberg's contribution.
The present efforts of Hawkins (1983, inter alia), Mallinson
and Blake (1981), Dryer (1984, 1985), and others continue to
expand and enrich the original themes developed by Greenberg.

THE PROBLEM AND AN OUTLINE OF THE EXPLANATION

This volume explores one specific problem within this
tradition. It was Greenberg who first observed that of the
six mathematically possible orderings of the three nuclear
constituents of a transitive clause, only three (SOV, SVO,
VSO) occur with any frequency as basic constituent orders
among the languages of the world (Greenberg 1966:77). Since
then additional research has shown that VOS languages clearly
occur, though with much less frequency (e.g. Malagasy:
Keenan 1976a, Pullum 1977). The evidence is also strong that
both kinds of object-initial languages exist (Derbyshire
1977, Derbyshire and Pullum 1981). Given, then, that all the
possible basic constituent order types do seem to occur, the
basic problem examined in this volume can be put into a
simple question:

(1) What are the relative frequencies of the six basic
    constituent order types and how are those
    frequencies to be explained?

There are two steps which must be taken to provide an
answer to this question, First, the frequency of occurrence
of each of the six basic constituent orders in the languages
of the world must be determined. At present, there is no
satisfactory statistical analysis of the frequency of
occurrence of the six mathematically possible orderings of
subject, object, and verb. All discussions of the relative
frequency of basic constituent orders are framed in terms of
simple dominances: "subject-initial languages predominate" or
"VOS languages are rare". All actual samples are
non-stratified convenience samples and are not reliable.
    Ultimately, what one would like to know is exactly how
frequent various constituent orders are. One would like to
know just how rarely VOS languages occur and what it means to
say that subject-initial languages predominate in the
languages of the world. Since the frequencies of various
orders may critically affect an explanation, Chapter 2

2

provides a detailed statistical analysis of the distribution of the six basic constituent order types in the languages of the world.

After the distribution of basic constituent orders has been determined, the second step can be taken. This step consists of providing an explanation for the relative frequencies of the various basic constituent order types. These relative frequencies are summarized in (2):

(2) SOV = SVO > VSO > VOS = OVS > OSV

The explanation proposed in this volume is a partial one, grounded in several fundamental cognitive principles of functional grammar, and can be briefly outlined as follows.

Typological explanation, to the extent it can be separated from areal, genetic, and historical influences, derives from universal principles of linguistic organization and processing. These principles derive from fundamental cognitive constraints on the processing of linguistic information during discourse production and comprehension. It is assumed here that grammars of human languages are organized functionally. Language specific syntactic alternations serve to signal specific semantic or pragmatic functions, which, in turn, reflect the language specific instantiation of general constraints on the representation, storage, and retrieval of information in the human mind. Neither the syntax of natural languages, nor typological facts related to syntax, can be properly understood when divorced from the psychological and, ultimately biological, constraints on the mind imposed both by its internal organization and structure and by the psycho-social context of human communication. Typological explanation, on the surface seemingly distant from the individual speaker, ultimately derives directly from the efforts of differing individuals engaged in communicative activity.

Two converging trends of language research detail this point of view. Within linguistics, the functional perspective has been developed in major works by Chafe (1970), Givón (1979, 1985), Dik (1978), Foley and Van Valin (1984), Halliday (1985), as well as through a great many specific studies by these and other linguists (e.g. Li (ed) 1976, Givón (ed) 1984, Li and Thompson 1976b, Chafe 1972, 1976, Hopper and Thompson 1980, and Tomlin 1983, 1985, 1986 (ed)).

Within psychology, the functional approach to language is best represented by the collaborative efforts of Bates and MacWhinney (MacWhinney and Bates 1978, Bates and MacWhinney 1979, Bates and MacWhinney 1981, Bates et al. 1982). In addition, work by Kintsch and van Dijk (Kintsch 1974, Kintsch and van Dijk 1978, van Dijk and Kintsch 1983) elaborates such a point of view in discourse processing. In his work on mental models Johnson-Llaird (1983) provides a very general cognitive framework for understanding the functional approach to language within psychology and linguistics.

The present explanation focuses on the interaction of three independently motivated functional principles. It is argued that those constituent orders which reflect the realization of those principles most fully occur with greater frequency than those which do not.

Each principle is motivated independently of the others, and is needed, as well, independently of the particular explanation offered here. They are independent of each other in that the data that underpin each principle are completely different. They are independent of the particular explanation offered here in that they are required to address linguistic problems other than the distribution of basic constituent orders.

The first principle is the Theme First Principle (TFP). This principle is an attempt to make more precise and explicit the informal idea that "old" information precedes "new" information. The relatively simplistic idea of "old" information is shown to involve at least two components. One component, *shared information*, involves the identification of referents which both speaker and hearer have in common. The other component, *thematic information, involves the signaling of information which is most salient to the development of the particular discourse. Both shared information and thematic information represent fundamental pragmatic notions grounded in cognitive processes. Shared information concerns the retrieval of referential information during discourse processing, ultimately requiring one consider its connection to memory (Chafe 1986). Thematic information concerns the focusing on important or salient information, ultimately requiring one consider its connection to attention (Tomlin 1985, 1986a).

It is thematic information that is connected with word order in natural language. Both direct evidence from psycholinguistic research and symptomatic evidence concerning the typology of movement rules and the relative positional tendencies of definite and indefinite NPs serve to motivate this principle. Further, it is shown that, with respect to basic sentences, thematic information correlates with subject.

The second principle is the principle of Verb-Object Bonding (VOB). The essential claim embodied by this principle is that the object of a transitive verb forms a more cohesive syntactic and semantic whole that does a transitive verb and its subject. Data from more than a dozen independent syntactic, semantic, and phonological domains are used to support this generalization, including data on noun incorporation, sentence adverbial placement, idiom structures, and stress placement.

4

The third principle is the Animated First Principle (AFP). This principle states that in basic transitive clauses the NP which is most "animated" will precede other NPs. Special care is taken to make as explicit as possible what the term "animated" refers to. Basically, the NP which is most animated will be the one which most closely approximates the prototypical agent -animate, active, volitional, and effective. This principle, like the others, is supported by data from several areas. And, like the TFP, it is shown that in basic sentences the most animated NP will tend to correlate with subject.

While the principle of VOB is comparatively new, both the TFP and the AFP have been discussed in the literature. A principle like the TFP is embodied in the approaches to theme taken by Daneš (1974) and Halliday (1967, 1968). A principle like the AFP can be found in the work of linguists like Hyman and Hawkinson (1974) whose work on the Natural Topic Hierarchy involves aspects of both agency and animateness. The essential difference between former discussions of the concepts and the discussion presented here are two. First, it is suggested that each of these principles derive from cognitive constraints on information processing in human language. And, second, the data in support of these language-general functional principles are drawn from a wider range of languages than traditionally has been the case.

The explanation for the distribution of basic constituent orders proposed here utilizes these three principles in a quite straightforward manner. Those constituent orders will be more frequent which permit more of the principles to be realized; those constituent orders will be less frequent which permit fewer of the principles to be realized. For instance, SOV and SVO are the most frequent basic constituent orders because these orders are the only orders which permit the maximal realization of the three principles. Since for basic sentences the most thematic information and the most animated NP correlate with subject, both the TFP and the AFP are realized for these orders because the subject comes first. Further, VOB is realized since the verb and object are juxtaposed in an SOV or SVO basic constituent order. Conversely, OSV languages are exceedingly rare, because none of these three fundamental principles is realized.

There are certain complicating factors which must be taken up in an explanation of the distribution of basic constituent orders, in particular the treatment of verb-initial languages and object-initial languages. But a discussion of these is better left until later. What is important to make clear at this point is that the distribution of basic constituent orders can be explained through the interaction of the three independently motivated functional principles described above.

5

Complicating Factors in Typological Explanation

The problem of explaining the relative frequency of basic
constituent orders in (2) is complicated by at least three
additional factors: genetic history, areal convergence, and
social history. These factors become problematic just in
case any one of them, or their combination, could
significantly affect the ordering relations presented in (2).

Genetic history refers to potentially differential rates
of language divergence over time. For instance, the fact
that SOV and SVO orders are the most common may be due in
part to the number of languages which diverged from a given
parent stock. Thus, SVO languages might be so frequent in
part because of the high frequency of Bantu (SVO) languages
splitting off from one another. Or, from a different angle,
SOV languages could have been more frequent had there been,
say, a greater rate of divergence among Dravidian languages,
all of which are SOV.

Further, it has been proposed (Givón 1979) that all
languages find SOV parent stocks sufficiently far back in
time. Givón's evidence comes from diachronic analysis of
word order change in Bantu, where Givón observes grammatical
fossils of SOV type in languages which are uniformly SVO.
Dryer (p.c.) has also pointed out that the greatest
proportion of language isolates, presumably final survivors
of near extinct stocks, are primarily SOV languages.

The relevant question to ask concerning genetic history
is whether the relative frequencies reported in (2) might
turn out to be different were it possible to factor out its
influence. The empirically conservative answer is
uncertainty, for with the information presently at hand, one
cannot really know. The more speculative answer seems to be
negative. In order to change the relative orderings in (2)
in such a way as to make object-initial languages most
frequent, or something equally dramatic, would require
pervasive changes of such magnitude that evidence of such
changes would surely be observable.

Smaller scale changes, for example VSO>VOS => VOS>VSO
seem, somewhat more plausible but still unlikely, except in
one case. The sample here reports SOV to be equally frequent
to SVO, where previous work identified SOV are the most
frequent order. Givón's historical argument and the
distribution of isolates lend credence to this point of view.
However, it should be kept in mind that all previous language
samples have been biased technically, resulting in an
unfortunate skewing in favor of SOV. For the moment, then,
it seems that considerably stronger evidence would be
required than is presently available to argue for even that
small possible change.

Areal convergence has clearly been responsible for some word order change. It is well known, for instance, that while SOV is the most common Uralic order, Finnish, surrounded by Indo-European languages of SVO order, has become an SVO language. Now if for some reason the principal areas of linguistic convergence were dominated by SOV or SVO languages, the proportion of languages of each type might be greater than it would be were no areal influence possible. Again, the pertinent question to ask is whether observable patterns of areal change could, if taken into account, result in a relative frequency ordering vastly different from that reported in (2). Again, the answer seems to be negative.

Social history could affect the relative frequencies in the following way. Independent of any linguistic reason, the lesser frequency of a given constituent order type may be due to the displacement of that type of language by some other type. For instance, perhaps VSO languages were once more frequent than they are now, because Celtic peoples (and thus Celtic languages) were more frequent, and had not yet been assimilated by non-Celtic (non-VSO) newcomers. Again, it is possible to speculate on the likelihood of social history drastically to alter the relative orderings reflected in (2); and, again, it seems implausible that such could be the case without massive observable evidence.

Other Explanations of Basic Constituent Order

While there has been a great deal of work done in linguistics concerning problems of order in general, there has been little work done concerning the basic question presented in (1). This section will deal only with that work.

The most recent major discussion dealing with the problem is found in Mallinson and Blake (1981:151ff). Mallinson and Blake assert that word order facts can be accounted for in terms of three general principles:

(3) Mallinson and Blake's three principles (1981:151)

   (a) more topical material tends to come nearer to the beginning of the clause (to the left) than non-topical material.

   (b) heavy material tends to come nearer to the end of the clause (to the right) than light material...

   (c) constituents tend to assume a fixed position in the clause according to their grammatical status or semantic relation or category status (noun, verb, prepositional phrase, etc.).

The first principle, (a), is essentially the same as the present TFP, though Mallinson and Blake do little to motivate it.

The second principle, (b), is well attested, and clearly relevant to the study of word order. However, it is not really relevant to the investigation of basic constituent orders, for the pertinent constituents considered are taken to be of the same general weight.

The final principle, (c), represents the observation that some languages exhibit relatively rigid word orders. As a principle for accounting for word order, principle (c) is not motivated at all. Exactly what its explanatory role could be is unclear, for its utility beyond dealing with word order variability seems negligible, making the principle appear *ad hoc*.

All in all, the Mallinson and Blake discussion is at best only a partial one, for the principles described do not receive sufficient or explicit motivation and their role in accounting for basic word orders is left only partially specified.

Krupa (1982) presents a very brief but elegant discussion of the precise question considered in this volume. His explanation also involves the interaction of three fundamental principles: (1) sentence depth, (2) the cognitive factor, and (3) the relative structural independence or S, O, and V.

Sentence depth involves the limited capacity of short term memory. Those orders are preferred which are least taxing to short-term memory, SOV and SVO. These orders appear to be least taxing because they are right branching where the remaining orders are not.

The cognitive factor reflects what might be called the natural iconicity of linguistic expression. Those elements are ordered earlier in the sentence which represent the earlier stages of the event described by the proposition. S should come first because (1) it is the cognitive theme or starting point of the utterance and (2) it is typically the agent, or initiator of the action. V should be second as the actional transition to the final O, which is changed through V. Thus, by the cognitive factor alone, SVO is the most preferred order, with SOV, VSO, VOS, and OSV partially consistent, and OVS inconsistent with this factor.

Relative structural independence concerns linearizing elements by their relative independence: V more independent than S and S more independent than O. Thus, VSO is most consistent with this principle; SOV, SVO VOS, OVS partially inconsistent .

By assigning ranks to the relative frequency of basic constituent orders and to the consistency of each basic order type to each of the three principles, Krupa shows a dramatically significant correlation (r=.94) holding between the frequency of orders and consistency with these principles.

Krupa's account is imaginative and quite consistent with the general argument presented here. However, the account has two problems. First, the basic constituent order frequencies which are assumed, in particular that SVO < SOV, that OVS = OSV, and that VOS > OVS, appear to be incorrect. Second, while the three principles are all intuitively attractive, none is particularly well motivated, either from a cognitive or cross-linguistic point of view.

Perhaps the most thorough work dealing with the basic problem is found in Pullum (1977). Pullum's explanation of the basic word order typology can be summarized as follows. Subject and object in basic sentences can be identified with the primitive grammatical relations *subject* (I) and *object* (II) in Relational Grammar (RG). In addition, RG has established independently the need for a hierarchy of grammatical relations: I>II>III>Non-terms (GRH) (Keenan and Comrie 1972). The basic word order for a language is determined by linearization rules which apply before any post-cyclic movement rules. The basic word order typology can be explained in terms of three linearization principles:

(3)   [Pullum (29)]
      The NP constituents of a clause are linearized in
      their GR hierarchy order, left to right.

(4)   [Pullum (30)] Verb placement.
      The verb of a clause may be placed in
      (a)   initial position in all clauses
      (b)   second position in all clauses
or   (c)   final position in all clauses.

(5)   [Pullum (31)] Optional.
      If placement of the verb by (30) leaves the subject
      NP non-initial, it can be assigned final position.

Pullum shows how these three principles predict the occurring orders and exclude the non-occurring ones:

(6)   [Pullum (32)]
      a.   V I II III NTs   (V initial, GRH maintained: VSO)
      b.   I V II III NTs   (V second, GRH maintained: SVO)
      c.   I II III NTs V   (V final, GRH maintained: SOV)
      d.   V II III NTs I   (V initial, (31) applied: VOS)

The first two linearization principles and their accompanying explanatory power are quite elegant. These two principles alone permit all the cases where subject precedes

9

object (which all exist), but do not permit any case where the object precedes the subject (though both VOS and OVS exist).

Because of the VOS cases Pullum is forced to posit the existence of a further linearization principle (found at (5)). This seems to be rather *ad hoc*, though it is mitigated somewhat by his noting its possible motivation in (i) the very widespread association "surface subject-theme" and (ii) the universal preference for themes to be in clause-peripheral positions (Pullum 1977:273).

But even with this mitigation the principle can be shown to be somewhat arbitrary. While (i) seems to be true within the limitations discussed below in Chapter 3, (ii) seems more limited. If it is the case that "themes" tend to be sentence peripheral, then there is an equal chance, *ceteris paribus*, for there to be OVS or VOS languages (note that both violate Pullum's principle found in (3)). That is, why should a language have final subjects only when the verb is initial? The motivation Pullum suggests for his third linearization principle is motivation only for the occurrence of final subjects. It cannot serve as motivation for his stronger claim that it is only verb initial languages that will have final subjects. Thus, his third linearization principle remains somewhat (though not completely) arbitrary.

The fourth major effort to explain the distribution of basic constituent orders is Diehl (1975). In a very ambitious undertaking, Diehl sets out to constrain not only the possible orderings of subject, object, and verb, but indirect objects and oblique NPs as well.

He does this by proposing five major factors which determine the order of elements in underlying linguistic structures: egodeictic iconicity, temporal iconicity, linkage iconicity, discourse structure, and model strings. Egodeictic iconicity states that the order of elements concerning four conceptual spaces (social space (people and things), spatial space (locations), temporal space (times), and logical space (ideas)) will parallel their order of acquisition in children. Thus, for instance, children acquire competence with respect to social space before they acquire competence with respect to temporal space, and ordinarily elements referring to things (e.g., subject and object) will form a tight inner nuclear core while time or location expressions occur outside of this core.

Temporal iconicity states that the order of elements in linguistic representation reflects the order of events in nonlinguistic cognitive experience. Thus, agent precedes patient, for instance, in order to match their order of involvement in the event. It also entails that agent precede dative and that source precede goal.

Linkage iconicity states that an element that relates, or links, two other elements conceptually will also link them by being ordered between them. This principle predicts that direct objects will occur between agent and dative NPs, giving S O IO or IO O S as the unmarked orderings of these constituents.

Discourse structure is quite straightforward. NPs which represent theme (in Halliday's sense) tend to occur at the periphery of clauses. Further, "old" information will tend to precede "new" information in unmarked structures.

Model strings deals with those aspects of word order which are in fact arbitrary. Those arbitrary facts include the relative order of verb and object and the relative order of verb and subject. Diehl proposes a set of four questions that deal with these aspects of word order.

Diehl uses these five factors to constrain the set of possible orderings of S, O, V, I (indirect object), and N (non-terms). There are 12 possible orderings of these elements. The application of the five factors reduces those 12 orders to six:

(7)   N S I O V
      N S I V O
      N S V O I
      S V O I N
      V S O I N
      V O S I N

Ignoring for a moment the N and I categories, one can see that, like Pullum, Diehl has constrained the possible orderings of S, O, and V to four: SOV, SVO, VSO, and VOS.

While the basic approach Diehl develops is both systematic and comprehensive, there are three problems with his analysis that reduce its utility. First, the motivation of the five factors is insufficient. With the exception of egodeictic iconicity, all of the principles Diehl uses are not motivated very well in his study. The primary difficulty is that little data is presented, and most of what is presented comes from English.

The second problem is that there is a great jump from the general factors to the specific ordering constraints they presumably entail. For instance, egodeictic iconicity entails that a patient NP (the direct object) be contiguous to its verb in basic orders. This seems to be a reasonable claim especially given the discussion of VOB in Chapter 4, but precisely how it is entailed by egodeictic iconicity is not made clear at all. The other factors have analogous problems.

The third problem is that Diehl's explanation seems to be wrong empirically. That is, his explanation excludes some orders which actually do occur. In particular, there are

Introduction

languages in which indirect object precedes direct object.
That is, the order SOIV and SVIO are both actually occurring
constituent orders (Blansitt 1973). In addition, Diehl's
explanation precludes OVS cases, but there appears to be at
least one well-documented case of an OVS language (Derbyshire
1977).
The only other work that deals specifically with an
explanation of basic constituent orders is Culicover and
Wexler (1974), which is carefully discussed in Pullum
(1977:270-271). Pullum states that Culicover and Wexler take
the split between subject and predicate as universal and also
make an assumption that "deep ergativity" exists. These
working assumptions produce a set of eight language types:

    (8)   a.   (Agent (Predicate-Patient))   Non-erg SVO
          b.   (Agent (Patient-Predicate))   Non-erg SOV
          c.   ((Predicate-Patient) Agent)   Non-erg VOS
          d.   ((Patient-Predicate) Agent)   Non-erg OVS
          e.   ((Agent-Predicate) Patient)   Erg SVO
          f.   ((Predicate-Agent) Patient)   Erg VSO
          g.   (Patient (Predicate-Agent))   Erg OVS
          h.   (Patient (Agent-Predicate))   Erg OSV

    Pullum questions the existence of the last five of
these, noting among other things that there exist many VSO
languages which are not ergative and that contrary to the
claim entailed at (b), there is strong evidence to suggest
that a subject-predicate split in SOV languages is
questionable (e.g. Schwartz 1974).
    The only other work that deals in some way with the
problem of basic constituent orders is the work connected
with universal underlying structure. For instance, it has
been suggested that all languages have VSO as an underlying
constituent order and that the set of occurring basic
constituent orders be constrained by positing the existence
of two rules (Subject-Formation and Verb-Final) (Bach
1974:276-277). This would be sufficient to produce SOV, SVO,
and VSO orders; Bach suspects that VOS languages are VSO
languages which have a thematization rule which moves
subjects to final position (1974:275n). The basic difficulty
with this sort of analysis is that it must add rules to deal
with new sorts of cases. First, that there are basic VOS
languages seems reasonable, especially given Pullum's (1977)
discussion. Second, there clearly are also OVS languages
(Derbyshire 1977). Both of these would require substantial
changes to the Bach hypothesis.
    Ultimately, the one important difference between prior
work and the explanation offered in this volume involves the
treatment of rare cases. Prior investigators limited their
examinations to considering the *existence* of constituent
orders and the non-existence of others. Thus, the discovery

12

of a new constituent order, first VOS and then OVS, requires a complete overhaul of these explanations. The explanation offered here deals with the relative frequencies of basic constituent orders, and thus avoids this difficulty.

ANALYTICAL FRAMEWORK

In this final introductory section it will be useful to discuss briefly some of the categories and terminology used, and the nature of the evidence and argumentation utilized in motivating the key principles.

Analytical Categories and Terminology

It is a fundamental assumption in typological research that the general analytical categories utilized do permit cross-linguistic comparison (cf. Hawkins 1983:11-12). But the comparability issue has two sides. The first side concerns the consistency and appropriateness of analysis when the single researcher engages in cross-linguistic comparison. This is a difficult issue, for it means on occasion either forcing some language-specific data into a badly fitting category or abandoning that data altogether. One can minimize the problem by providing the most explicit possible definitions for key categories. Some of these definitions follow.

Subject

It is well beyond the scope of the present volume to recapitulate the extensive discussion of this notion within even recent linguistic history (Keenan 1976b, Li (ed) 1976, Schachter 1976, Foley and van Valin 1977, Tomlin 1983, etc.). Subject will be taken here to refer to the primary syntactic relation borne by a NP with respect to the verb. It is generally identifiable through syntactic alternations of agreement and voice. None of the following represent either features of subject or its identifying characteristics: semantic role; position; theme, topic, or so-called old information. Subject is strictly a syntactic category; it has no semantic or pragmatic attributes. It does have semantic and pragmatic correlates, but since these are partly to be demonstrated through the principles motivated here, it is not permissible to include them in identification procedures.

Object

The syntactic relation of object is even more elusive to define than subject, for ultimately it exhibits less independence from the verb than do other primary grammatical

13

relations. It is interesting to note, for example, that in Postal's comprehensive discussion of Raising (1974), not a single argument hinges on identification of object *per se* but rather only on showing that a NP was no longer a subject.

For this volume, object will be taken to refer to the secondary grammatical relation borne by a NP with respect to the verb. Following Postal's lead, if a given NP is nuclear to a transitive clause and *not* the subject, one has identified the object. The syntactic relation of object does not include semantic role (patient) as either a defining or identifying characteristic.

Verb

The verb is taken here to a totally straightforward category. *Verb* should be taken to refer to the verb root and any bound morphemes may include tense, aspect, agreement markers, pronominal clitics, directional markers, and so on. Certain problematic cases, like English phrasal verbs (e.g., *eat up*, *sit on*), will be treated as single verbs, but in no case does any argument for VOB rest on data that includes a controversial treatment of such problematic cases.

The definition of other categories, particularly the discourse and semantic categories used in motivating the three principles, is delayed until the relevant chapter.

The second side of the comparability issue involves the researcher's interpretation of other linguists' uses of critical terms in their own work. In a study such as this, one examines the work of literally scores of other linguists spanning periods of as much as 100 years. The question arises how one is to resolve their use of a particular term with the use that is explicitly stipulated for it here. First, the individuals who provided the descriptions consulted were trained within the same general tradition, despite differing theoretical frameworks. Thus, one does not expect their use of a term to vary drastically from those stipulated. Second, when the use of a term does seem to vary from the use intended for it, it tends to vary in reasonably predictable ways. Within this framework, the usual variation is to use terms limited here to syntactic concerns for semantic roles or discourse phenomena. Thus, for example, some writers use *subject* for *agent* or *object* for *patient*. When discovered, such variation could be recast into the present terminology with little trouble; otherwise, the information was used as presented. And if there were reason to doubt that the use was sufficiently close to that intended the information was not used.

Evidence and Argumentation

Direct and symptomatic evidence

Two distinct classes of evidence can be used to motivate the functional principles: *direct evidence* and *symptomatic evidence*. Direct evidence derives from the immediate identification of a pragmatic or semantic relation and its correlation with linguistic structure. For example, direct evidence for the principle that theme is coded by position in a particular language requires that thematic arguments be identified directly, through semantic definitions or psycholinguistic testing, and then correlated with syntactic facts of order. Structural or semantic correlates of theme, such as definiteness, do not provide direct evidence for this functional principle.

Symptomatic evidence derives from the systematic observation of reliable syntactic or semantic correlates to direct evidence. The stronger the correlation used, the more certain the conclusions to be drawn from such evidence.

Perhaps the best example of symptomatic evidence for a functional principle is the role of definiteness in arguing about theme and word order. While the correlation is by no means absolute, there is a clear tendency for definite NPs to represent clause level themes and for referential indefinite NPs *not* to do so. Thus, investigating the relative order of definite versus indefinite NPs in transitive clauses provides very reliable indirect, or symptomatic, evidence in favor of the principle that thematic information comes first.

Almost all argumentation for functional principles in so-called functional or typological approaches to grammar depend on symptomatic evidence. Symptomatic evidence is of value, for it is relatively easy to identify and collect, at the cost of being less reliable. Direct evidence is of value, for it is extremely reliable, though it is difficult to obtain.

The present volume draws on both types of evidence. Where it is available direct evidence is used to motivate each of the three functional principles, especially to support the assertion that these principles have a cognitive basis. Symptomatic evidence is used both to motivate the principles and to demonstrate their cross-linguistic validity.

Argumentation

While each of the three functional principles described below differs in its detail, the general outline for the argumentation for each remains the same. Each principle represents a claim that certain linguistic facts are distributed in language use in some particular and non-random manner. It must be demonstrated across a diverse set of languages that the essential claim embodied by each principle is true. Conversely, in order to invalidate a principle, it must be demonstrated that in a diverse set of languages the essential claim does not hold, either by the linguistic facts being distributed randomly, as for example it would were theme distributed evenly within the sentence, or by the facts being distributed in some way differently than predicted.

It should be emphasized here that in order to compromise a given functional principle, its failure must be demonstrated generally. The observation of an isolated counterexample, or an isolated exceptional language, cannot of itself invalidate a principle. The reason for this is straightforward. The approach taken here permits the interaction of principles, which under some kinds of circumstances might block the realization of one or another principle. So, for example, the explanation offered here permits the possibility that some VOS and OVS languages might represent exceptions to the TFP, which it turns out is correct for at least one clear case (Tomlin and Rhodes 1979).

At this point, it is useful to recapitulate the question examined in this volume:

(1) What are the relative frequencies of the six basic constituent order types and how are those frequencies to be explained?

The next chapter provides the answer to the first half of this question by presenting a statistical analysis of the frequency of each of the six basis word order types. The following three chapters motivate each of the three functional principles: Theme First Principle, Verb Object Bonding, and the Animated First Principle. The final chapter articulates how these principles explain the relative frequency distribution discussed in Chapter 2. Finally, several appendices are presented to provide others with the database and references from which this effort proceeded.

Chapter 2

THE FREQUENCY OF BASIC CONSTITUENT ORDERS

INTRODUCTION

This chapter addresses two problems in typological research.
First, it presents a statistical analysis of the frequencies
of the six mathematically possible orders of the nuclear
constituents of basic transitive clauses--subject (S), object
(O), and verb (V)--for a representative sample of the
languages of the world. Second, it considers the broader
problem of producing adequate language samples for
typological research as one instance of the need for greater
empiricism and methodological rigor in linguistic typology.
    Several recent articles have strongly criticized
empirical and methodological weaknesses in linguistic
research. Gross (1979) criticizes generative grammar for too
much concern with the construction of abstract theoretical
apparatus and an unfortunate disregard for the systematic
collection of linguistic data pertinent to and necessary for
empirical investigations. Hurford (1977) explores the
concept of linguistically significant generalization,
demonstrating that not all supposedly significant
generalizations are in fact so, and arguing that a more
rigorous probabilistic methodology would permit linguists to
test the significance of proposed claims. Bell (1978) argues
convincingly for the need for increased sensitivity on the
part of typological researchers to the quality of the samples
on which typological claims are based.
    These criticisms seem especially pertinent for those
engaged in typological research, for there one seeks to make
perhaps the most general of generalizations about language
and intend that they be taken as particularly important for
understanding human linguistic organization. Yet the
empirical basis for many typological claims is weak;
generalizations are regularly made on untested convenience
samples of fewer than 50 languages (and usually considerably
fewer). Even the most appealing work in syntactic typology,
for example Hopper and Thompson (1980) or Givón (1981), would

17

be strengthened by a more systematic discussion of the database used in the research. This criticism by no means implies that the generalizations are false ones, or that no insight into the nature of language is to be drawn from the work; but it does mean that the reliability and the validity of their claims is compromised to some extent.

The present chapter deals with one relatively simple problem in linguistic typology in an empirically and methodologically more rigorous manner. At present it is not known with what frequencies basic constituent orders actually occur in the languages of the world. Hopefully, this chapter provides a useful answer to that question. Further, in trying to deal with this relatively simple problem several deeper methodological issues are raised which must be faced if efforts in typological research are to transcend simple, if exciting, speculation.

The Problem

The simple typological problem addressed here can be posed as in (1):

(1) With what frequency does each of the mathematically possible orders of S, O, and V occur in the languages of the world?

Table (1) below displays the results of a statistical analysis of the frequencies of the six possible constituent orders. The frequencies were determined by obtaining the proportion of each possible order from a reasonably representative sample of the world's languages. The final sample was produced through the systematic collection of data on more than 1000 languages (1063 in the database in Appendix A) and through comparison of the genetic and areal characteristics of subsamples of that data with the genetic and areal characteristics of the world's languages as represented by the Voegelin and Voegelin (1977) reference work. The final sample used here was one whose genetic and areal characteristics did not differ significantly (as measured by the Kolmogrov goodness-of-fit test) from those of Voegelin and Voegelin (1977).

Other samples

Other language samples produced have been used, or can be used, to determine the frequency of the six basic constituent order types. Most are considerably narrower in scope than the one attempted here; and, it is important to note, most were designed to address different issues.

The seminal work on word order correlations is Greenberg (1963). He provides a 30 language judgment sample as the basis for his proposed language universals. It is possible to determine the frequencies of each of the six basic constituent order types using that sample:

(2) | SOV | SVO | VSO | VOS | OVS | OSV |
     |-------|-------|-------|------|------|------|
     | 37.0% | 43.0% | 20.0% | 0.0% | 0.0% | 0.0% |

However, the sample suffers from two weaknesses that compromise the reliability and the validity of these figures. First, the sample is not representative of the genetic distribution of the world's languages. For example, six languages, or 20% of the sample, are Indo-European; yet Indo-European comprises only some 3% of the world's languages. Furthermore, there are no languages at all from the large Indo-Pacific macro-phylum, even though languages in that macro-phylum constitute at least 15% of the world's languages. Second, the sample is not representative of the areal distribution of the world's languages. For instance, there is no language in the sample from New Guinea or Melanesia even though there are more than 1000 languages in that area, or more than 20% of the estimated total.

While the reliability and the validity of the Greenberg sample are reduced by these weaknesses, there are three mitigating factors which must temper this criticism. First, the purpose of the sample was to investigate correlations between basic constituent order and the order of other elements, and not to determine the frequency of basic constituent order types. Second, Greenberg himself acknowledged that the sample was biased (1966:75). Third, as Bell (1978:131) also notes, a significantly larger body of data is presented in Appendix II (1966:108-110).

Ultan (1969) provides a language sample complete with a frequency breakdown for basic constituent order types:

(3) | SOV | SVO | VSO | VOS | OVS | OSV |
     |-------|-------|-------|------|------|------|
     | 44.0% | 34.6% | 18.6% | 2.6% | 0.0% | 0.0% |

Ultan's figures are derived from a 75 language convenience sample. But this sample, like the Greenberg sample, is not representative of the world's languages either genetically or areally.

Ruhlen's (1975) survey of the languages of the world includes constituent order information for 427 languages, with which it is possible to calculate frequencies for each of the six types:

(4) | SOV | SVO | VSO | VOS | OVS | OSV |
     |-------|-------|-------|------|------|------|
     | 51.5% | 35.6% | 10.5% | 2.1% | 0.0% | 0.2% |

If Ruhlen's data were in some sense taken to be as a representative sample of the world's languages, it, too, would suffer from genetic and areal distortions. However, the information is presented simply as descriptive data. Perhaps it can serve as an example that size alone cannot guarantee sample representativeness.

Perkins (1980) contains a 50 language sample drawn from the set of 1213 cultures listed in Murdock (1967, 1967-71). Perkins uses stratifications produced by Kenny (1974) to divide Murdock's list into linguistic groups (based on Voegelin and Voegelin's linguistic phyla) and culture groups (based on Kenny's measures of cultural similarity), which he then randomly sampled to derive his final sample of fifty.

Though Perkin's sample may be representative of the diversity of languages (and cultures), it is not representative of the universe of natural languages. For instance, Perkin's sample includes a single language for all of Niger-Congo, 2% of his final sample, even though there are more than 1000 Niger-Congo languages, or approximately 20% of the Voegelin and Voegelin total. Similarly, the sample contains 17 languages from the North American continent (including Central America), 34% of the final sample, yet languages from that area represent at most some 8% of the estimated world total. Thus, while Perkin's sample, like Greenberg's, is useful for exploring correlations among variables of interest, it is not useful for estimating the frequency of basic constituent orders in the universe of natural languages.

Mallinson and Blake (1981) provide a 100 language convenience sample which includes a frequency breakdown for constituent order types:

(5) SOV   SVO   VSO   VOS   OVS   OSV   Unclass.
    41.0%   35.0%   9.0%   2.0%   1.0%   1.0%   11.0%

A close examination of the Mallinson and Blake sample shows that it is not a representative sample of the world's languages, thereby making problematic their frequency figures. The sample is biased genetically. For instance, Indo-European represents 10% of the Mallinson and Blake sample, but only 3% of the estimated total population. Nilo-Saharan represents 9% of the Mallinson and Blake sample, but only 2.5% of the world total. Large groups like Niger-Kordofanian or Austronesian are systematically undersampled, Niger-Kordofanian representing 9% rather than 20% of the estimated total, Austronesian 8% rather than 16%. In fact, only a few groups, Sino-Tibetan for example, approximate their estimated proportions in the languages of the world. The sample shows similar biases with respect to areal distributions.

Finally, Tomlin (1979) provides a direct and reasonably detailed discussion of the distribution of basic constituent orders. The results reported there put the frequencies at:

(6) SOV   SVO   VSO   VOS   OVS   OSV
     45.8%   41.5%   11.0%   1.5%   0.3%   0.0%

While the final sample used to produce these figures still appears to be a good one, there are still two major weaknesses in that attempt. First, though that sample overall remains a valid one, several errors were made in the use and interpretation of the chi-square statistic. Second, there are a large number of clerical errors apparent in the database. The present study corrects those errors and increases substantially the size of the database (45%) from which the final sample is drawn.

The remainder of this chapter details the results of the statistical analysis, the procedures followed in reaching those results, and the problems and implications for typological research a study such as this raises. The next section, RESULTS AND DATA, presents the final results of the analysis along with a discussion of the ways these results may and may not be interpreted. The following section, METHODOLOGY, describes the specific procedures used to produce the final sample. It also discusses the logic of tests of goodness of fit and the general rationale for using statistics in language sampling. The final section, DISCUSSION, considers a number of problems which threaten the validity of the analysis presented here as well as general theoretical implications of this study.

RESULTS AND DATA

Results

Table (1) displays the results of the statistical analysis of the frequency of each of the mathematically possible orderings of subject, object, and verb. The frequencies represent the proportion of each possible order in a representative sample of the languages of the world. The final sample used was corrected for genetic and areal bias by using the Kolmogrov test to measure the goodness of fit between the final sample and a standard derived from Voegelin and Voegelin (1977) (see METHODOLOGY for discussion).

21

	Constituent Order	Number of Languages	Frequency in Final Sample
-V	SOV	180	44.78
	OSV	0	0.00
-V-	SVO	168	41.79
	OVS	5	1.24
V-	VSO	37	9.20
	VOS	12	2.99
Totals		402	100.00

Table (1). The frequencies of basic constituent orders in a representative sample of the languages of the world.

While Table (1) indicates clearly the frequency of each of the basic constituent orders in the final sample, it does not indicate explicitly the significance of the relative frequencies. The significance of the relative frequencies is presented in (7):

(7) SOV = SVO > VSO > VOS = OVS > OSV

What this means is that while there is some slight difference in the final sample in the frequencies of SOV and SVO, that difference is not statistically a significant one. That is, the comparative frequencies of SOV and SVO are essentially the same, with the differences in the absolute figures being attributable to chance. The same holds for the relative frequency of VOS to OVS but with two hedges. First, even though the chi-square sum was significant at the .05 level, the small number of objects considered (5 OVS and 12 VOS) makes a single sample claim more questionable than would a larger number of objects. Second, it is still not clear that the reported OVS cases (all from Derbyshire and Pullum 1981) are as unequivocal as one might like (cf. Dryer 1983 for related discussions).

Limits on Interpretation

It should be made clear that certain limitations must be placed on the interpretation and use of these figures. From a conservative statistical point of view no true statistical inference can be made from the stratified sample produced by this method of analysis about the actual typological frequencies of basic constituent orders in the languages of the world; true statistical inference can be made only from random sampling. Had several hundred cases been randomly selected from Voegelin and Voegelin (1977) and frequencies determined from that sample, one could than make a more valid statistical inference.

But this sample is not a random one. Since it is not random, it necessarily suffers from numerous biases. The two most serious ones have been adjusted for: genetic and areal affiliation. Yet other possible biases remain; and, what is worse, it is technically not possible to account for them all. Consequently, from the more conservative point of view one cannot generalize from the final sample produced here to the languages of the world.

A less conservative point of view permits some general inference to be made, but that inference should not be confused as statistical inference. Having controlled the sample for the worst sources of bias, one can plausibly infer from the sample results the frequencies of basic constituent order types in the general population because other potential sources of bias seem (to the linguist) extremely unlikely to be significant.

The most likely sources of additional bias for this study include library bias (sources available), research bias (which languages have actually been researched), language of publication bias, and historical bias. Of these only historical bias seems even a remotely plausible candidate for having any significant effect on the sample. Historical bias would occur if one failed to count languages or language families which are extinct. Thus, for example, there may have been at some point in the past many more VSO languages than are included in the sample results because peoples who spoke VSO languages may have been more numerous. Or, perhaps at some earlier stage in history there were more SOV languages than there are currently, since only at this point in time has sufficient time passed to permit much SOV to SVO change. This source of bias can be dealt with only after much more research has been done on historical change.

Thus, the claim made here is that the figures in Table (1) do represent the frequencies of each constituent order type in the languages of the world. But that claim is not, nor can it ever really be, a true statistical inference. It is a weaker claim than that, though on reflection additional sources of bias seem unlikely sources of significant error.

The Data

Because of the problems inherent in this task (see DISCUSSION), it is useful to describe briefly the database from which the final sample was drawn. The database in Appendix A contains information on the basic constituent

23

order of 1063 of the world's languages. Each entry includes information on the language name, basic constituent order, areal location, genetic affiliation, and source references. The genetic affiliations follow closely the classifications in Voegelin and Voegelin (1977).

METHODOLOGY

Rationale

Bell (1978) has argued convincingly the need for good sampling in typological research. Simply put, both the validity and the reliability of any claims made in typological research depend, in part, upon the representativeness of the sample on which the typological claims are based. A poor sample necessarily diminishes the plausibility of specific argumentation; a good sample provides the firm empirical foundation on which convincing argumentation must ultimately rest.

In order to determine the frequency of each basic constituent order in the languages of the world, it is not sufficient merely to collect a large number of cases and determine proportional frequencies within that collection. If the sample collected is not representative, the proposed frequencies derived from that sample will be skewed to the extent to which the sample varies from the general population. Increasing the size of the sample does not guarantee that the sample will be any more representative (Bell, 1978). As will be seen below, the 1063 language database is in no way a representative sample of the world's languages, even though the database contains nearly 20% of the total number of languages.

Perhaps an analogy can make the sampling problem clearer. Let us say that someone has accepted the task of deciding whether a given batch of vegetable soup is "just like Mom used to make". Let us assume that this woman kept good records, so we know that a given volume of soup should contain a certain proportion of broth and of each of six vegetables: carrots, potatoes, celery, cabbage, peas, and tomatoes. Suppose further that the person examining the soup must make his determination based on a single dip of a one-cup ladle.

Ideally, what should happen is that when the examiner evaluates the ladle of soup, he should find (if the soup is like "Mom's") a proportion of each vegetable equal to the proportion for that vegetable in Mom's original recipe. He should also find an equivalent proportion of vegetables to broth. If the proportions are the same for each vegetable, the soup (ceteris paribus) will be just like Mom's; if the proportions are different, the soup will be different.

24

It should be clear that merely dipping the ladle into the soup is not likely to produce a reliable sample. The soup may have been sitting for awhile so that the vegetables have all settled. Dipping the ladle too shallowly will result in too much broth; dipping the ladle too deeply will result in too many vegetables. In either case the sample would not be representative of the actual soup examined. The sample would be biased in some way, and this bias could result in a mistaken inference about whether or not the soup is "just like Mom's". Note that increasing the size of the sample by increasing the size of the ladle does little itself toward removing the biases.

Clearly, what must be done in this case is to give the soup a good stir in order to put all of the vegetables into suspension. A sample of this suspension will yield a much more accurate picture of the proportion of each vegetable. The stirring, then, represents a sampling technique that will ensure a representative sample of soup, which may then be compared with Mom's original recipe.

In typological research one faces a similar problem. It is at best risky to base language-general claims on samples of languages collected by convenience. Some effort must be made to assure the representativeness of the samples used. And, in the long run, only by adoption of careful sampling procedures can one insure the maximum representativeness of typological samples.

Goodness-of-fit

The particular kind of statistical measurement performed in this study is referred to as goodness-of-fit. The best way to explain how goodness-of-fit testing works is to consider an example. Suppose one wants to determine whether or not a particular coin is fair. In a goodness-of-fit test, one compares the theoretical distribution for some given number of throws with the observed results one gets throwing the coin the given number of times. So, one might compare the expected frequency of heads versus tails for 1000 throws, the theoretical distribution being 500 heads and 500 tails, with the actual results one obtained after throwing the coin 1000 times, the observed distribution being, say, 492 heads and 508 tails.

Clearly, the closer the observed occurrence of heads and tails is to the predicted theoretical distribution, the more likely it is that the coin is fair. If there is no difference at all between the observed and the theoretical distribution, then the fit between the sample and the theoretical distribution of that population will be perfect, and the coin will be evaluated as fair. Conversely, if the differences are dramatic, as they would be in this case if there were, say 999 heads and 1 tail, the coin would be evaluated as crooked. The various statistics available provide a precise measure of the extent and the significance of such differences, and, importantly, permit one to evaluate the goodness-of-fit when the extent and the significance of the differences between the observed sample distribution and the theoretical distribution is not obvious.

The problem faced here is producing a sample of languages representative, genetically and areally, of the world's languages. Goodness-of-fit testing is helpful here for one can compare the genetic and areal characteristics of a given sample of languages to the genetic and areal characteristics of the languages of the world. For each genetic or areal class represented in the languages of the world, one would like to include in the sample a number of languages equal to the number of languages predicted for that class given the proportion of that class in the languages of the world. Crudely, if 1% of the world's languages are Burmese-Lolo, then a sample of 400 languages should contain four Burmese-Lolo languages; if .5% are Semitic, one would expect to find two Semitic languages; and so on. Since in the actual sampling some genetic and areal classes are almost inevitably overrepresented or underrepresented, one must find some way to determine whether the overall variation in the sample is so great the sample is not representative. Goodness-of-fit testing permits that determination.

Two common statistical tests were considered for this study: the Pearson chi-square statistic and the Kolmogrov goodness-of-fit test. Each test can be used and is widely used to measure goodness of fit. Each test demands, as do all statistical tests, that specific assumptions be met in order to utilize the test felicitously. While it is possible to meet the essential assumptions for each statistical test, meeting the assumptions for the chi-square statistic resulted in a comparatively cruder final sample than the final sample possible using the Kolmogrov goodness-of-fit test. Thus, the Kolmogrov goodness-of-fit (K-test) was used to check the representativeness of the final sample.

The Kolmogrov test is an effective one for this task, for it requires minimal assumptions and it is easily computed. There are two assumptions for the K-test. First, it assumes that each observation in the observed frequency distribution is independent of all others. This assumption has been met here, for each of the objects included in the final sample is an independent human language and its inclusion into a particular cell of either contingency table is in no way dependent on the inclusion of other objects in other cells. Second, it assumes that the theoretical distribution is mathematically continuous. However, Marascuilo and McSweeney (1977:249) observe that it is common, especially in working with behavioral data, for this assumption to be relaxed. When this assumption is relaxed,

26

the K-test becomes more conservative. The second assumption for the K-test is relaxed in this study; the significance of this is that the final sample is somewhat more certainly representative than is technically claimed.

Determining the Theoretical Distribution

In a good deal of goodness-of-fit testing determining the theoretical distribution of some population is a simple matter for it can be computed mathematically. For a thousand throws of a coin, one expects 500 heads and 500 tails because on each throw there is a .50 probability of a head and a .50 probability of a tail. However, not all populations are distributed probabilistically, and in such a case the determination of the theoretical distribution can be considerably more difficult. One must determine the theoretical distribution empirically, examining the distribution of the relevant characteristics in the general population in order to establish a standard against which the sample population can eventually be compared.

Since the goal here is a sample of languages which is representative of the world's languages genetically and areally, it is necessary to determine the theoretical genetic distribution and the theoretical areal distribution of the languages of the world. This, in turn, requires the creation of two independent classifications, or 'frames', for the world's languages. Fortunately, there is one major reference work, Voegelin and Voegelin (1977), which provides sufficient information on the genetic affiliation and areal locations of the world's languages to permit the creation of useful genetic and areal frames.

The production of the genetic frame required that the languages of the world be divided into reasonably comparable genetic groups. Ideally, each cell in the frame should be comparable in time depth or level of classification to all the other cells in the frame. The specific frame used in this study can be found in Appendix B. Most of the cells represent genetic groups of approximately the level of Italic/Romance of Indo-European.

Choosing such a level of classification resulted in the finest frame that was still practically manageable. Still, some adjustments to the frame were necessary to accommodate smaller genetic groups. In particular, it was necessary to have at least 10 objects in each cell of the theoretical distribution in order to guarantee that at least one language be required for that cell in the final sample. Therefore, in most cases groups of less than 10 languages were combined into either the next highest level of classification or into those groups designated in Appendix B as "Other" classifications.

27

For example, the approximately Romance-level groups of Oto-Manguean include Chinantecan with seven languages, Otomian with six, Popolocan with four, Zapotecan with two, Mixtecan with three, Manguean with two, and two ungrouped languages. The requirements discussed above resulted in moving to the next highest level of classification for this case--Oto-Manguean.

The second method of combination can be illustrated with Indo-European. Some Indo-European groups were quite manageable; but other groups, like Baltic and Slavic, were too small to stand alone. Since the next highest level of classification was Indo-European, and since some of the divisions within Indo-European were manageable, Slavic and Baltic were combined into an *ad hoc* group, "Slavic-Baltic". Isolates and small families each were combined into a single group.

Combining groups in these ways is not as *ad hoc* as it may seem; the combinations were required only to facilitate the use of the K-test. Though the combinations do permit it, they do not necessitate even minor genetic distortion in the sample. To make this clear, let us consider Oto-Manguean again. This phylum represents only 0.5% of the world's languages. Therefore, for a final sample size of 402 languages, two should be Oto-Manguean. The combination of Chinantecan with the other small groups of Oto-Manguean permits, but does not necessitate, the following small distortion. It would be possible for both of the needed Oto-Manguean languages to be chosen from Chinantecan to the exclusion of the other small groups. However, there is nothing in the combinations or in the use of the K-test itself that requires one take two Chinantecan languages. And, in fact, the random selection of two languages from the nine collected resulted in one Otomian language (Mazahua) and one Zapotecan language (Zapotec).

The production of the areal frame parallels the production of the genetic frame. The areal frame requires that each and every language fall into one and only one areal cell. This, in turn, requires that the world be divided into a number of linguistic areas. Appendix C displays the specific areal frame used in this study.

Dividing the world into linguistic areas could be done in a number of ways. One could lay an arbitrary grid over the world such that each and every language fell into one and only one segment of the grid. This would work perfectly well for the K-test and introduces no distortions into the picture at all. It is, however, impractical.

One could also follow Bell's suggestion (1978:147n) to use Murdock's culture areas (Murdock 1966, 1967) as the basis for constructing the frame. However, this proved impractical as well. First, Murdock's set of culture areas number over 100; this is simply too fine a frame for this study. Second,

28

Murdock does not provide circumscriptions of his culture
areas; rather he pinpoints one or two particular cultures for
each of the areas.

The method used to construct the present areal frame is
relatively simple. First, those areas of the world were used
which are generally recognized to be non-controversial
linguistic or culture areas. For instance, it is generally
accepted that South Africa forms a unified linguistic area
(Masica 1976); consequently South Asian cell was incorporated
into the areal frame. Second, where no specific linguistic
or culture areas are generally recognized, areas were defined
negatively. For instance, after the areas Southeast Asia,
East Asia, Europe, and Mid Central Asia were circumscribed,
there remained a large area to which was assigned the cell
North and Northeastern Asia.

When geographical features, such as major mountain
ranges or rivers, were not adequate to circumscribe an area,
current political boundaries were used. If these were not
useful, then an arbitrary latitude or longitude was used.
The kinds of decisions made in circumscribing the areas for
the area frame raise no problems for the use of the K-test.
All that is needed is some sort of grid, even an arbitrary
one, from which one can compute expected and observed
frequencies. It is simpler, and more congruent with common
linguistic thinking, to circumscribe areas in the manner
described above than to toil with either of the others. The
present areal frame permits a complete and non-distorted use
of the K-test.

Production of the Final Sample

The end result sought in creating the final 402 language
sample was a single sample whose total genetic and areal
distortion was not statistically significant when compared to
the genetic and areal characteristics of the standard
prepared from Voegelin and Voegelin (1977). The 1063
language database could not itself serve as a final sample,
for measurement of the genetic and areal characteristics of
the database revealed quite significant variation from the
standard. Some genetic groups, like Altaic and Caucasian,
were grossly overrepresented; other genetic groups, like
Macro-Ge, were grossly underrepresented. Similar problems
existed for the areal groupings.

Consequently, the 1063 language database was selectively
subsampled to produce a final sample. Each subsampling was
measured with the K-test to determine the extent of its
variation from the characteristics of the standard. When a
subsampling was found whose total variation from the

theoretical genetic and areal distributions of the standard was not statistically significant, that subsample became the final sample.

Following Bell's suggestions (1978), it becomes necessary to state explicitly certain assumptions that underlie the sampling performed here. First, the universe of objects represented by the sample is the set of natural human languages. It includes extinct languages for which there is limited data (eg. Tocharian B), but excludes non-existent possible human languages (eg. Proto-Oceanic) and created languages (eg. Esperanto) or language analogs (eg. FORTRAN). Second, the field from which the sample and the database were drawn includes references from the research libraries at the Universities of Michigan and Oregon as well as the personal libraries of numerous Michigan and Oregon colleagues.

Four hundred two languages were chosen as the optimum number for the final sample. This number represented the largest number of languages that could be included practically in the sample given the size of the database. Languages were chosen randomly from those collected in the database for each of the cells in the genetic frame. For those cells for which an insufficient number of languages had been collected, additional languages were chosen randomly from the remaining languages in the database to bring the total number of languages in the sample to 402. This sample was then measured twice with the K-test, once against the theoretical genetic distribution of languages and once against the theoretical areal distribution.

Selective adjustments were made to the contents of particular cells in both the genetic and areal contingency tables in order to bring the sample as closely into alignment with the standard as possible. For instance, the penultimate subsampling still exhibited unacceptable areal bias; in particular, there were too many languages in the South Asia cell and too few in the Western Africa cell. Consequently, a new subsample was produced in which the number of languages in the South Asia cell was reduced, while the number of languages in the Western Africa cell was increased. The particular languages chosen in each instance were randomly selected from those available.

This final sample was then measured twice and in each case the maximum K-value fell below the threshold for rejecting the null hypotheses.

The final genetic test ran as follows. The null hypothesis, H was tested against the alternative, H' , using the Kolmogrov test to measure the goodness of fit between the observed genetic distribution in the sample and the theoretical distribution of the prepared standard.

(8) H : The observed genetic distribution of languages
in the sample is **equivalent** to the theoretical
genetic distribution of languages in the
standard prepared from Voegelin and Voegelin
(1977).

H' : The observed genetic distribution of languages
in the sample is **not equivalent** to the
theoretical genetic distribution of languages
in the standard prepared from Voegelin and
Voegelin (1977).

For this test, the significance of the test result can
be pinpointed on the following continuum:

(9) Test value: 0.00-.061 .061-.068 .068-.081 .081-.150
    Sig level: 1.00-.1   .1-.05   .05-.01   .01-.00
    Interp: Non-sig   Marg sig Sig   Highly sig

The null hypothesis in this case will be rejected if the
maximum value of the K-test is .061 or greater. The maximum
value computed was .028. This value has a corresponding
significance level of .68, which statistically is
unequivocably non-significant. What this means for the study
is that there is no reason to conclude that there is a
difference in the genetic distribution between the final
sample and the theoretical distribution. That is, the null
hypothesis is not rejected and one can infer that the sample
genetic distribution does not vary from the theoretical
genetic distribution of the standard. If the standard is a
fair one, and if the possible distortions discussed are not
in themselves significant, then one can further infer that
the final sample is not biased genetically.

The final areal test follows the same pattern. The null
hypothesis, H , was tested against the alternative, H', using
the Kolmogrov test:

(10) H : The observed areal distribution of languages in
the sample is **equivalent** to the theoretical
areal distribution of languages in the standard
prepared from Voegelin and Voegelin (1977).

H': The observed areal distribution of languages in
the sample is **not equivalent** to the theoretical
areal distribution of languages in the standard
prepared from Voegelin and Voegelin (1977).

The significance of the test result here, too, can be
pinpointed on the continuum in (9). The null hypothesis in
this case will be rejected if the maximum value of the K-test
is .061 or greater. The maximum value computed was .018.

31

This result is also unequivocably non-significant, and again the null hypothesis is not rejected. Thus, given the same limitations noted above, one can infer that the final sample is not biased areally.

Finally, since the sampling techniques described here reduce significantly both genetic and areal biases in the final sample, and since no additional sources of bias appear likely to affect the sample in any significant way, the final sample does appear to be representative of the languages of the world.

DISCUSSION

There are a number of problems, both theoretical and practical, which threaten the validity of a study such as this. The threat to the study consists of possible conflicts between the ideal requirements on an adequate statistical treatment of the problem and the theoretical and practical limitations which prevent meeting this ideal.

All of the problems discussed below are connected to one primary requirement on the felicitous use of the Kolmogrov test. The K-test requires, as do all such tests, that each of the objects included in the sample be drawn independently from the population. What this means is that each object in the sample must be independent of, equivalent to, and comparable to every other object in the sample. As will be seen below, there are a number of problems which threaten to compromise the independence, equivalence, and comparability of the objects in the sample produced here.

Included in the discussion of each problem below is consideration of how the problem threatens the study and what practical steps were taken in the resolution of that problem. It is beyond the scope of this volume to consider any of these problems in much detail. However, it is essential to recognize the problems and to explain the difficulties they pose, for these same problems threaten the validity of all typological claims, even those made without consideration of sampling problems. Finally, it should be made explicit that the ultimate validity of the figures presented in Table (1) hinges on an appropriate resolution of these problems.

Problem 1: The comparability of linguistic claims

Ideally, in order to assure the independence of the objects within the sample and the database, each object should be described and selected using uniform procedures and explicit criteria. To the extent this is not possible the representativeness of the database population is compromised, and the ultimate validity of the statistical study is compromised as well.

This particular problem has both a practical and a theoretical side. The practical side of the problem is that the terms and procedures used to identify the basic constituent order of a particular language are not consistent from case to case. The data reported here are derived from the examination of some 400 references by nearly 350 linguists and writers writing within numerous theoretical and descriptive traditions over a span of 100 years.

The use of basic descriptive terms obviously varies among different writers. For instance, subject is sometimes used to refer to a syntactic category, it is sometimes used to refer to the sentence- or clause-level theme or topic, and it is sometimes used to refer to the semantic role of agent. The basic, and usually implicit, procedures used to determine basic constituent orders also vary. Sometimes basic order is determined simply through frequency of use; sometimes it is determined through the complexity of structure. In some instances inappropriate data is used, such as clauses with pronominal NPs. These practical problems complicate the evaluation and selection of data for inclusion in the database.

The theoretical side of the problem is that it is not clear whether or not in principle it is possible to make comparable cross-linguistic descriptions. For this to be possible, each descriptive term needs to be well-motivated and well-placed within some sort of theory of typological description. However, it is clear that none of the descriptive terms relevant to the task here has the necessary grounding. The obvious example is the notion "subject".

The resolutions to these problems taken in this volume are straightforward. Since the theoretical side of the problem is not resolved, one can only make some sort of assumption regarding the ultimate possibility of genuine cross-linguistic comparison. Obviously, the assumption made here is that cross-linguistic comparison is both possible and feasible.

Given that assumption, the practical side of the problem was dealt with as follows. The claims and statements made by the numerous linguistic writers concerning the basic constituent order of specific languages were evaluated according to specific guidelines. First, referenced claims were used as presented unless concrete evidence existed in the reference to cast doubt on the claim. So, for instance, Tucker & Bryan (1966:55) describe Mamvu (Nilo-Saharan: C Sudanic: Mangbutu-Efe) as an OSV language. However, the illustrative data includes only sentences with pronominal NPs. Such data does not permit one to infer a basic constituent order, consequently the Tucker & Bryan statement has not been incorporated into the database. Second, where doubts concerning the validity of a particular basic constituent order were raised, the claim was checked either

33

through independent verification in an additional source or through the examination of text or sentence data elsewhere in the work. Those claims that were verified were included in the database. Those claims for which alternative orders seemed more plausible were reinterpreted and included. And those claims for which doubts remained were excluded. Finally, in any case where conflicting orders were proposed in different sources, an attempt was made to resolve the conflict through additional verification or reinterpretation. When such efforts failed, the language was not included in the database. In all, about 100 cases were excluded from the database for one or another reason.

Problem 2: The determination of basic constituent order

Ideally, the procedures followed to determine the basic constituent order for each of the languages used in the sample should be the same. Yet a number of difficulties and issues preclude this.

First, there is the theoretical issue of whether every language in fact has a basic constituent order. Basicness is a property assigned to linguistic structures through some subset of the properties of frequency, predictability, and complexity. It may be the case, for instance, that some languages could have two candidates for basic constituent order, each of which was equally frequent, predictable, and complex. In such a case, the determination of basic constituent order would be exceedingly difficult. Similarly, if it were possible to have a free (i.e., random) word order language, the determination of a basic constituent order might be impossible.

The practical decisions taken here with regard to the determination of basic constituent order follow. First, it is assumed that no language has free, or random, constituent order. Second, it is assumed that every language has one order which is more basic. 'Basic" here does not mean a fixed or rigid constituent order, as English is a rigid SVO language or Japanese a rigid SOV language, rather it means unmarked or prototypical constituent order, as Spanish is prototypically SVO, despite the high frequency of VS structures in narrative test (Givón, p.c.). Both of these assertions must be treated as assumptions since no clear theoretical resolution to either exists.

Third, the claim of the source cited was used unless there was some specific reason to doubt it. In such cases the procedures for resolving problems were used as described for problem 1.

Problem 3: The dialect-language problem

Ideally, each object included in the database and in the final sample clearly should be a separate and independent language. In addition, each object listed as a language in Voegelin and Voegelin (1977) should be a separate and independent language. If not enough care is taken to guarantee that each object is in fact an independent language, the expected and observed proportions of specific cells in the genetic and areal frames will be distorted to some extent. This, in turn, would result in a certain amount of genetic and areal bias despite the sampling efforts. Thus, it is important to determine whether a particular object is an independent language or whether it is a dialect of some particular language.

Unfortunately, the theoretical resolution of this problem is not at hand. The primary criterion by which the problem might be resolved, mutual intelligibility, seems of dubious value, for social and political factors merge with and cloud more idealized linguistic issues. Other possible criteria, --lexical or phonological for example --, seem primarily to be elaborations of one or another aspect of mutual intelligibility and must, ultimately, share its fate.

The practical resolution to the problem for the present study is to make consistent use of Voegelin and Voegelin (1977). Only those objects which are listed as independent languages (specifically those objects which are numbered) are counted as languages in this study. And, only one object is included in the database for each independent language. So, for instance, Voegelin and Voegelin (1977:133) list Netsilik and West Greenlandic as dialects of Inuit; thus, there is one and only one entry in the database (Inupik) to represent this cluster of dialects. Further, to be consistent, even cases which are ordinarily widely treated as separate languages in the literature are treated as single entries if they are listed as such by Voegelin and Voegelin (1977). Thus, German, Dutch, Afrikaans, and Yiddish are not included as separate languages in the database despite ordinary linguistic practice, since they are all included under Netherlandic-German in the Voegelin and Voegelin reference (1977:146).

Conclusions

To the limited empirical question proposed in (1) this volume offers a reasonable and appropriate solution. Through the careful production of a more representative sample, this study offers more firmly grounded figures on basic

35

constituent order frequency than can be produced using less demanding non-stratified convenience samples. And, it is important to note, it provides results which are different from those produced through convenience counts of languages.

Still, the problems discussed above clearly do threaten the validity and reliability of the claims incorporated in Table (1). further, the practical resolutions described here do not fully address the issues raised by these problems. But, it is critical to see these same problems threaten all typological claims.

Thus, the implications of this kind of typological effort are somewhat paradoxical. First, it would have been desirable to claim that the effort presented here exemplifies what ought to be a primary kind of research effort in typology. That is, before one even begins to propose some sort of language general typological statement, one should be responsible to produce an appropriately representative sample of language data. As Bell points out (1978:129-135), some typological work is sensitive to the problem of representativeness in the data samples used. Still, most typological work today proceeds from remarkably small and universally untested data samples. This is represented in part by the data presented below to motivate the three functional principles used in the explanation offered in this volume.

Despite, however, any desire to make the claim described above, these is a second and paradoxical implication to this study. The testing procedures utilized here demand that the objects included in the sample be comparable, but the problems considered above raise serious questions about the ultimate comparability of that data and of typological data in general. Thus, the second implication is that progress in typological research will be hindered until the theoretical issues which impinge on typological research receive systematic theoretical treatment.

Chapter 3

THE THEME FIRST PRINCIPLE

INTRODUCTION

This chapter describes, motivates, and limits a first
functional principle of grammatical organization: the Theme
First Principle (TFP). This principle is a generalization
about the distribution of one kind of pragmatic information
in sentences or clauses. The general thrust of this
principle is that in sentences or clauses information that is
more "thematic" tends to precede information that is less
"thematic". Thematic information, in turn, represents the
psycholinguistic reflex of more general processes of
attention in cognition.

In order to motivate this principle there are a number
of necessary steps to be taken; each of these comprises one
section of the chapter. The first section presents a
discussion of 'thematic information' (TI). It argues that in
order to describe the distribution of information in
sentences and clauses it is critical to distinguish
information the speaker and hearer merely hold in common
(what will be here called *shared information* (SI)) from
information which they have in common but which is also
connected in a specific manner to the 'goal' of the discourse
(what will be called here *thematic information* (TI)).
Further, the distinction between TI and SI will be stipulated
in such a way as to reduce the problems inherent in the
typical semantic definitions of corresponding notions, (e.g.,
Halliday's contrast between "given" and "theme," 1967, 1968).

The second section discusses the argumentation for the
TFP. It is necessary to demonstrate that more thematic
information tends to precede less thematic in simple main
clauses. This can be done in two ways. First, *direct
evidence* can be provided by examining the role of attention
in discourse production and the resultant distribution of TI
in text artifacts. Second, *symptomatic evidence* can be
provided by examining the distribution of predictive
correlates of TI in sentence level grammar:

The third section presents the evidence for the TFP. A limited amount of direct evidence is provided. Extensive symptomatic evidence is also presented.

The final section discusses two limitations on the TFP. One limitation concerns the relation of TI to 'subject.' TI is not necessarily identifiable with subject in particular languages--especially if all sentence types are examined. However, in basic sentences in most languages there exists a significant correlation between TI and subject. Since it is primarily basic sentences that are used to determine basic constituent order, and since there is a correlation between TI and subject in basic sentences, it is appropriate and reasonable to link TI to subject when discussing basic constituent order in general. However, the linking of TI to subject is limited to a general discussion of basic constituent orders in the manner described above.

The second limitation that the TFP represents an abstraction about language in general, an abstraction garnered from data concerning the distribution of information in texts. It is not offered as an absolute language universal. It is offered, rather, as one of three fundamental functional principles that shape language specific grammars, and, as such it may work with or in opposition to other forces.

THEMATIC INFORMATION IN DISCOURSE AND TEXT

In order to contextualize properly the specific treatment of thematic information taken up below, it is necessary to consider several background issues. The discussion of these issues involves making explicit two distinct orientations on discourse matters taken in linguistics and cognitive science.

The first distinction to draw is that *discourse* and *text* are different, and that *discourse analysis* is consequently a different enterprise than *text analysis*. *Discourse* represents the entire spectrum of linguistic, cognitive, and social processes involved in the cooperative enterprise of speech communication. *Text* represents the specific *artifact* produced during the process of discourse creation. Thus, the text artifact, or simply *text*, is the product of a larger set of active processes grounded in the psycholinguistic makeup of the discourse participants and the sociolinguistic conventions under which they interact.

Text analysis seeks to understand the organization of the text artifact through the description of semantic and pragmatic parameters revealed by the linguistic structure of the artifact itself. Two superior examples of this approach are Halliday and Hasan's (1976) work on textual cohesion and Givón's (1984) collection of articles on topic continuity.

38

Discourse analysis, on the other hand, seeks to identify and explain those linguistic, cognitive, and social processes through which communication is effected and the text artifact produced and comprehended. It looks outside the text artifact for explanation. Clear examples of discourse analysis include Chafe's (1986) paper on the activation of information in memory in discourse and Tomlin's (1986a) description of the syntax of reference.

The second distinction to draw is between developing a theory of discourse processing and developing a reliable methodology for text analysis. The first, and larger enterprise has as its central task the identification and description of the component linguistic and cognitive processes which govern the use of syntactic alternations during the on-line production and comprehension of discourse. The second, and narrower, enterprise has as its central task the identification of particular instances of correlating function and form in extent text data, and depends primarily upon structural information for that identification.

In what follows below the notion of thematic information will be motivated theoretically as a pragmatic function from the point of view of discourse analysis. In turn, techniques for text analysis will be presented for the data analysis on which the motivation hinges.

Thematic Information and Shared Information

It is essential to draw a distinction at the clause and sentence level between two general pragmatic notions: *shared information* and *thematic information*. A definition for each is found in (1):

(1) *Shared Information*: information in an expression is shared to the extent the speaker assumes the hearer is able to identify the referent of the expression.

Thematic Information: information in an expression is thematic to the extent the speaker assumes the hearer attends to the referent of the expression.

The difference between these two general notions is an important one, and one which is often blurred in linguistic discussion. Shared information is concerned with establishing and maintaining reference in discourse production and comprehension. Linguistically, it is connected to issues of definiteness (du Bois 1980, Clancy 1980), pronominalization, and the syntax of reference. Psycholinguistically, it appears to be connected to cognitive processes of information retrieval, or activation, in memory (Chafe 1986).

39

Thematic information is concerned with the selective
focus of attention on information during discourse production
and comprehension. Thematic information appears to help the
hearer orient attention to specific information within the
hearer's current mental model (Johnson-Llaird 1983) of the
events or subject matter under discussion. Thematic
information in this sense seems to *frame* the unfolding
discourse by directing the hearer to specific points in his
mental representation of events about which additional
elaboration is to be provided. The information which serves
as the frame may do so either because it is particularly
important to the speaker, given the specific discourse task
at hand, or because it is particularly salient in the events
or subject matter being described.

Thematic information at the clause or sentence level is
a function of the higher level theme or purpose of the event
or paragraph in which the sentence occurs. The more general
goal of the higher level paragraph, what van Dijk and Kintsch
(1983) call the macroproposition, controls thematic
information at the lower level. Tomlin (1986b) demonstrates
clearly that the assignment of thematic arguments to subject
in English is controlled at the local paragraph level and
neither at the episodic or global levels of discourse
organization. This has important implications for the
identification of theme in text, as discussed below.

Linguistically, thematic information is connected to
issues of voice (Tomlin 1983), word order, and sentence
prosody (Chafe 1976, 1986). Psycholinguistically, it appears
to be connected to cognitive processes of selective attention
during discourse production and comprehension (Tomlin and
Kellogg 1986).

It is important to emphasize that shared and thematic
information represent independent pragmatic notions.
Information which is shared is not necessarily thematic,
information which is thematic is not necessarily shared,
though there is a significant correlation in this direction.

These notions can be illustrated by considering the
following text fragment.

(2): Text fragment I: from Clavell, James. 1966.
Tai-pan. New York: Dell Publishing Co. p. 521.

That afternoon **Struan** went aboard *China Cloud*. *He*
sent *Captain Orlov* to one of the lorchas and
Zergeyev to spacious quarters in Resting Cloud.
He ordered *all sails* set and *the moorings* let go
and *he* fled *the harbor* into the deep...
He stayed on *the quarterdeck* all day and part of
the night and once more *he* slept. At dawn *he* shot
the sun and *∅* marked *the chart* and again *∅* ordered
the ship home to...

From the point of view of shared information, all of the italicized NPs represent entities which the speaker believes the hearer can identify. The particular expressions utilized, pronouns and proper names, represent the typical and well-understood devices for coding shared information in English.

From the point of view of thematic information, all of the boldfaced NPs represent entities on which the speaker intends to focus the attention of the hearer. The overall passage is thematically *about* Struan and a set of actions he takes as captain of the China Cloud. It makes sense that this general paragraph level theme is framed around Struan, the principal character. One can see this post-hoc through the frequency with which Struan was mentioned within the passage as compared to other characters. But, it is due to the syntactic treatment of references to Struan (syntactic subject) that attention is directed to Struan as the most salient, and therefore thematic, character *during* the on-line course of discourse production and comprehension.

The Identification of Thematic Information

It is very much the tradition in linguistic research on discourse to provide some semantic description of theme or topic or old information and then to be satisfied with applying those definitions introspectively to text data of interest or with using structural information of one kind or another to identify instances of the particular pragmatic notion in text data. Neither an introspective approach nor a structural approach are ultimately suited to the task of identifying thematic information in discourse data (Tomlin 1985). Without some suitable method for identifying thematic information in discourse and text the theoretical description of this notion provided above is of little practical use.

There are at least three separate ways one can go about identifying thematic information in discourse and text: (1) experimentally, through the manipulation of attention in discourse production or comprehension; (2) descriptively, through the analysis of text goals by informed subjects; and (3) descriptively, through the statistical analysis of text artifacts.

Experimental Identification

Since thematic information at the sentence level represents the linguistic reflection of attention allocation during discourse production, it follows that if one were to

41

manipulate in some way the allocation of attention for a
particular linguistic task, one could determine how attention
allocation was manifested in language use. More simply put,
if one can manipulate attention as an independent variable,
one can observe dependent language use changes in the
behavior of human subjects. While this kind of effort is
both difficult and expensive, it does provide very good
evidence for examining thematic information and its
functional coding in syntax. Tomlin and Kellogg (1986),
discussed below, represents one instance of manipulating
attention directly during discourse comprehension in order to
investigate the role of order in coding thematic information.

Text Goal Hierarchies

A second way to identify clause and sentence level thematic
information in discourse is to establish the relative
thematicity of referents within a relevant stretch of text
data. Competing referents are ranked in importance with
respect to the goal of the discourse introspectively either
by an expert subject or by multiple subjects.
     The precise procedure is presented in (3):

  (3) *Establishing a text goal thematic hierarchy.*

       (1) Parse text into relevant structural units
           (paragraphs).
       (2) Determine the rhetorical goal of the text
           (describe, narrate, etc.).
       (3) Isolate the clause and sentence level
           referents.
       (4) Rank the referents as centers of attention with
           respect to (2).
       (5) Use the resulting hierarchy to identify the
           most thematic referent.

     As described below, Tomlin (1983) uses this procedure to
investigate the interaction of syntactic subject, thematic
information, and agent in hockey play-by-play produced in
English. It has also been used by Pettinari (1983) to
investigate the thematic structure of surgical reports, and
by Tomlin and Rhodes (1979) to investigate information
structure in Ojibwa.

Measurement of Referential Density

The final means of identifying thematic information in text,
not utilized directly here, is to measure the cumulative
referential density of the various referents within a
relevant domain of discourse (Tomlin 1986b). It seems
reasonable that referents which are more important, more

42

central to the discourse being produced, should occur with greater frequency than less central referents. With an objective, quantitative means to measure this density, one would have a reliable way to compare the thematic ranking of competing referents.

The specific method for computing cumulative referential density is specified in (4). This method represents a variation on text measurement techniques developed by Givón (1984). Givón's techniques for measuring what he calls *topic continuity*, measuring referential distance and referential persistence, are essentially linear. Tomlin (1986a) and Fox (1986) each argue in part that these linear measurements are not sensitive to the hierarchical organization of discourse. The present technique is responsive to that hierarchical organization: clause and sentence level thematic information is determined at the paragraph level. Tomlin (1986b) demonstrates that clause level themes are determined at a local level of discourse organization and not at more global levels.

(4)   *Computation of cumulative referential density*

    (1)   Divide text into paragraph units.
    (2)   Divide text into clauses.
    (3)   Identify referents in each clause.
    (4)   Compute cumulative referential density (RD).
            RD=*Total cumulative references*
                Total cumulative clauses
    (5)   Rank order referents in hierarchy

An example will make this measurement technique clearer. Consider the paragraph in (5):

(5) The man walked into the store, picked up a newspaper and put it on the counter. He took out a quarter and handed it to the clerk, who put it in the cash register. The man walked out.

This text fragment contains a single paragraph, so the first step is taken care of. The next two steps are to divide the text into clauses and identify the referents of each clause. This is displayed in (6).

(6)   *Clause*   *Text (referents in bold)*

      1   *The **man*** walked into *the **store*,**
      2   *(MAN)* picked up **a newspaper**
      3   *(MAN)* put **it** on **the counter**
      4   *(MAN)* took out **a quarter**
      5   and *(MAN)* handed **it** to **the clerk**,
      6   **who** put **it** in **the cash register**.

43

7   *The man* walked out.

Computing the referential density for each referent at each clause requires taking the number of references to the given referent at a given point in the paragraph and dividing that by the number of clauses to that that point in the paragraph.
The cumulative frequency for each referent at each clause, the comparative thematic ranking of each referent at each clause, and a global summary are presented in (7) and (8).

(7) *Referential Density of Referents over Seven Clauses*

	MAN	CLERK	PAPER	QUARTER	STORE	REG	COUNTER
1	1.00	.00	.00	.00	1.00	.00	.00
2	1.00	.00	.50	.00	.50	.00	.00
3	1.00	.00	.67	.00	.33	.00	.33
4	1.00	.00	.50	.25	.25	.00	.25
5	1.00	.20	.40	.40	.20	.00	.20
6	.83	.33	.33	.33	.17	.17	.17
7	.86	.29	.29	.29	.14	.14	.14

(8) *Resulting Thematic Rankings: Clause by Clause*

Clause	Ranking
1	M = S > CL,P,Q,R,C
2	M > S,P > CL,Q,R,C
3	M > P > S,C > CL,Q,R
4	M > P > Q,S,C > CL,R
5	M > P,Q > CL,S,C > R
6	M > CL,P,Q > S,R,C
7	M > CL,P,Q >S,R,C
Overall	M > CL,P,Q > S,R,C

With these measurements it is possible to identify the most thematic argument in any given clause, with which one can investigate how that most thematic information is realized syntactically. In the fragment presented above, the most thematic NP (represented by italicized boldface) is consistently the syntactic subject.

PREVIOUS RESEARCH INTO THEMATIC INFORMATION

It would be incorrect to suggest that the distinctions between TI and SI offered here are completely unique. All of the major writers on information structure in discourse and text have noted and discussed some difference between information that is merely shared and information which is critical to the development of the discourse. While a full discussion of those works is beyond the scope of this volume, excellent detailed summaries can be found in Daneš (1974) and Jones (1977). However, two writers do seem particularly sensitive to it: Daneš and Halliday.

Daneš (1974, 1970) offers a bipartite definition of "theme". Theme for Daneš was, first, what the utterance is about, and, second, old or given information which serves as the starting point of the utterance.

Halliday (1967, 1968) discusses what he calls the thematic structure of English clauses. Two of the three independent information structure he distinguishes are of interest here: 'information focus' and 'thematization.' Information focus is concerned with the distribution of "given" and "new" information, "new" information being the element receiving the heaviest stress. "Given" information is characterized (1967) as "that which has been talked about." Thematization, on the other hand, is concerned with the distribution of "theme" and "rheme," the "theme" being "what is being talked about, the point of departure for the clause as a message" (1968:212).

For both writers it is important to distinguish the information held in common by the speaker and hearer from information which is used to frame or develop the text. The critical difference between the approaches to information distribution offered by Daneš and Halliday and that presented here lies in their relative utility for actual text analysis. The following text fragments can be used to illustrate the differences.

(9) Text fragment II: from a Detroit-Boston hockey game (Tomlin 1983)

...Firing it out to center ice, here's John Wensink and Reed Larsen digging after it. *It's picked up by McNab.* McNab tried to send it back, but he's checked by Reed Larsen. Knocked it away from Cashman, *picked it up a second time*, a nifty move in the corner to play it over the left side to Maloney. Danny Maloney. Tried to work by Park, but couldn't do it...

(10) Text fragment III: from a New York-New York hockey game (Tomlin 1983)

...Down into the Ranger zone. Coming back for it is Don Awrey. Teams changing on the fly. Awrey at his own blue line. Got it to Vickers. Vickers takes the turn at the line. Out on the right wing side to Vadnais. Vadnais handed it right to Nystrom. Bob Nystrom back to Persson. Persson up the left side ahead of Bourne. Bourne brings it

around the defence right it. Shoots! Blocked by
Thomas and the rebound came off the stick of
Vickers...

These two fragments are typical of the play-by-play
reporting of the movement of the puck down the ice during a
hockey game. In the behavioral situation, the puck (ideally)
is passed from offensive player to offensive player in an
attempt to get open in order to shoot the puck into the goal
net. The defense attempts to interfere with this either by
intercepting the puck or by checking (blocking with one's
body) the player controlling the puck.

Rather than provide a complete analysis of each
fragment, let us consider instead one alternation in the text
fragments. Consider the two clauses in context underlined in
(9). In the one case there is a passive clause with agent,
in the other case the same behavioral event is reported by an
active clause with the same predicate. The question to
consider is why the one case is a passive and the other an
active.

It is not entirely clear, but it seems that an analysis
using either Daneš or Halliday would identify the four
nuclear NPs as "given" information: all four NPs have been
previously identified in the text (including prior text).
Therefore, either the alternation is random or it is
conditioned by some other factor.

If one examines the passive clause, one can ask what the
theme of the clause is. Under a Daneš-type of analysis, the
theme is what the utterance is about; under a Halliday-type
of analysis, it is what is being talked about. Is the
utterance in the first clause about the puck or about McNab
or about a picking-up event? In the second clause the same
questions can be asked: is the utterance about the puck,
Larsen, or a picking-up event? In one sense the answer is
clear; in the passive clause the sentence seems to be about
the puck, in the active clause the sentence is about Larsen.
It may be the case that Larsen is the theme of the active
clause because this clause is the second of a string that
describes the actions of Larsen. But such a determination is
not possible for the passive clause. In these cases it seems
that the specification of the theme for each clause is
dependent upon the experience or intuition of the analyst.
But having identified the theme of each clause, it seems
reasonable to propose that the alternation between the active
and the passive is determined by some sort of rule that
places the theme in the subject.

The analysis of these fragments offered in Tomlin (1983)
results in what is basically the "same" analysis. However,
the route to the analysis is much more explicit. As with the
Daneš and Halliday approaches, all four NPs are identified as
"given"; that is, they are determined to be shared

information for the announcer and the hearer (the analyst) in that the examination of the videotaped events showed that the referents were all identifiable to both announcer and hearer.

The determination of what information is more thematic and which is less thematic is likewise explicit. As discussed above, it is possible to construct independently or any particular text a hierarchy of thematic information for use in the analysis of play-by-play descriptions of bringing the puck down the ice.

(11) player in > puck > player > other
    control of   without
    puck   puck

Turning to the two clauses, one can quickly see that in the first clause the reference to the puck contains information that is more thematic than that in the reference to McNab (who has not had any control of the puck). In the second clause, the reference to Larsen is more thematic than the reference to the puck, because Larsen has had control of the puck. The alternation of the clauses can be explained by a hypothesis that states that more thematic information will occur in syntactic subject.

The difference between this last analysis and the kind of analysis one can produce using the Daneš or Halliday definitions is primarily a difference in explicitness. The thematic information hierarchy, while linked to the text, is established independently of the text through an understanding of the behavioral situation. Thus, the determination of what is more thematic information can proceed independently of any cues from the syntax. One might suspect that the identification of the theme in the first analysis was due as much to the fact that the analyst was influenced by his naive knowledge of English syntax (that syntactic subject tends to hold "theme") than by the clarity of the definitions in either Daneš (1970a) or Halliday (1967, 1968a).

The point of this section, however, has not been to criticize Daneš or Halliday. Their work has obviously influenced the approach offered here. Rather, this section illustrates what is meant by TI and what is involved in this approach in general. This has been done in part by briefly examining several text fragments and in part by contrasting the present offering with similar predecessors.

ARGUMENTATION FOR THE TFP

The Theme First Principle, or TFP, is formally stated in (12):

(12) The Theme First Principle: in clauses information
that is relatively more thematic precedes
information that is less so.

Given the discussion of TI in the previous section, the
principle should need little further discussion. Basically,
it is a small refinement of the common working assumption
that "old" information precedes "new" information. The TFP,
however, is somewhat more precise in that the identification
of what is more thematic has been made more explicit, and
thus the principle is subject to more rigorous empirical
testing. Further, since a distinction has been made between
TI as opposed to SI, the claim embodied in the TFP is a
narrower one than that embodied in the claim that "old"
precedes "new," where no such distinction is made.
    The nature of the evidence to support the TFP is simple.
It must be demonstrated that in a diverse set of languages
the unmarked distribution of information is such that
information that is more thematic tends to precede
information that is less thematic. It is necessary to
restrict the permissible data to the unmarked cases of
information distribution in order to eliminate certain
rule-produced "counterevidence." For instance, if it is
demonstrated that the unmarked distribution of information in
English is consistent with the TFP, certain marked
clauses--those with heavy primary stress on the initial
element--would appear to be counterevidence. However, since
the distribution of such clauses is both limited and
reasonably predictable--they occur primarily in contrastive
environments--they seem not to be so much genuine exception
as rule-governed exception which can be explained.
    The nature of the counterevidence for the TFP is
likewise simple. For the TFP to be invalidated as one of the
major forces that shape the grammars of natural languages, it
must be demonstrated in a diverse set of languages that the
unmarked distribution of information is something other than
more thematic information preceding less thematic. Thus,
either less thematic information must generally precede more
thematic information or the distribution must be random.
    The basic argument that will be used here to support the
TFP is as follows. In particular languages one can observe a
tendency for more thematic information to precede less in
simple main clauses. It seems that in almost every case
examined--both directly and symptomatically--more thematic
information does precede less thematic. The TFP is
represents a generalization about this general distribution
of information in languages. Failure to make such a
generalization embodies the (at least implicit) claim that
the observed pattern of distribution of information in
natural languages is accidental. But the TFP claims that the
general linear distribution of information is not accidental,

and predicts that newly discovered or newly examined languages stand a significant chance of having more thematic information precede less thematic information in simple main clauses.

EVIDENCE FOR THE TFP

Direct Evidence for the TFP.

This section presents a limited amount of direct evidence for the TFP. The studies described involve the direct manipulation of attention in discourse comprehension or the direct identification of thematic information in text data. Thematic information so identified is then correlated with syntactic structure to reveal a general tendency for thematic information to come earlier in the sentence or clause. The principal limitation of the present studies is that they deal exclusively with English.

Tomlin and Kellogg (1986) investigate the function of preposed information in procedural discourse by having subjects perform mapping tasks under differing attentional primes. Subjects were asked to map letters onto colored boxes in response to oral commands either of the form "Put the E in the blue box" or "In the blue box put the E". Subjects were placed into two groups, which were given different attention priming instructions. One group was primed to think about letters by being told that their global task was to manipulate letters and that their specific task was to manipulate a particular set of letters; no mention of boxes occurred. The other group was primed to think about colored boxes by being told that their global task was to manipulate boxes and that their specific task was to manipulate a particular set of colored boxes. Thus, the first group had their attention oriented toward letters, and the second group had their attention oriented toward boxes.

If thematic information serves to frame the ensuing discourse by orienting the attention of the hearer, and if initial position is a primary syntactic code for doing this, then one would expect there might be differing performance on a letter to box matching task, if the form of instructions given were sometimes compatible with and sometimes incompatible with the original attentional priming. Consider (13):

(13)   Mapping experiment

	TASK PRIMING	
	Toward BOXES	Toward LETTERS
Put the E in the blue box.	Incompatible	Compatible
FORM		
In the blue box put the E.	Compatible	Incompatible

If the locative expression occurs at the end of the sentence, then its placement is incompatible with attention to the mapping task oriented toward locations, or boxes. But if the locative expression is preposed, then its placement is compatible with an orientation towards boxes and incompatible with an orientation towards letters. In trying to map letters onto boxes subjects should, if order is connected to attention, perform the mapping task more quickly or more accurately when the form of the linguistic expression is compatible with the task priming they received than if it is not. The results of the experiment show that this is exactly the case. Subjects performed more quickly and more accurately when given instructions compatible with their task orientation than when given incompatible instructions. Thus, to the extent that thematic information does reflect attention allocation in discourse production and comprehension, this experiment provides direct evidence that earlier ordering of thematic information facilitates comprehension while later ordering inhibits it.

Tomlin (1983) investigates the function of syntactic subject in English. This paper argues that the function of syntactic subject in English is a dual one: it codes as its primary function clause level thematic information and as a secondary function the semantic role of agent. What this means is that when two NPs compete for the subject relation the one which is more thematic always wins. If, however, the relative thematic rankings of the two competing NPs are equal, then subject codes its secondary function, agent.

The evidence for this derives from the analysis of sixteen hours of transcripts taken of ice hockey play-by-play discourse. These texts were analyzed following the procedure outlined in (4) above . Each text was initially divided into relevant structural units. In the case of hockey play-by-play the primary unit was the description of the action of **bringing the puck down the ice** or **shooting on goal**, both principal event types occurring in hockey action.

Next, the goal of hockey play-by-play was determined to be to provide an accurate description of the events unfolding on the ice. It specifically is not to evaluate the play or to provide history or background in which to construe the play. Only discourse which meets the goal of play-by-play was considered.

Third, all of the available referents were isolated in the transcribed passages.

Fourth, for each passage the referents were competitively ranked in terms of their placement on a hierarchy of attentional importance. In hockey play-by-play, for the action of **bringing the puck down the ice**, there are two principal centers of attention: the puck and the players. The puck is a center of attention because without it there is no game at all and when it leaves the rink the game stops. The players are a center of attention because they are the ones that move the puck around thereby producing the game, and because the spectators want to know who performed well, who poorly, and so on. These centers of attention are not linguistic but behavioral. Even naive viewers will follow the puck (when they can see it) and the players around it.

Since both the announcer and the viewers find their attention focused in essentially the same way, the announcer uses those general centers of attention to frame his particular description of the action on the ice. While attention to the players is an important feature of viewing hockey action, it is not as important as following the puck. Everyone--the announcers, the audience, the cameras, even the players--follows the puck around the rink. The course of the puck determines the outcome of the games. Sometimes, however, a particular player takes control of the puck. When this happens the two centers of attention coincide for a while. Thus, if one were to set up a working hierarchy of TI for play-by-play descriptions, of bringing the puck down the ice, references to a player controlling the puck would be more thematic than references to other things. Since attention to the puck is the primary center of attention, references to the puck, while less thematic than references to a player controlling the puck, will be more thematic than references to a player without the puck. These, in turn, will be more thematic than references to other things. This particular working hierarchy of TI then can be summarized as in (14):

(14)   player in   >   puck   >   player   >   other
       control of   without
       puck   puck

With such a hierarchy one can go to any particular text and determine the manner in which TI is distributed, how it is treated syntactically, and what syntactic, semantic, or pragmatic factors correlate with it.

51

While the evidence in both these studies is restricted to English and therefore cannot really be generalized across languages without replication, it does constitute strong direct evidence for the TFP. And, since the description of the TFP is grounded in cognitive processes of attention in discourse production and comprehension, and since there is little reason to expect those processes to be drastically different among human beings, it is reasonable to speculate that replication of the above studies with speakers of other languages would yield similar results.

Symptomatic Evidence for the TFP

This section presents data from independent syntactic domains which individually and collectively support the TFP as described above. The domains of data include the examination of constraints on movement rules, constraints on the position of independent pronominal elements, as well as a class of discourse conditioned rules.

Constraints on Movement Rules

These data comprise the primary symptomatic argument for the TFP. There are some movement rules which can move around any sort of NP, definite or indefinite. However, there are other movement rules which are restricted in their ability to move NPs. Some movement rules in some languages are constrained to some degree to moving only definite (or generic) NPs. Other movement rules in some languages are constrained to moving only indefinite NPs. The distribution of these rules is constrained in a manner consistent with the TFP.

The diagram in (15) represents the distribution of movement rules as evidenced in part by the data below. The cells in the diagram represent the logical possibilities for movement rules. The horizontal dimension represents the two directions an element may move: toward the beginning of a sentence (left), or toward the end of a sentence (right). The vertical dimension contains the possible combinations of definite and indefinite. As one can easily see, for two of the cells there is a positive correlation between definiteness and the direction of movement. In addition, two of the cells are empty.

(15) Distribution of movement rules.

	LEFT DEFINITE	RIGHT INDEFINITE
DEFINITE	YES	NO
INDEFINITE	NO	YES

A principle like the TFP is needed to account for the correlations and for the empty cells. As (15) illustrates, if a language has a movement rule which is restricted to definite NPs only, then that rule will move the NP toward the beginning of the sentence. There is in general no movement rule which moves an NP toward the beginning of a sentence which requires that the element moved be indefinite only. Conversely, if a language has a movement rule which is restricted to moving indefinite NPs only, then that rule will move those indefinite NPs toward the end of the sentence. There is no movement rule which moves an element to the end of a sentence which is restricted to moving definite NPs only.

The approach to the distribution of information embodied in the TFP is supported well by these observations. If an NP represent TI, it will tend to be definite. Thus, a rule restricted to definites is likely to move such NPs to the place where TI belongs. Further, since most of these rules are traditionally described as optional, some factor other than their definiteness must condition the application of the rule at a level higher than the sentence. Similarly, a rule restricted to indefinites is more likely to move such NPs toward the end of a sentence, since indefinite NPs tend not to be TI and will not be treated syntactically as such.

The data is presented below, divided into two classes: rules which move only definites left, and rules which move only indefinites right.

Movement rules which move only definite NPs leftward
The first cases are cases in which the alternations necessary to demonstrate the restrictions conclusively were available.

Indonesian (Chung 1976). In Indonesian there is a secondary passivization rule Chung names Object Preposing which restricts the NPs promoted and moved to definite NPs. Attempts to use Object Preposing with indefinite NPs result in ungrammatical sentences:

(16) dokter   itu   saja   periksa
     doctor   the   1sg   examined
     The doctor, I examined.
(17) *medja   saja   pegang
      table   1sg   touch

A table, I touched.

(18) *seorang   laki   saja   akanbunuh
     human   man   1sg   fut-kill
     A man, I will kill.

In addition, Chung observes that there is a left-dislocation rule with the same restriction:

(19) anak   itu   dia   mem-beli   sepatu
     child   the   2sg   act-buy   shoes
     The child, he bought shoes (for).
(20) *anak   dia   mem-beli   sepatu
     child   2sg   act-buy   shoes
     A child, he bought shoes (for).

Indonesian also has an ordinary passive. This transformation promotes an object to subject, with the result that the former object moves leftward. This rule is also restricted to definite NPs:

(21) Ali   mem-beli   buku
     Ali   act-buy   book
     Ali buys a book.
(22) Ali   mem-beli   buku   itu
     Ali   act-buy   book   def
     Ali buys the book.
(23) buku   itu   di-beli   Ali
     book   def   is bought   Ali
     The book is bought by Ali.
(24) *buku   di-beli   Ali
     book (indef) is bought by Ali
     A book is bought by Ali.

English. Left-dislocation is restricted to definite NPs:

(25) His father, Tom respects him.
(26) The beans, they're in the third aisle.
(27) *A newspaper, John wants to read it/one.

Tough-movement is also restricted to definite NPs (or generic NPs) (Morgan 1968, Lasnik and Fiengo 1974):

(28) That assignment was hard to do.
(29) *An assignment was hard to do.
(30) My dog is easy to train.
(31) *A dog is easy to train. (non-generic reading)

Passivization, strictly speaking, is not restricted to definite NPs, but there is still a strong tendency for the NP in subject to be definite. Sentences with indefinite NPs preceding definite ones are less preferred:

(32) A stranger cut down the old oak.
(33) The old oak was cut down by a stranger.
(34) The stranger cut down an old oak.
(35) ?An old oak was cut down by the stranger.

Thai. In Thai there is a rule which fronts NPs which also severely restricts the NPs fronted to definite NPs. NPs are usually not marked for definiteness or indefiniteness. Thus, the sentences in (36) and (37) can occur in a text in which the object NP is either shared information or non-shared information:

(36)	khon	níi	kàt	mǎa
	man	this	bite	dog
	This man bit		a	dog.
				the

(37)	dèk	khon	nán	hěn	nǎŋsʉ̌ʉ
	child	class	that	see	book
	That child saw the book.				
			a		

However, if the object is moved before the subject, the only possible reading is one in which the object is either definite or generic:

(38)	mǎa	khon	níi	kàt
	dog	man	this	bit
	The dog, this man bit.			

(39)	nǎŋsʉ̌ʉ	dèk	khon	nán	hěn
	book	child	class	that	see
	The book that child saw (it).				

It is possible in Thai to more fully specify an NP. An NP that occurs with a demonstrative will always be definite; an NP can be made overtly indefinite by quantifying it with the number 'one' /nʉŋ/. Though such sentences occur less frequently than those in (36) - (37), they exhibit overtly the restriction described above:

(40)	khon	níi	kàt	mǎa	tua	nán
	man	this	bite	dog	class	that
	This man bit that dog.					

(41)	mǎa	tua	nán	khon	níi	kàt
	dog	class	that	man	this	bit
	That dog, this man bit.					

(42)	khon	níi	kàt	mǎa	tua	nʉŋ
	man	this	bit	dog	class	one

(43)*?	mǎa	tua	nʉŋ	khon	níi	kàt
	dog	class	one	man	this	bit
	A dog, this man bit.					

Bitransitive clauses in Thai. The most common way to construct bitransitive clauses in Thai is with a serial verb construction as in (44). It is also possible with a limited set of verbs, including /hây/ 'give,' to use a construction like that in (45):

(44) khon   ʔau   nǎŋsʉ̌ʉ   hây   dèk
     man   take   book   give   child
     The man gave the book to the child.

(45) khon   hây   nǎŋsʉ̌ʉ   dèk
     man   give   book   child
     The man gave the book to the child.

It is possible to prepose either the object or the indirect object in either case, but as (46) - (55) illustrate, the fronted NP must still be definite:

(46) khon   níi   ʔau   nǎŋsʉ̌ʉ   lêm   níi
     man   this   take   book   class   this
     hây   dèk   khon   nán
     give   child   class   that
     This man gave this book to that child.

(47) nǎŋsʉ̌ʉ   lêm   níi   khon   níi   ʔau   hây
     book   class this   man   this   take   give
     dèk   khon   nán
     child class that
     This book, this man gave to that child.
     [definite object has been fronted]

(48) dèk   khon   nán   khon   níi   ʔau   nǎŋsʉ̌ʉ
     child   class   that   man   this   take   book
     lêm   níi   hây
     class   this   gave
     That child, this man gave this book to.
     [definite indirect object fronted]

(49) *ʔnǎŋsʉ̌ʉ lêm   nɯŋ   khon   níi   ʔau
     book   class one   man   this   take
     hây   dèk   khon   nán
     give   child class that
     *A book, this man gave to that child.
     [indefinite object fronted]

(50) *ʔdèk   khon   nɯŋ   khon   níi   ʔau   nǎŋ sʉ̌ʉ
     child class one   man   this   take   book
     lêm   níi   hây
     class   this   give
     *A child, this man gave that book to.
     [indefinite indirect object fronted]

(51) khon   hây   nǎŋsʉ̌ʉ lêm   níi   dèk
     man   give   book   class this   child
     khon   nán

56

```
            class   that
            The man gave this book to that child.
  (52)  năŋsúɯɯ  lêm    níi     khon    hây    dèk
         book    class  this    man     give   child
         khon    nán
         class   that
         This book, the man gave to the child.
            [definite object fronted]
  (53)  dèk    khon    nán    khon   hây   năŋsúɯɯ
         child class   that   man    give  book
         lêm    níi
         class this
         That child, the man gave this book to.
            [definite indirect object fronted]
  (54) *?năŋsúɯɯ lêm   nɯŋ    khon   hây   dèk
         book    class one    man    give  child
         khon    nán
         class   that
         A book the man gave to that child.
            [indefinite object fronted]
  (55)*?dèk   khon    nɯŋ    khon   hây   năŋsúɯɯ
         child class   one    man    give  book
         lêm    níi
         class  this
         A child the man gave the book to.
            [indefinite indirect object fronted]
```

Kinyarwanda (Kimenyi 1976). Kimenyi reports that all
subjects in Kinyarwanda must be definite (1976:258). Since
Kinyarwanda is an SVO language, all transformations that
promote non-subjects to subject will move such an NP leftward
and will be restricted to definite NPs only. In particular
Kimenyi states that passivization is restricted to definite
objects only; indefinite or unspecified objects cannot be
passivized (1976:259).

```
  (56)  umwaána    a-ra-som-a            igitabo
         child      3sg-pres-read-asp    book
         The child is reading the book.
  (57)  igitabo    cyi-ra-som-w-a          n'úmwaána
         book       it-pres-read-pass-asp   by-child
```

Haya (Byarushengo and Tenenbaum 1976). Haya is a Lake Bantu
language with basic SVO order. Definite objects (both direct
and indirect) are distinguished from indefinite objects by
the presence of an object agreement clitic in the verbal
complex. Definite objects have them; indefinite objects do
not. There is a left-dislocation rule which can move objects
NPs to pre-verbal position. The NPs so moved must be
definite; that is, there must be an object agreement clitic
in the verbal complex:

(58) abakázi   ba-gi-mu-cumb-il-a
      women   they-it-him-cook-app-md
      kakûlw'   énkôko
      kakulu   chicken
      The women cook chicken for Kakulu.
(59) abakázi *kakûlw'* ba-gi-*mu*-cumb-il-a énkôko
(60) *abakázi *kakûlw'* ba-gi-Ø-cumb-il-a énkôko

Givón (1975) and (1976) report similar constraints in other Bantu languages, Rwanda and Swahili. Mould (1974) also reports this constraint for Lugunda. Horton (1949) reports it for Luvale.

The data presented in the cases above is critical for the establishment of the TFP. The particular alternations presented demonstrate quite clearly the explanatory power of the TFP. But there is an additional class of data that can be presented. This data, presented below, is data consistent with the TFP, but for which the alternations are not available necessary to demonstrate convincingly the need for the TFP. Such data can be found in older grammars or in more recent work whose primary concern is focused on some other sort of problem. Therefore, though this class of data is offered with some reservation for it is not conclusive, yet it remains consistent with the TFP.

Wappo (Li and Thompson 1976a). Wappo has SOV for its basic constituent order, but other orders are possible. In particular, an object can be fronted if it is "focused." Every case of "focused" elements presented involve definite NPs:

(61) ce   šaw-i   lakhuh   nuh-khe?
      that bread-subj   focus   steal-pass
      It's the bread that got stolen.
(62) ?ah   lakhuh   ce   naw-ta?
      1sg   focus   that   see-past
      It's I who saw that.
(63) ce   chica   ?ah   t'a-ta?
      that bear   1sg   kill-past
      That bear, I killed.
(64) [ce   k'ew   chica-ta-ta?]   ?ah   hatiskhi?
      [that man   bear kill-past] 1sg   know
      I know that the man killed the bear.

Gude (Hoskison 1975). The basic order of elements in the Gude clause is VSO (Hoskison 1975:228). There is a left-dislocation rule in Gude which permits the fronting of any constituent if it has been "pre-mentioned." The fronted

constituent is followed by a functional pause and may be
precede by a 'topic' marker /ma/. All of the cases presented
are consistent with the TFP.

> (65) agi   bələ-n nə john tə bwaya   ndzii
>   aspect kill- sm john   leopard now
>   John is killing a leopard now.
>
> (66) (ma) john (-a), agi bələ-n nə ci tə
>   john   asp kill- sm he
>   bwaya   ndzii
>   leopard now
>   John, he is killing the leopard now.
>
> (67) (ma) bwaya   (-a), agi bələ-n nə john tə
>   leopard   asp kill- sm john
>   ci   ndzii
>   he   now
>   The leopard, John is killing it now.

Mokilese (Harrison 1976). Like many other languages,
Mokilese has a left-dislocation rule which fronts various NPs
and leaves a pronoun copy behind. Though Harrison does not
explicitly state that this rule is restricted to definite
NPs, all of the cases he presents involve definite NPs:

> (68) nihra jerimweinno, ara kadarla ih pohnpei
>   their son   they sent   him Ponape
>   Their son, they sent him to Ponape.
>
> (69) woalmeno,   ngoah   kiahki
>   that man,   I   don't like
>   That man, I don't like.
>
> (70) bob,   ih   kin   poki   pahioahu
>   Bob,   he   beats his   wife
>   Bob, he beats his wife.

Hausa (Jaggar 1978). Jaggar provides a detailed discussion
of Hausa and a left-dislocation process in Hausa. Like the
Mokilese case, all of the data provided involve definite NPs
only:

> (71) yâaraa suh   kai   wà   muusaa   kaayaa
>   boy   they took to   Musa   loads
>   The boy took the loads to Musa.
>
> (72) yâarân (dai), suh   kai wà muusaa kaayaa
>   boys   they took to Musa   loads
>   The boys, they took the loads to Musa.
>
> (73) muusaa (dai), suh dai màsa   kaayaa
>   Musa   they took to him loads
>   Musa, they took the loads to him.
>
> (74) kaayân (dua), yâaraa suh dai wà muusaa suu
>   loads   boys   they took to Musa   them
>   The loads, the boys took them to Musa.

Movement rules which move only indefinite NPs rightward

French (Perlmutter and Postal 1975). There is a rule in
French which replaces an indefinite subject with a dummy *il*
and moves the former subject to clause final position. The
NP moved is necessarily indefinite:

(75)	trois	femmes	ont	étés	tuées
	three	women	have	been	killed

Three women have been killed.

(76)	il	a	été	tué	trois	femmes
	it	has	been	killed	three	women

Three women have been killed.

(77)	*il	a	été	tué	les trois femmes	que	vous
	it	has	been	killed	the three women	that	you
	avez	vues
	have	seen

English. *There*-insertion moves a subject NP to postverbal
position and replaces the former subject with the dummy
there. The NP moved must be indefinite:

(78) There's a man in the garage.
(79) *There's the man in the garage.

Lithuanian. There is a movement rule in Lithuanian which
moves an indefinite subject to the right of the verb. No
dummy replaces the former subject. But in this case, too,
the NP moved must be indefinite:

(80)	žmogus	yra	sode
	person	be	in garden

Someone is in the garden.

(81)	yra	žmogus	sode
	be	person	in garden

There is someone in the garden.

(82)	tas	žmogus	yra	sode
	that	person	be	in garden

That person is in the garden.

(83)	*yra	tas	žmogus	sode
	be	that	person	in the garden

German (Breckenridge 1975). Breckenridge discusses a rule
in German she calls *es*-insertion. When *es*-insertion applies,
a subject is moved to the end of a clause and a dummy *es*
replaces it. The NP moved must be indefinite:

(84)	es	steurte	sie	eine	böse	Hexe bei
	it	contributed	them	a	wicked	witch

A wicked witch contributed them.

(85) es   weden   hier   Schuhe   repariert
     it   become   here   shoes   repaired
     Shoes are repaired here.
(86)*es stieß ihn der Soldat von der Brücke
     it pushed him the soldier off the bridge

Chinese (Li and Thompson 1976c). Li and Thompson report that, with some qualifications, it is the case that in Chinese an NP that occurs before the verb will be interpreted as definite while an NP that occurs after the verb will be interpreted as indefinite.

(87) rén   lái   le
     people   come   asp
     The people have come.
(88) lái   rén   le
     come   people   asp
     Some people have come.
(89) háizi   děi   tàng   yifu
     child   must   iron   clothes
     The child must iron clothes.
(90) yifu   háizi   děi   tàng
     clothes   child   must   iron
     The child must iron the clothes.

Russian (Li and Thompson 1976c). The same article reports that it is also the case in Russian that an NP before the verb is interpreted as definite while an NP after the verb is interpreted as indefinite:

(91) v   komnate   drovaty
     in   room   bed
     In the room is a bed.
(92) krovaty   v   komnate
     bed   in   room
     The bed is in the room.
(93) v   komnate   vošla   ženščina
     in   room   came   woman
     Into the room came a woman.
(94) ženščina   vošla   v   komnatu
     woman   came   in   room
     The woman came into the room.

Right-Dislocations. There does exist one class of transformations which are exceptional to the observation that in general there are no rightward movement rules restricted only to definite NPs. This is the class of Right-Dislocations. In English, Right-Dislocation moves an

NP to the end of a sentence, and leaves a pronominal copy in the NP's original position. The NP moved is usually definite:

(95) My brother bought a Rabbit.
(96) He bought a Rabbit, my brother.
(97) A man was here to see you last night.
(98)??He was here to see you last night, a man.

This rule, then, stands as an exception to the observation in (15) that there are no movement rules restricted primarily to definite NPs which move the NP to the end of a sentence. It can be shown, however, that though this may be the case, Right-Dislocation in English is not a counterexample to the TFP.

In order to demonstrate this it must be shown that the function of Right-Dislocation is something other than to move TI to the end of a sentence. The primary function of Right-Dislocation seems to be to self-correct potentially defective texts. One way in which a text can fail is for the speaker to assume incorrectly that the way he refers to some entity will serve for the hearer to identify the entity when in fact it will not. Thus, in the actual text fragment below, the speaker used the phrase *that book* to refer to a particular book the experience of which he believed he shared with the hearer. Since this phrase was not sufficient for the hearer to pick out the intended referent, the text breaks down for a moment, and the hearer initiates a side sequence to repair the text. After the repair is completed, the text continues:

(99) Text Fragment IV.
    a B: ...D brought me *that book*. It's really good.
      A: Which one?
      B: It's called "How to Survive the Loss of a
          Love."
      A: Oh ya.
      B: It's really good.

This same text could have been repaired by the speaker himself. At point a, had he anticipated the possible failure of the phrase that book to identify the intended referent, he could have self-corrected the text by uttering:

(100) ...D brought me that book, "How to Survive the
      Loss of a Love."

This would have accomplished the same thing that the side sequence did. The frequency of Right-Dislocations may be attributable to the preference of speakers to self-correct faulty texts (Schegloff, Jefferson, and Sacks 1977, Moerman 1977).

Further, the use of Right-Dislocation is not restricted in any way to NPs which represent TI. It is restricted primarily to the domain of shared and non-shared information. That is, the use of Right-Dislocation is conditioned primarily by the anticipation of a failure to identify some referent, not with a failure to see the connection of that referent to the goal of the text. Only if the latter were true would Right-Dislocation have anything to do directly with TI.

In addition, there are at least three sentence level syntactic constraints that demonstrate that the function of Right-Dislocation is different from the function of either Topicalization or Left-Dislocation (which tend to deal with TI), and that it is the same as hearer-initiated side sequence. The first constraint involves the use of the phrase *I mean*. In the hypothetical text fragment presented in (101), the hearer-initiated side sequence *Who?* can be ended by the speaker's reply *John, I mean*.

(101) A: He came over again last night.
       B: Who?
       A: John, I mean.
       B: Oh, I see.

The phrase *I mean* can just as easily be appended to the end of a Right-Dislocation that serves the same function. Notice also that the phrase cannot be appended (with the same meaning) to a non-Right-Dislocated sentence:

(102) John came over again last night.
(103) He came over again last night, John, I mean.
(104) ?John came over again last night, I mean.

Further, *I mean* cannot be used with Topicalization and Left- Dislocation:

(105) *John, I mean, he came over again last night.
(106) *My brother, I mean, my father doesn't like him.

The second constraint involves the use of the phrase *that is*. If the functions of Right and Left Dislocations were the same, then each should be able to take the same parenthetical qualifiers. But *that is* can only occur with Right-Dislocations:

(107) He came over again last night, John that is.

(108) I just can't stand them, the Smiths that is.
(109) *John that is, he came over again last night.
(110) *My brother that is, my father doesn't like him.

The final constraint involves the use of the phrase you know /yənó/. This phrase can be used after the fronted NP in a Left-Dislocation or Topicalization, but not after the dislocated NP in a Right-Dislocation:

(111) John, you know, he came over again last night.
(112) My brother, you know, my father doesn't like him.
(113) *He came over again last night, John you know.
(114) *I just can't stand them, the Smiths you know.

The discussion of the syntactic constraints on Right-versus Left-Dislocation challenges the hypothesis that both rules have an essentially similar function. The comparison of the Right-Dislocation has nothing to do directly with TI. Thus, the function of Right-Dislocation in English is not to move TI to the end of a sentence.

Therefore, while Right-Dislocation in English is exceptional to the observation presented in (15), it is clearly not a counterexample to the claim embodied by the TFP. It remains to be seen whether Right-Dislocations in other languages have a similar function. Byarushengo and Haya (1976) report the function of Right-Dislocation in Haya to be similar to that described for English, for instance. Let it stand as a prediction that in any language sensitive in other respects to the TFP, any right-movement rule involving only, or primarily, definite NPs will not have a function that deals directly with TI, and that one likely function for such rules is to self-correct potentially defective texts.

The Position of Independent Pronominal Elements

This section presents data which demonstrate that independent pronominal elements in diverse languages are either permitted or required to take an earlier position in a sentence than are nominal NPs in corresponding sentences. This observation (though stated somewhat differently) was first made by Greenberg (1966) in his Universal 25:

(115) Universal 25: If the pronominal object follows the
       verb, so does the nominal object (Greenberg
       1966:91).

Further, it can be inferred from the data below that there are likely to be few languages in which an independent pronoun must take a position later in a sentence than a nominal NP in a corresponding sentence.

It must be made clear that only pronominal elements which occur as independent words at the sentence level are considered here. Purposely excluded are clitic pronouns which are bound to the verb stem, as occur for instance in Persian or Spanish. These are not sentence level constituents and thus are not relevant for the analysis of sentence level phenomena.

The first set of data includes those cases in which pronominal elements obligatorily take an earlier position in a sentence or clause than do nominal elements in corresponding sentences.

Norwegian (Haga 1976). Norwegian, an SVO language, has a minor movement rule Haga names Light-Pronoun Shift. This rule obligatorily moves an object pronoun over an adverbial into post-verbal position.

> (116) Winston utbedret visst skaden ved dugnad
> Winston repaired "I think" the damage through volunteer work
> Winston repaired the damage through volunteer work.
> (117) Winston utbedret den visst ved dugnad
> Winston repaired it I think through volunteer work.
> Winston repaired it I think through volunteer work.
> (118) *Winston utbedret visst den ved dugnad

Welsh (Awbery 1976). The basic constituent order in Welsh is VSO. In simple sentences the position of nominal and pronominal object is the same:

> (119) gwelodd   y   dyn   gi
> saw   the   man   dog
> The man saw a dog.
> (120) gwelodd   y   dyn   ef
> saw   the   man   it
> The man saw it.

However, the inflected form of the verb in the simple sentences is not able to carry all combinations of tense and aspect. To express these other combinations of tense and aspect, a different verb form, what Awbery calls the periphrastic form, is used. In the periphrastic form of a sentence an inflected form of the verb *to be* is followed by the subject, then by an aspect marker, then by the main verb in an uninflected form and finally by the nominal object (Awbery 1976:13):

> (121) mae'r   dyn   wedi   gweld   y   ci

```
is      man    after   see      the  dog
The man has seen the dog.
```

When the object is pronominal, however, it must precede the uninflected main verb:

```
(122)  mae'r   dyn    wedi    ei     weld     (ef)
       is      man    after   his    seeing   (him)
       The man has seen him.
(123) *mae'r   dyn    wedi    gweld   ef
       is      man    after   see     him
```

Ila (Smith 1907). The basic constituent order of Ila is SVO, when the object is nominal. When the object is pronominal, the order is SOV.

Karen (Jones 1961). Jones reports that in Karen a pronominal object always precedes other objects.

Masai (Greenberg 1963). With nominal subject and object the word order in Masai can be either VSO or VOS. But when the object is pronominal, the order is obligatorily VOS.

The second set of data is like the first except that the restriction is not absolute. That is, the pronominal element may occur more toward the beginning of a sentence or clause than the nominal element, but does not have to.

Yidiñ (Dixon 1977). While there is no absolute constraint on the position of pronominal elements relative to that of nominal ones, Dixon observes that the order of constituents is affected in part by a preference for pronouns to come "as near as possible to the beginning of a sentence" (1977:268). He observes further that a pronominal object is less likely to occur post-verbally than a nominal object. A nominal dative NP usually follows the verb, but a pronominal dative is found before the verb more frequently than after it. And, a pronominal dative will often precede a pronominal object.

```
(124)  ŋundu    gana    ŋanda    guman     wiwin
       you-SA-part      I-dat    one-abs   give-imp
       You give me (just) one (shell).
(125)  ŋanʸdʸi:nʸ bama:ɪ   guga:ɪ   mayi:gu
       us-acc     person   call     veg. food
       A man called us to eat vegetable food.
```

Hilagaynon (Wolfendon 1971:236-237). While all other nominals may be fronted by a rule of topicalization, nominal agents may not. But if an agent is pronominal, topicalization is permitted:

(126) ginkihad niya   ang ahos   sa lamesa
       sliced   by her the garlic at the table
       She sliced the garlic at the table.
       V S O Loc
(127) niya ginkihad ang ahos sa lamesa
       S V O Loc
(128) ang ahos ginkihad niya sa lamesa
       O V S Loc
(129) sa lamesa ginkihad niya ang ahos
       Loc V S O
(130) ginkihad ni puring ang ahos   sa lamesa
       sliced   by Puring the garlic at the table
       Puring sliced the garlic at the table.
(131) *ni Puring ginkihad ang ahos sa lamesa
(132) ang ahos ginkihad ni Puring sa lamesa
(133) sa lamesa ginkihad ni Puring ang ahos

The third set of data includes two cases in which the
rightward movement of independent pronominal elements is
constrained.

Kusaiean (Lee 1975). In Kusaiean the unmarked order for
predicate adjective constructions is S-V:

(134) mwet   sac   arulac   puhlaik
       man   the   very   brave
       The man is very brave.

With nominal NPs the alternate V-S order is possible:

(135) arulac   puhlaik   mwet   sac
       very   brave   man   the
       Very brave is the man.

But when the subject is pronominal, the inversion is
blocked:

(136) el   arulac   fuhng
       he   very   brave
       He is very brave.
(137) *arulac   fuhng   el
(138) nga   marsrinsracl
       I   hungry
       I am hungry.
(139) *marscrinsracl   nga

Tondano (Sneddon 1975). Tondano is basically VSO, and like
many other Austronesian languages, allows the two NP
constituents to be permuted. However, if the subject is
pronominal, the permutation is blocked. This is schematized
in (140):

67

(140) V S O   V O S
       nom   nom
       V S O   *V O S
       pro   pro

Discourse-Conditioned Syntax

This section presents data which demonstrate that certain
syntactic alternations in various languages are triggered by
discourse phenomena. In these cases the triggering is
constrained completely by the TFP.

English (Tomlin 1976). *Dative Movement.* Dative movement is
a transformation whi·h relates sentences like (141) to those
like (142):

(141) I gave the flowers to Mary.
(142) I gave Mary the flowers.

However, when the direct object is a pronoun, Dative
Movement is forbidden:

(143) *I gave Mary them.

These facts are consistent with the TFP, but not
necessarily compelling. Compelling evidence for the TFP
comes from examining the use of Dative Movement in
discourses. Native speakers prefer dative-moved sentences
embedded in paragraphs where the text prior to the
dative-moved sentence dealt with possible recipients.
Conversely, when prior text deals with objects for giving,
dative-moved sentences were not preferred (Tomlin 1976). Only
a discourse constraint on syntax like the TFP can capture the
underlying generalization in such data.

Particle Shift (Ross 1967). Particle Shift describes the
surface alternation in (144) and (145):

(144) Mary ate up her lunch.
(145) Mary ate her lunch up.

Here, too, there is a restriction when the object is
pronominal. But in this class of cases the rule applies
obligatorily. Failure to apply Particle Shift when the
object is pronominal results in ungrammatical sentences:

(146) Mary ate it up.
(147) *Mary ate up it.

Further, with indefinite nominal objects non-particle shifted sentences seem better than those in which Particle Shift has applied (though both are grammatical):

(148) ?Mary gobbled a whole turkey down.
(149) Mary gobbled down a whole turkey.

Kusaiean (Lee 1975). In Kusaiean there is a Dative-Movement-like rule that moves an indirect object before the direct object under unspecified conditions:

(150) el   tolma   pohl   sas   nuh   sihk
      he   threw   ball   the   to   me
      He threw the ball to me.

(151) el   tolma   nuh   sihk   pohl   sac
      he   threw   to   me   ball   the
      He threw me the ball.

(152) sogn el molelah nuknuk fohn se nuh sihk
      John he bought shirt the for me
      John bought the shirt for me.

(153) sohn el molelah nuh sihk nuknuk foh se
      John he bought for me   shirt the
      John bought for me the shirt.

But when the object is pronominal, this inversion is not permitted. Thus, while (154) is acceptable:

(154) Kuhn el sinuhkihn yuh nuh yohrohl ninac
      Kuhn he pushed   me to mother
      Kuhn pushed me to mother.

the inverted sentence is (155) is not:

(155) *kuhn el sinukihn nuh yohrohl ninac yuh.

Ngarinjn (Coate and Oates 1970). The basic constituent order of Ngarinjn is unclear; it is another possible OVS case, but the data concerning constituent order is unclear. However, this order is not relevant for the following discussion.
    Ngarinjn has a passive construction. If the passive agent is a proper noun, it follows the verb:

(156) bada   ŋawiŋga   Wattira
      hit   I-act-ref Watti-by
      I was hit by Watti.

But when the passive agent is a pronoun, it *precedes* the verb:

(157) miriŋun   andura   wondidj   birwiŋga

                    everything him-by   made   they-act-ref past
                    Everything was made by him.

Mokilese (Harrison 1976). In Mokilese, sentential
complements are commonly extraposed to the end of the
sentence:

    (158) kapwurramwei pwa ih pe   pwili sukuhl
           surprising   comp he still going school
           It is surprising that he is still going to
           school.
    (159) mwehu   pwa   arai   pirin   kijoudo
           good   comp   they   aux   coming
           It's good that they are coming.

Thus, it is not surprising that the nominalized complement of
an intransitive verb also tends to follow the verb:

    (160) dahrla   ah   kijou
           faster   his   running
           He ran faster.

However, when the nominalized complement refers to a definite
event (as signalled by the definite determiner), the
complement usually precedes the verb:

    (161) inenin pispis as   kodkod (Extraposed)
           very   quick his   husking
           He husks very quickly.
    (162) ah kodkod-do   inenin   pispis (not Extraposed)
           his husking-def very   quick
           That husking he did was very quick.

LIMITS ON THE TFP

The first limit is that the TFP is not presented as an
"absolute" language universal. Such 'universals' are
notoriously dubious as universals either because of a lack of
precision in their formulation or because of the relatively
easy establishment of counterevidence. The TFP is offered
here instead as one of three fundamental functional
principles that shape the grammars of natural languages. As
such, this principle may interact with others. The
interaction may result in the augmentation, reduction, or
elimination of the effect that the TFP has on the grammar of
some particular language (see the discussion of Ojibwa in
Chapter 6).
    The second limit involves the relation of TI to the
'subject' of basic constituent orders. It is very crucial to
make clear the manner in which TI and subject are related.
First, it is not being claimed that all subjects represent

TI, or that TI is always realized as subject. What is being claimed is that within the domain of objects examined in this volume (basic constituent orders), TI *coincides* with subject.

The justification for this comes primarily from Keenan and his work toward a universal definition of subject (Keenan 1976b). Several of his properties, particularly the definiteness property and the old information property, are directly translatable into terms consistent with the TFP. The subjects of basic constituent orders tend to be definite because TI tends to be definite and TI tends to come first. Old information in its more casual usage is a conflation of shared knowledge and TI.

However, TI is not a *property* of subjects, for such a statement needlessly conflates a semantic/pragmatic phenomenon with a syntactic device which may (or may not) encode it.

Now while TI is a not *property* of subjects (even in basic sentences), TI and subject do *correlate* in basic sentences (and thus in basic constituent orders). An example should make this clearer. Tomlin (1983) draws a distinction between two coding devices for English: initial position and syntactic subject. Initial position is identified by observing that there are significant alternations in English involving initial position (Topicalized versus non-Topicalized sentences, for instance). Syntactic subject is identified by observing significant alternations that pick out a unified class of NPs (passive versus non-passive or subject-verb agreement, for instance). Now if these two syntactic encoding devices are independent (as the discussion of their motivation would suggest), then it would be confusing to say that one "property" of "subject" was "initial position." Initial position is initial position; and subject is subject. However, the two do correlate strongly.

Another way to put this would be that not all initial NPs in English are subjects; neither are all subjects in English initial NPs. Thus, the two coding devices are independent. However, sometimes the NP which is in initial position is the same NP that is the syntactic subject. In such a case the two independent coding devices would coincide.

Framing the relation between TI and subject in terms of correlation instead of properties enables one to avoid a difficulty raised by Schachter (1976). Schachter has shown that the class of transformations that isolates a single unified class of NPs in English isolates two syntactically independent classes in Tagalog. One class of NPs is picked out by role (agent) related transformations; the other class is isolated by reference (discourse) related transformations.

Now this is a problem for the *property* approach to subject, for one cannot tell precisely what is to be counted when as subject or not. However, under the correlation approach described here, there is no such problem. The various "properties" are recognized as independent linguistic factors which may correlate or not. In English certain syntactic and semantic factors correlate strongly which in Tagalog do not always do so.

However, for the purposes of this volume, the difficulties described so well by Schachter are not immediately relevant. This is because in basic sentences numerous coding devices and semantic/pragmatic functions coincide. For example, the S in SVO is in initial position, it is the subject, it is definite (shared) and so on for all those "properties" that Keenan has so carefully catalogued (1976b). Thus, for Tagalog the role and reference properties that Schachter isolates (using non-basic sentences) will tend to coincide in basic sentences.

One of the properties that correlates significantly with subject in basic sentences is TI. This is the only sense in which are related TI and the subject of basic constituent orders. The same argument can be extended to subject and "animatedness" in Chapter 5 below.

Chapter 4

VERB-OBJECT BONDING

INTRODUCTION
This chapter motivates, describes, and limits a second
functional principle that shapes the grammars of natural
languages: Verb-Object Bonding (VOB). VOB is a
generalization about the relationship of the object of a
transitive clause to the verb. In general the object of a
transitive clause is syntactically and semantically more
tightly "bound" to the verb than is the subject of a
transitive clause.
    The sections of this chapter reflect the steps necessary
to achieve this goal. The next section considers the precise
claim being proposed in the VOB principle. The claim is that
in general in transitive clauses it is more difficult to
interfere with the syntactic juxtaposition and semantic unity
of the verb and object than it is to interfere with that of
the verb and subject. Various independent syntactic,
semantic, and even phonological processes appear to conspire
to prevent the separation of the object from the verb; and
these same processes often permit separation of the subject
from the verb in order to maintain the bond between the verb
and object.
    The form of argumentation for VOB is identical to that
used to motivate the other principles. The cross-linguistic
data examined consistently show a substantial syntactic and
semantic link between the object of a transitive clause and
the verb which is not paralleled by the subject of a
transitive clause. If these observations are not accidental,
only some principle like VOB will successfully capture the
generalization.
    The third section presents the data that underpin the
VOB. The data reveal that a variety of independent
syntactic, semantic, and phonological processes all seem
constrained in their application to preserve the cohesiveness
of transitive verb and object.

73

Finally, the limits on the principle are considered briefly. One limitation is similar to one offered for the TFP. VOB is not to be taken as an absolute language universal, but rather as another fundamental principle that may shape natural languages. A second limitation is that the principle should not be construed as any sort of principle about VP-constituency.

THE PRINCIPLE AND ITS INTERPRETATIONS

The principle of Verb-Object Bonding is presented in (1):

(1) Verb-Object Bonding (VOB): the object of a transitive verb is more tightly bonded to the verb than is its subject.

This principle claims that a transitive verb and its object form a more cohesive, unified syntactic and semantic whole than do a transitive verb and its subject. The data presented below show that it is more difficult to interfere with the syntactic unity of the verb and its object, by attempting syntactic insertions, movements, and so on, than it is to interfere with any such possible unity between the verb and subject. They show further that there is also a greater semantic unity between verb and object than between verb and subject.

Exactly why there should be such a bond between a transitive verb and its object is not entirely clear, though Keenan (1984) offers one plausible direction to investigate. Yet the evidence in support of the principle is quite persuasive. Across a reasonably diverse set of languages, one find from language to language a systematic maintenance of the integrity of the verb-object bond. The data vary from the preferences of speakers not to separate a verb and its object to clear and absolute grammatical constraints on such separation.

Characterization of the Parts of the Principle

In order to be more explicit about the intended interpretation of the principle, it will be useful to characterize briefly the critical parts of the principle: transitive and bonding.

Transitive

The traditional definition of transitive verb is a verb that takes an object complement in addition to its subject. Though the issues raised in defining transitivity in grammar (Hopper

and Thompson 1980) are particularly difficult and important
theoretical issues, this more traditional approach is the one
that will be used here.

Bonding

The more formal notion of bonding that underlies (1) is not
unlike the common non-technical understanding of the term.
For 'bonding' of any kind to exist, two independent entities
must be brought together in such a way that it is difficult
to separate them. The more difficult it is to separate the
two elements, the stronger the bond between them is said to
be.

The prototypical case of grammatical bonding is the
relation of bound morpheme to verb root. A bound morpheme
can never stand 'alone'; that is, it can never be separated
from some other morpheme. Neither can independent material
be inserted between a bound morpheme and its associated stem.
For instance, as the example in (2) illustrates, the bond
between the English past tense morpheme {-d} and the verb
stem cannot be broken (at the word level):

(2) John walk-ed quickly to town.
     *John walk quickly ed to town.
     *ed John walk quickly to town.

The principle of VOB states that the object of a
transitive verb is bound more tightly to the verb than is the
subject.

Besides discussions of bound morphemes, the discussion
of bonding in general has been not very extensive. Foley
(1976) discusses a hierarchy of bondedness for NPs in
Austronesian languages. This hierarchy describes the
distribution of ligatures for certain NP types in
Austronesian languages (Foley 1976:19):

(3) Foley's Bondedness Hierarchy

	articles + noun
	deictic + noun
strength of	interrogative + noun
bonding de-	quantifiers/indefinites + noun
creases	adjectives + noun
	participles + noun
	relative clauses + noun

If at any point on the hierarchy a given Austronesian
language requires the use of a ligature between the noun and
its adjunct, the language will also require the use of a
ligature at every point below that point. So, if a language
requires the use of a ligature for interrogative+noun NPs, it

75

will require one for adjective+noun as well, but not
necessarily for deictic + noun. Foley appeals to an
otherwise undefined notion of "strength of a syntactic bond"
(Foley 1976:20) as an explanation for the hierarchy.
Nevertheless, it is clear that the required insertion of
material (the ligature) between two independent elements in
contrast to optional or obligatory non-insertion of material
between other elements satisfies the characterization of
bonding presented here. The concept of bonding for the
principle of VOB is thus quite similar to the concept of
bonding discussed by Foley.

Prior Discussions of Verb-Object Bonding

Unlike the other two principles considered in this volume,
there has been only limited discussion in the literature of a
principle like VOB. One brief mention occurs in Bese et al.
(1970) where the writers speculate that some special
relationship between verb and object might account for the
existence of VOS languages. It is also reported in Sedlak
(1975) that Osgood has argued in two unpublished manuscripts
for the existence of a stronger bond between verb and object
than between verb and indirect object.

In his work on word order Vennemann (1974) cites the
contribution of Otto Behaghel whose laws contain a principle
quite similar to the principle of VOB offered here. This
principle is reported as follows:

(5) Behaghel's First Law: "Das oberste Gesetz ist
dieses, da daß geistig eng Zusammengehörege auch
eng zusammengestellt wird" (p.4): "The most
important law is that what belongs together
mentally [semantically] is placed close together
[syntactically]." (Vennemann 1974:339).

Vennemann provides no further discussion of this
principle except to claim that Behaghel's principle had been
made more precise in Bartsch's Principle of Natural
Constituent Structure (1974:340):

(6) If $\Phi(\xi)$ is a function-argument relationship in
the semantic representation of a sentence (where
semantic representations are formulas of a
properly extended predicate logic), and if A, B are
the lexical realizations of Φ and ξ in that
sentence, then A and B appear, in the natural case,
juxtaposed rather than at a distance - in that
sentence.

Though more general in scope, this principle seems quite similar to that proposed here. Its strength is its explicitness and its place in Bartsch's and Vennemann's general work in syntax--including their work on word order (Bartsch and Vennemann 1972, Vennemann 1973, 1974).

Bazell (1953) includes two separate principles which together approximate that captured by VOB. The first principle is that of adhesion, which deals with the insertion of material between two elements:

(7) A unit is in close adhesion if no simple units can be intercalated between them. It is in relatively close adhesion if few simple units, or no units of small complexity, can be intercalated (1953:36).

The second principle is that of cohesion, which deals with the substitutability of units:

(8) The cohesion between units depends on the frequency with which they are commutable with a single unit. (1953:35-36).

Finally, any argument for the existence of a VP constituent can be translated into an argument for VOB. Thus, in a sense, observations and argumentation for a VP constituent in general can be taken as some sort of discussion of VOB. However, Schwartz (1974) has shown that the evidence for a VP constituent in SOV and VSO languages is considerably weaker than that for SVO languages, and concludes it is so weak that a VP constituent for SOV and VSO languages does not exist. However, VOB embodies no claim about constituency whatever, only that the bond between verb and object is stronger than that between verb and subject. Thus, the data presented below, which include data from both SOV languages and VSO languages, are intended to motivate only the weaker claim embodied in the principle of VOB.

THE FORM OF ARGUMENTATION FOR VOB

The evidence needed to confirm the VOB principle must satisfy the following condition. It must be demonstrated in a diverse set of languages that in general the verb and object of a transitive clause form a more cohesive unit than do the subject and verb.

This can be done in one of two principal ways: syntactically or semantically. It can be done syntactically by demonstrating that it is more difficult to insert material between verb and object than between verb and subject, or that it is more difficult to move the object from the verb than the subject from the verb. It can be done semantically by demonstrating that the object and verb form an immutable

whole while the verb and subject do not. Thus, the data
below can be divided into two main classes--a class of
syntactic data and a class of semantic data. In addition,
there is some phonological evidence supportive of VOB.

The evidence needed to deny the VOB principle is
likewise straightforward. It must be demonstrated that in a
diverse set of languages the object and verb do not form a
cohesive unit in contrast to the verb and subject in a
transitive clause. Either the verb and subject must form
such a cohesive unit, or it must be demonstrated that there
is no observable pattern of syntactic or semantic cohesion
exhibited by either the subject and verb or the object and
verb.

It is important to point out again the relativistic
nature of the VOB principle. It involves a comparison of the
grammatical behavior of the object and verb with the
grammatical behavior of the subject and verb. Thus, no
counterevidence is discovered if it is observed only that
some material can be inserted between the object and verb.
Such data constitute counterevidence to VOB only in the
further event that the material in question cannot be
inserted between the verb and subject in that language.

Having outlined the framework in which the data in below
are to be considered, all that remains to be done in this
section is to consider the basic argument for the VOB
principle. The data below demonstrate that in a diverse set
of languages there exist independent kinds of syntactic,
semantic, and phonological behavior which are constrained to
maintain more fully the cohesiveness of the verb and object
of a transitive clause than any cohesiveness exhibited by the
verb and subject of a transitive clause. The VOB principle
captures this generalization. Failure to make such a
generalization for a theory for cross-linguistic comparison
entails a claim that the similarity in behavior exhibited
across this diverse set of languages is accidental. The VOB
principle claims that the observed syntactic behavior is not
accidental, and predicts the general nature of the
verb-object versus verb-subject relationship in newly
discovered or newly analyzed languages.

DATA FOR VOB

This section presents data from more than a dozen independent
syntactic and semantic domains which individually and
collectively argue for a principle of verb-object bonding.

Noun Incorporation

Noun incorporation has been most extensively discussed in
connection with American languages (Kroeber 1909, Sapir 1911,
Woodbury 1975, Merlan 1976, etc.). However, noun

incorporation occurs in languages throughout the world. Basically, the phenomenon involves an alternation between constructions involving an NP, usually a non-referential indefinite noun object (but not always, cf. Sapir 1911), and the verb. The incorporated NP loses syntactic signs of independence --independent particles, for instance--and becomes a part of the verbal complex as evidenced, for example, by its presence inside bound verbal affixes or by phonological reduction (Mardirussian 1975).

In the data considered here it is the case that object NPs can be incorporated into the verbal complex of the languages presented, but subjects NPs cannot be. There are some cases of incorporation of noun subjects, for instance in Sora (Dryer, p.c.). However, it seems to be the case that if a language permits subject incorporation, as does Sora, it will also have object incorporation. That is, if a language has noun incorporation at all, it will have object incorporation. Thus, noun incorporation, a process which tightly binds an NP to a verb, must in general bind an object to a verb in a language if anything is so bound.

Mokilese. In Mokilese (Micronesian-SVO) there is a set of verbs into which an indefinite object may be incorporated (Harrison 1976). Mokilese verbs in general are marked for aspect by suffixes on the verb. When the verb is transitive, a definite object follows:

(9)   ngoah   audoh-la   rimeh-i
        1sg   fill-perf bottle-this
        I filled this bottle.
(10)   ngoah   poadok-di suhkoah-i
        1sg   plant-perf tree-this
        I planted this tree.

But with indefinite objects incorporation occurs, and the object moves inside the aspect marker:

(11)   ngoah   audoh-rimeh-la
        1sg   fill-bottle-perf
        I filled bottles.
(12)   ngoah   poad-suhkoah-di
        1sg   plant-tree-perf
        I planted trees.

Onondaga. Similarly, in Onondaga there is an alternation between non-incorporated object NPs occurring outside a bound morpheme and incorporated forms with the object inside the bound morpheme (Woodbury 1975):

(13)   wa?hahninú?   ne?   oyɛ́? kwa?
        tns-he/it buy asp. nm. part. it-tobacco-n.s.

He bought the tobacco.
(14) wa?hayɛ?kwahni:nu?
tns-he/it-tobacco-buy-asp
He bought tobacco.

There are some additional examples discussed in Mardirussian (1975). They include:

Kitonemuk
(15) a-kɘm   a-hō-j
3sg-make   3sg-hole-obj   [def. obj., no
                                            incorporation]
He digs his hole.
(16) a-hō-kɘm
3sg-hole-make   [indef. obj., incorp.]
He digs holes.

Chukchee (from Comrie 1973)
(17) tumg-e   na-ntɘwat-ɘn   kupre-n
friends-erg set   net   [def. obj., no incorp.]
(18) tumg-ɘt   kopra-ntɘwat-g?at
friends-nom net-set   [indef. obj., incorp.]
The friends set the nets.

Nahuatl
(19) ni-k-čiwa   tamal-li
1sg-obj-make   tamale-abs
I make the tamale.
(20) ni-tamal-čiwa
1sg-tamale-make
I am tamale-making.

Some further cases are presented by Sedlak in his discussion of a greater bond between object and verb than between indirect object and verb (Sedlak 1975). Sedlak does not provide the alternation between incorporated and non-incorporated forms, but the examples, drawn from Sapir (1911), do contain good morphological glosses:

Southern Paiute
(21) gam'U-yaai-nUm-pUγa'
rabbit-hunt-usitive-remote past
He used to hunt jackrabbits.

Takelma (from Sapir 1911)
(22) xã-p:iⁱ-nóᵘa-k'wa
back-fire-warm (aorist) -one's own
He was warming his back.

And, finally, there are two more examples, not discussed by Sedlak or Mardirussian, taken from Sapir (1911):

Oneida
(23) lun-d-nagla'sl-ezaks-gwɛɛ
3m sg sub-pass-village-search-imperf
They searched for villages.

Pawnee
(24) táhĭkst^{uɛn} tát-rĭks-st$^{u-ɛn}$
1sg-arrow-make-temp
I make an arrow.

The incorporation of the object into the verbal complex
is also an active process in Gunbalung, Yana, Tongan,
Malagasy, Fijian, Sora (Mardirussian 1975), Iroquois,
Shoshonean, Tsimshian (Sedlak 1975, Sapir 1911), Otomi,
Mohawk (Merlan 1976), Nass-Gitksan (Rigsby 1975), Mojave
(Munro 1976), as well as Kusaisean, Tsou, Ponapean, Tiwi,
Ojibwa, and Turkish.

Sentence Qualifier Placement (Lehmann 1973)

Sentence qualifier is a term used by Lehmann to class
together a number of grammatical morphemes that share the
property of modifying the primary predication of a sentence.
The major qualifiers are negation markers and interrogative
markers, but others include markers of reflexive,
desiderative, and potential. Lehmann observes that sentence
qualifiers occur on the side of the verb opposite the object.
That is, such markers occur before the verb in consistent VO
languages (Qualifier V O) and after the verb in consistent OV
languages (O V Qualifier).

It is possible to construct a strong argument for VOB
using Lehmann's observations. Logically speaking, it is just
as likely that a sentence qualifier will separate object and
verb as it is likely to separate subject and verb. However,
the data presented below demonstrate that though there is no
prior reason why such qualifiers should not separate the
object from the verb, they tend not to do so. A principle
like VOB can provide a general constraint on the relationship
of verb and object that can explain Lehmann's observation of
the distribution of these elements. In addition one can see
that there are some cases in which Lehmann's observations do
not hold, but in which placement of qualifiers still does not
violate the principle of VOB.

The first set of examples below present data consistent
with both VOB and the observations that Lehmann makes. In
each case a sentence qualifier appears on the side of the
verb opposite the object. Thus, for instance, in Hebrew the

unmarked order of verb and object is VO. The question
marker, /ha-/, is attached to the left side of the verb, the
side opposite the direct object:

Hebrew
(25) ka:tab   seper
      write   book (indef)   V O
      He wrote a book.
(26) ha-ka:tab   seper
      Q-write   book (indef)   Q V O
      Did he write a book?

The additional examples below are similarly supportive
of VOB:

Sanketi (Lehmann 1973)
(27) huḍugu   pošu   pār-aṇ-ā
      boy   cow   see-pres-3sg   S O V
      The boy sees a cow.
(28) huḍugu   pošu   pār-aṇ-an-ā
      boy   cow   see-pres-3sg-Q   S O V Q
      Does the boy see a cow?

Japanese
(29) shōnen wa bōru o nageta
      boy   WA ball O threw   S O V
      The boy threw the ball.
(30) shōnen wa bōru o nageta ka
      boy   WA ball O threw Q   S O V Q
      Did the boy throw the ball?
(31) shōnen wa bōru o nage-ne-katta
      boy   WA ball O throw-NEG-past   S O V NEG
      The boy didn't throw the ball.
(32) shōnen wa bōru o nage-ne-katta ka
      boy   WA ball O throw-NEG-past Q   S O V NEG Q
      Didn't the boy throw the ball?

Toba Batak
(33) manembak ursa si jon di tombak
      act-hunt deer art John in forest   V O S Loc
      John hunts deer in the forest.
(34) ngang manembak ursa si jon di tombak
      NEG   act-hunt deer SI John in forest
                                         NEG V O S Loc
      John doesn't hunt deer in the forest.

English
(35) John cooked the fish.   S V O
(36) John did not cook the fish. S NEG V O
(37) Did John cook the fish?   Q S V O

Yagaria
(38) a'i de-ma'   gayale-di hao-di-i-vie
      that man-?   pig-my   shoot-past-3sg-Q
                                                    S O V Q

      Did that man shoot my pig?

Grebo (Innes 1966). Innes observes that in Grebo, an SVO
language, the position of what he calls adjuncts, which
includes both adverbs and sentence qualifiers, is outside the
verb-object combination.

(39) ɔduda   bla ne tɔ
      he-pound-past rice ne well   S V O Adv
      He pounded the rice well.
(40) ne yida   bla du Mɔle
      I   neg-past rice pound Monday   S NEG V O
      I did not pound rice on Monday.

There are some languages which do not follow exactly the
pattern described by Lehmann. But even in these languages
the sentence qualifiers do not separate the object and the
verb (though they may separate the subject and verb):

Thai
(41) khǎw kin khaâw
      he   eat rice   S V O
      He eats rice.
(42) khǎw yàag kin khaâw
      he   desid eat rice   S DESID V O
      He wants to eat rice.
(43) khǎw mǎy yàag kin khaâw
      he   NEG desid eat rice   S NEG DESID V O
      He doesn't want to eat rice.
(44) khǎw kin khaâw mǎy
      he   eat rice   Q   S V O Q

Malagasy (Keenan 1976a)
(45) nanome vola   an-dRabe ve ianao
      give   money acc-Rabe Q   you   V O IO Q S

In the case of Thai, the interrogative marker should
precede the verb (probably coming initially) if Thai were a
consistent VO language. Similarly, the question marker in
Malagasy should also precede the verb. However, they do not.
These cases are not counterexamples to Lehmann's claims,
since it may be the case that neither is a consistent VO
language. However, while the markers occur somewhere other
than in their expected places, these other positions are
constrained by the principle of VOB. Other examples of this
include Gidabal, Kru, and Saramaccan.

83

Gidabal (Geytenbeek and Geytenbeek 1971). In Gidabal the basic order of constituents is SVO. Ordinarily, polar interrogatives are produced merely by using a marked intonation. However, there is an optional interrogative marker. This marker does not break up the verb and object:

> (46) njang wailu yang-:nj ngudumbunj-a: baya:nj
>   Q   you   go-fut Woodenbong-to today   Q S V
>   Are you going to Woodenbong today?
> (47) njang darbang gawa-le-:n   njulangam
>   Q   sticks break-rep-past they   Q O V S
>   Were they breaking sticks?

Kru (Lord 1977). Kru has SOV as its basic constituent order. If Kru was a consistent OV language, one would expect that the negative marker should follow the verb as it does in Japanese, for instance. However, the negative marker in Kru precedes the verb. And when the verb is transitive, the negative marker will precede both the verb and its object, even if the object is definite (examples from Hyman 1974):

> (48) ɔ́ sé kɔ̀ nǎ dí
>   he NEG rice neg eat   S NEG O V
>   He didn't eat the rice.
> (49) ɔ́ sé kɔ̀ jù   nǎ tè à nǎ dí
>   he NEG rice child def bought rel def eat
>   He didn't eat the rice the child bought.
>   S NEG V O

Saramaccan. Saramaccan, like Thai, is SVO, but polar questions are signaled by a sentence final particle, /nó/ (Glock 1972).

Sentence Adverbial Placement

All languages have constraints on the placement of sentence adverbials. The positions taken by sentence adverbials in any language are not determined randomly but in some principled manner. There seems to be a tendency, for instance, for time and location adverbials to occur at either end of a clause, in the case of preposed adverbials to thematically frame the setting. Sentence adverbials can, however, occur in other places. But these other positions seem to be constrained in a manner sensitive to the VOB principle.

In the cases below, sentence adverbials are not permitted to intervene between the verb and object though they are all permitted to separate the verb and subject. Thus, the data presented below support the following argument for VOB: It is equally possible, logically speaking, for a sentence adverbial to occur between verb and object or

between verb and subject. However, in the observed data,
sentence adverbials are constrained from separating verb and
object but not from separating verb and subject. If such
constraints are not accidental, the principle of VOB provides
at least a partial explanation for such constraints.

Some languages have an obligatory constraint that
prohibits sentence adverbials from occurring between the verb
and object. These same languages will usually permit such
adverbials to break up the subject and verb:

> *English*
> (50) Unfortunately, John cooked the fish.   Adv S V O
> (51) John unfortunately cooked the fish.   S Adv V
> (52) *John cooked unfortunately the fish.   *S V Adv O
> (53) John cooked the fish unfortunately.   S V O Adv

Indonesian (reported with English examples in Schwartz 1974).
With intransitive verbs, sentence adverbials like /kəmarin/
'yesterday' can precede, separate, or follow the subject and
verb:

> (54) kəmarin   pasien itu mati   Adv S V
>   yesterday patient def die
>   Yesterday, the patient died.
> (55) pasien itu kəmarin mati   S Adv V
> (56) pasien itu mati kəmarin   S V Adv

However, when the verb is transitive, the adverbial can
occur in any position but between the verb and object:

> (57) kəmarin   pasien itu mənulis   surat   AdvSVO
>   yesterday patient def act-write letter
>   Yesterday the patient wrote a letter.
> (58) pasien itu kəmarin mənulis surat   SAdvVO
> (59) *pasien itu mənulis kəmarin surat   *SVAdvO
> (60) pasien itu mənulis surat kəmarin   SVOAdv

Toba Batak. Again, in this typically VOS language, the
adverbial can occur in any position with intransitive verbs:

> (61) manogotnogot   laho   si jon tu   onan
>   in the morning go   John to   market
>   John goes to market in the morning.   Adv V S Loc
> (62) laho manogotnogot si jon tu onan   V Adv S Loc
> (63) laho si jon manogotnogot tu onan   V S Adv Loc
> (64) laho si jon tun onan manogotnogot   V S Loc Adv

But with transitive verbs the adverbial is prohibited
from occurring between the verb and object:

> (65) manogotnogot   manembak   ursa si jon di tombak

```
                        in the morning act-shoot deer John   in forest
                        In the morning John shoots deer in the forest.
                                             Adv V O S Loc
      (66) *manembak manogotnogot ursa si jon di tombak
                                             *V Adv O S Loc
      (67)  manembak ursa manogotnogot si jon di tombak
                                             V O Adv S Loc
      (68)  manembak ursa si jon di tombak manogotnogot
                                             V O S Adv Loc
      (69)  manembak ursa si jon di tombak manogotnogot
                                             V O S Loc Adv
```

Schwartz (1974) reports that similar restrictions can be found in Mandarin and Tera.

The cases presented above were crucial ones in that there was an absolute constraint on the position of sentence adverbials. In other languages it may be possible for sentence adverbials to separate the object and verb, but such placements may be less grammatical than placement either initially or finally, and, in any case, less common than the separation of subject and verb.

Japanese. For intransitive verbs there are only two possible positions for sentence adverbials (since Japanese is rigidly SOV). Both are equally acceptable:

```
      (70)  zannen nagara shōnen wa shinda      Adv S V
            unfortunately boy     WA died
            Unfortunately, the boy died.
      (71)  shōnen wa zannen nagara shinda      S Adv V
```

With transitive verbs there is an additional possibility, but it results in sentences with a lower grammatical acceptability:

```
      (72)  zannen nagara shōnen wa bōru o nageta   AdvSOV
            unfortunately boy     WA ball O threw
            Unfortunately, the boy threw the ball.
      (73)  shōnen wa zannen nagara boru o nageta   SAdvOV
      (74) ?shōnen wa bōru o zannen nagara nageta  ?SOAdvV
```

It should also be noted that just as there were no cases observed in which a sentence adverbial obligatorily broke up a transitive verb and its object, so was it the case that no observations were made of any preference in any language for a sentence adverbial to break up a transitive verb and its object.

Modal Placement

Steele (1975) presents a detailed discussion of the placement of modal elements in natural languages. Her observations can be recast into a strong argument for VOB. If there were no special relationship between verb and object in transitive clauses, modal elements would separate the verb from the object or the verb from the subject with equal frequency. However, as Steele's work demonstrates, the distribution of modal elements is such that in general the object is not separated from the verb, though the subject may be. And in those few cases where the object is separated from the verb, the subject is also separated from the verb. The principle of VOB captures this generalization.

In SVO and SOV languages, placement of modals that would separate the object from the verb are forbidden. English can be used to illustrate the general pattern:

> *English*
> (75) John drives the car.   S V O
> (76) John may drive the car.   S Mod V O

Steele catalogues a substantial number of SVO languages that follow this pattern:

> (77) S Modal V O: Chrau, Vietnamese, Swazi, Thai, Albanian, English, Diola-Fogney, Gbaya, Lunda, Yoruba, Nguna, Indonesian, Snohomish, Wichita, Mandarin, Tera.
> (78) *S V Modal O

Modal placement in SOV languages tends also to be consistent with VOB:

> (79) S O V Modal: Mojave, Quechua, Khalka, Korean, Tamil, Lahu, Navajo, Washo, Burmese, Eskimo, Marathi, Kashaya, Pomo, Japanese.
> (80) *S O Modal V

However, in VSO languages, modal elements may sometimes, as in (82), separate the object from the verb. But if modal elements do separate the object from the verb in some language, they also separate the subject and verb:

> (81) Modal V S O: Kapampangan, Ulithian, Wolio.
> (82) V Modal S O: Fox, Rarotongan
> (83) *V S Modal O

Steele provides no data concerning VOS languages, but in Toba Batak modals precede the verb obligatorily:

Toba Batak
(84) boi do manembak ursa si jon di tombak   Mod V O S
      able part act-hunt deer John   in forest
      John can hunt deer in the forest.
(85) *manembak boi (do) ursa si jon di tombak *V Mod O S

Finally, Steele's analysis of Thai is not complete.
While most modals in Thai do precede the verb, there are
several which may follow it. However, these modal elements
must follow the entire VO complex. Thus, the one example
that varies from the general patterns Steele observes varies
from those patterns in a manner totally consistent with VOB.

Thai (John Grima, p.c.)
(86) khon nán khàp rót daây   S V O Mod
      man   that drive car able
      That man can drive the car.
(87) khon nán daây khàp rót   *S Mod V O
(88) khon nàn khap daây rot   *S V Mod O

Proverbal Replacements

It is possible in some languages to replace a verb+object
phrase by a proverbal form. In no case has it been observed
that a proverbal form can replace a subject+verb phrase in a
transitive clause. If there were no special syntactic
relationship between object and verb, there should be an
equal possibility of observing either verb-object or
verb-subject proverbal replacements. The data reveal,
however, that there is not an equal possibility for each type
of proverbal replacement. Therefore, some special
relationship must exist between verb and object. The VOB
principle states what the relationship is.
    Illustrative data for proverbal replacement comes from
English:

English
(89) John caught a fish and May did, too.
(90) The bird watched the cat and so did the dog.

Movement Constraints

The data presented in this section demonstrate the
cohesiveness of verb and object (as opposed to verb and
subject) with respect to their sensitivity to movement rules.
In the case below there is a movement rule sensitive to the
bond between object and verb, but no parallel evidence of any
such sensitivity to a verb-subject relationship. As in the
cases above, this behavior can be explained by the VOB
principle.

The movement constraint occurs in Toba Batak (VOS). There are two movement rules to consider. One rule is a topicalization transformation, T, which can move most constituents to initial position. The second rule is a clefting rule, C, which also can move most constituents to initial position, but differs from T in that a particle /do/ follows the fronted constituent.

Any constituent of a sentence with an intransitive verb may be fronted by either rule:

(91)	laho	si jon	tu onan			V S Loc
	go	John	to market			
	John goes to the market.					
(92)	T:	si jon laho	tu onan			S V Loc
(93)	C:	si jon do laho	tu onan			S do V Loc
(94)	T:	tu onan laho	si jon			Loc V S
(95)	C:	tu onan do laho	si jon			Loc do V S

However, when the verb is transitive, one cannot move the object NP, though all other constituents may still be fronted:

(96)	manembak ursa si jon di tombak	V O S Loc
	act-hunt deer John in forest	
	John hunts deer in the forest.	
(97)	T: si jon manembak ursa di tombak	S V O Loc
(98)	C: si jon do manembak ursa di tombak	S do V O Loc
(99)	T: di tombak manembak ursa si jon	Loc V O S
(100)	C: di tombak do manembak ursa si jon	Loc do V O S
(101)	T: *ursa manembak si jon di tombak	*O V S Loc
(102)	C: *ursa do manembak si jon di tombak	*O do V S

Thus, in Toba Batak it has been shown that there are two movement rules which can move away from its unmarked position any constituent except the object, which remains firmly bonded to its verb.

Idioms

There are two possible idiom structures of interest for this study: those of the form verb-subject and those of the form verb-object. If in some particular language the number of verb-object idioms is significantly greater than the number of verb-subject idioms, one can argue that there must be some special relationship between verb and object in that particular language, and that the principle of VOB captures that relationship. Further, if such observations hold across languages, then one can construct a general argument along the same lines.

Verb-Object Bonding

There are two significant collections of idioms, one of them informal, which means there is insufficient evidence to offer the general argument with much conviction. However, in both cases below the evidence for VOB is compelling. In both cases idioms of the form verb-subject are rare.

English
(103)

verb-object	verb-subject
bury the hatchet	the ax fell on
face the music	the cards are stacked against
shoot the breeze	
blow the whistle	
smell a rat	
climb the wall	

McCawley's informal list of English idioms (McCawley 1972) contains 313 idioms of either the form verb-object or verb-subject. Of these 313, 310 are of the form verb-object; only three are of the form verb-subject (a bit less than one percent).

Vietnamese (Nguyễn 1970)
(104)

verb-object	verb-subject
an cháo dá bát eat soup kick bowl to be ungrateful	cát dâp sóng vùi sand buries water covers to disappear in the water
bay diều dặt chuyên invent items, create topics to lie	voi gày ngụ'a dạp elephant smashes, horse steps on to maltreat
bẻ hành bẻ tỏi pick onion pick garlic to criticize people for small imperfections	
choc trò'i khuấ'y nu'ó'c tickle sky stir up water to be powerful	
bàn ngnag tán dọc discuss width talk about length to speak at random	
so't ngọt xẻ bòi share sweet divide tasty to share the good things of life	

90

Nguyễn's study of four syllable idiomatic expressions
in Vietnamese is quite useful. He observes that there exist
approximately 3,000 such expressions, which are used both in
speaking and in writing. He catalogues 825 of those
expressions which he states are fairly well-known to the
average Vietnamese. Of the 825 expressions in his
collection, 299 are of either the form verb-object or
verb-subject. Verb-object idioms constitute a fraction of
the 299 significantly greater than chance would predict--214
of the 299 (72%).

In addition to the major collections discussed above,
additional information on idioms in other languages was
collected, though with some difficulty. When informants for
the particular languages below could produce any idioms at
all, they were always of the form verb-object.

Thai
(105)   object-verb
           thɯg   kɔɛ   kam
           arrive goal   karma
           to die

           chak   waw
           fly   kite
           to masturbate

Toba Batak
(106)   object-verb
           mangallang pisang
           act-eat   banana
           to attend an engagement ceremony

           mangkunti   pagar
           act-carry on head pagar (??)
           to be pregnant

Malay
(107)   object-verb
           main   sabun
           play   soap
           to masturbate in the shower

Finnish and Japanese idioms tend also to be of the form
verb-object.

Paraphrases, Compounds, and Cognate Objects

It is common to find in some languages paraphrases of verbs
or verbal compounds of the form verb-object or to find
objects cognate to some verb. Since verb-subject paraphrases

91

or compounds or cognate subjects are extremely rare, the
observations below constitute additional evidence for greater
bonding between object and verb than between subject and
verb. The paraphrase data include:

English
(108)   shower   take a shower
        anchor   drop anchor
        bomb   drop bombs on
        fine   impose a fine on

Thai
(109)   riən naŋsɯɯ   riən
        study books   study

        kin khaâw   kin
        eat rice   eat

The cognate object data include:

English
(110)   sing a song
        do a deed
        die a (glorious) death
        dream a dream
        sleep the sleep (of the dead)
        breathe (his last) breath

Luvale
(111)   kukina ngoma
        dance   dance, drum
        dance a dance

        kwimba mwaso
        sing   song
        to sing

        kuvulumuna mulonga
        offend   offense
        to offend

Asmat (Ajam dialect)   (Lang 1975)
(112)   mbetsj mbetsj-
        a weep to weep
        to weep

        mbui   mbui-
        a bath to bathe
        to bathe

        ndi   ndi

```
            a dance to dance
            to dance

            wu     wu-
            a bundle to bundle
            to wrap in a palm leaf

            utsj   otsj-
            a laugh to laugh
            to laugh
```

Nebak (Lang 1975's report of data from Fabian and Fabian
1971:80f).
(113) sandi   tasandin
      urine   prog-urinate-he-pres
      He is urinating.

      meluk   tawan
      sleep   prog-sleep-he-pres (sleep a sleep)
      He is sleeping.

      si   susuping
      cry   cry-cry-neg   (cry a cry)
      Don't cry.

The compounding data include:

Yoruba (Bamgbose 1964)
(114)   V   N

        še [do]   ɛbɔ [sacrifice]
                 ɛdá [creation]
                 ɛ̀fɛ̀ [ridicule]
                 ɔ̀fɔ̀ [mourning]

        V + N

        šɛ̀bɔ   make a sacrifice
        s'ɛ̀dá   to create
        s'ɛ̀fɛ̀ to ridicule
        s'ɔ̀fɔ̀   to mourn

Yagaria (Renck 1975). According to Renck about half of the
verbs in Yagaria are compounds, and about half of these are
of the form "adjunct + auxiliary." These compounds consist of
one non-inflected word (adjunct), which carries the essential
meaning of the compound, and an inflected verb ("auxiliary")
which may lose its independent meaning. These compounds
cannot be easily distinguished from sequences of object and
verb and may have derived from them.
    Some adjuncts occur only in compound form:

(115) gigi hu - to laugh
       vuyu hu - to pull

Others occur in compounds, buy may have independent use
as well:

(116) aepa hu - to begin   aepa (beginning)
       bina fei - to buy   bina (price)
       eigava ei - to wake up   eigava (new)
       eida ho - to spit   eidana (saliva)
       haku ei - to fly   haku (wing)
       Note: /hu/ = be, do, say and /ei/ = hit

Compounding also occurs in Asmat, Oksapmin, Kewa,
Kaugel, Melpa, Wahgi, Karam, Kapau, Kate, Waffa (Lang 1975).

Borrowing

One common borrowing strategy utilized in many languages is
to borrow a noun from the host language and combine it with
the borrowing language's verb for *do* or *make*. The
combinations so formed are always of the form object plus
verb, and seldom, if ever, of the form subject plus verb.

Azerbaijani
(117)   N   N + V (V-ed, to do)
       baehs   baehs-ed
       (discussion)   (to discuss)

       hæram   hæram-ed
       (taboo)   (to spoil)

       hærækæt   hærækæt-ed
       (movement)   (to move)

       ištiraak   ištiraak-ed
       (participation)   (to participate)

Hindi
(118)   N   N + V (V=kərna, to make)
       xətəm   xətəm kərnā
       (finish)   (to finish)

       košıš   košıš kərnā
       (attempt)   (to try)

       ıntəzām   ıntəzām kərnā
       (arrange)   (to arrange)

       usər   usər kərnā

(influence)   (to influence)

Japanese
(119)   N   N + V
         (Chinese)   (V=suru, to do)

         benkyō   benkyō (o) suru
         (study)   (to study)

         rikai   rikai suro
         (understanding) (to understand)

         shokuji   shokuji (o) suru
         (meals)   (to take meals)

Enga (Lang 1975)
(120)   N   N + V
         (Tok Pisin)   (V=pingi, to hit or lénge, to
                          utter)

         Ióko   Ióko pingi
         (lock)   (to lock)

         pépa   pépa pingi
         (paper)   (to write)

         kása   kása lenge
         (cards)   (to gamble)

         bóta   bóta lenge
         (vote)   (to vote)

Telefol (Lang 1975's report of data from Healey 1965).
(121)   N   N + V
         (Tok Pisin   (V=keemin, do, be)
         or English)

         súkul   súkul keemin
         (school)   (attend school)

Oksapmin (Lang 1975's report of data from Lawrence
1971).
(122)   N   N + V
         (source not   (V=hapaat, do, make)
         given)
         sukul   sukul hapaat
         (school)   (attend school)

         sukul   sukul hahapaat
         (school)   (teaches me, does to me)

```
            waratu              waratu hapaat
            (worship?)          (worships)
```

Conjunction Reduction

There are three ways in which coordinate transitive clauses
can be reduced, (Bokamba 1975, Tai 1969, Sanders 1970). In
all cases the element reduced must be identical to an element
in the sister clause. English can serve to illustrate the
three reductions. There are subject-reduced clauses:

> (123) Tom hit the ball and threw the bat.
>   From: Tom hit the ball and Tom threw the ball.

There are VP reduced clauses:

> (124) Tom and Harry hit the ball.
>   From: Tom hit the ball and Harry hit the ball.

And there are object-reduced clauses:

> (125) Tom threw and Harry hit the ball.
>   From: Tom threw the ball and Harry hit the ball.

It has been observed by Koutsoudas that all languages
permit subject-reduced and VP-reduced clauses. However, it
is the case that some languages do not permit object-reduced
clauses. Some examples follow.

> *Chinese* (Bokamba 1975)
> (126) wang dále nánháizi wang tile nyúhaizi
>   wang hit boy   wang hit girl
>   Wang hit the boy and Wang kicked the girl.
> (127) wang dále nánháizi Ø tile nyúhaizi
>   wang hit boy   kick girl
>   Wang hit the boy and kicked the girl.
>   [subject-reduced case grammatical]
> (128) wang gen lee dále nánháizi
>   wang and lee hit boy
>   Wang and Lee hit the boy.
>   [VP-reduced case grammatical]
> (129) *wang dále lee tile nánháizi
>   *wang hit lee kick boy
>   *Wang hit and Lee kicked the boy.
>   [Object-reduced case ungrammatical]
> (130) *wang dále nánháizi lee tile
>   *wang hit boy   lee kick
>   *Wang hit the boy and Lee kicked.
>   [Object-reduced case ungrammatical]
```
```

These observations also hold for Arabic, Thai, and Lango (Watson 1974).

Without a generalization of the sort embodied in VOB, there exists no reason why there should not be languages in which there are object-reduced and VP-reduced clauses but not subject-reduced or in which there are subject-reduced and object-reduced clauses but not VP-reduced. However, if V and O form a more cohesive syntactic unit in general, then it is not surprising that there are some languages which require that the V + O unit be reduced as a unit or not at all.

Phonological Arguments

The following section contains a number of phonological arguments for VOB. Each one makes use of the following general form. In a transitive clause there exists some sort of clause-level phonological behavior--reductions or sandhis--which occur between object and verb but not between subject and verb. This phonological behavior parallels the phonological behavior one observes in the same language between elements whose bonded relationship is not controversial, usually that of the constituent formed by possessor and possessed. If the behaviors are the same, then it is inferred that the bonding is parallel as well. If it is different, then that case provides no evidence either for or against VOB. There will be evidence against VOB just in case there is phonological behavior between subject and transitive verb that parallels that between possessor and possessed which is not also paralleled by object and verb.

Lake Miwok (Silva 1973). Lake Miwok has SOV as its basic constituent order. It also has a rule which shifts word stress from non-final to final syllable in certain circumstances. It is normally the case for both noun and verb roots to be stressed on the first syllable. However, when suffixes are added to such a root, the stress shifts to the second (final) syllable of the root:

(131) ʔáje + -npa + t----------->ʔajénpat
      stick+onto+allative   to the stick

(132) túmaj + ṭu--------------> tumájṭu
      stick+inst   with a stick

(133) ʔélaj + -ak------------->ʔelájak
      baby+to possess   to have a baby

Bound morphemes and their roots were discussed above as prototypical examples of grammatical bonding. At the phrase level with (at least) two sorts of NPs--adjective + noun and quantifier + noun--the stress shift will occur:

(134) /ʔáde / to be big, large

?itikut   se ?ade
his teeth also be big
His teeth are also big.
    [pred. adj.: no shift occurs]

?adée   putúukon
large black ants
large black ants
    [adj. + noun: shift occurs]

(135)   /cáne/   to be numerous

jómin cáne
reservation-subj be numerous
There are many reservations.
    [pred. adj.: no shift occurs]

canée   koócan
many   people
many people
    [quantifier + noun: shift occurs]

The bonding between these elements, like that of the
affix and root cases, is not controversial. But object
nominals in transitive clauses also undergo stress shift.
Subject nominals do not (Silva 1973:66):

(136)   /wíki/   battery

wikíi   konṣíkan?ina
battery they-charge-fut-n ina
They're going to charge the battery.
    [shift occurs]

wíki-n j óok
battery-subj be dead
The battery is dead.
    [shift does not occur]

French Selkirk (1972). Selkirk shows that while the object
of a transitive verb undergoes liaison, the indirect object
does not. Thus, the object of a transitive verb is bonded to
the verb to a greater extent than is the indirect object.
    What is needed for this study is evidence to show that
liaison does not work with the subjects of transitive verbs.
The data below show that liaison does not occur between the
subject of a transitive verb and the verb:

(137)   le   žã   ašet   boku   dǝ sa
        les gens achetent beaucoup de ça

The people buy a lot of that.
    [no liaison]

(138) *le žã zašet boku dɔ sa
      [*liaison]

(139) lez om   ɛm   sa
      les hommes aiment ça
      Men like that.
      [no liaison]

(140) *lez om zɛm sa
      [liaison]

However, liaison does occur between a transitive verb and its object:

(141) nu   dɔnɔrõ zun   pɔm a notr mer
      nous donnerons une pomme à notre mère
      We will give an apple to our mother.
      [liaison]

Thus, French liaison comprises additional support for VOB.

Yoruba (Bamgbose 1964). There are phonological processes in Yoruba which apply to certain two-word phrases when the second word begins with a vowel. There are various cases reported, and among these are several verb + object sequences:

(142) V́ + N ----> V́   gbé odó ----> gbódó
                                   lift the mortar
      V́ + Ǹ ----> V́   mú ìwé ----> múwé
                                   take a book
      V + Ǹ ----> V̀   ka ìwé ----> kàwé
                                   read a book

While there are other cases described, there are no cases of a transitive nominal subject undergoing the same process.

Maninka (Spears 1967). There is a tone dissimilation process in Maninka which applies only to the objects of transitive verbs and to the objects of prepositions. Subjects of both transitive and intransitive verbs do not undergo the dissimilation.

Ga'anda (Newman 1971). There is a downstep tone process in Ga'anda which applies to certain two-word sequences. While the data are unclear, due in part to the variety of circumstances under which the process is active, it is still the case that the process applies to noun+noun sequences

which semantically are cases of inalienable possession and to
verb+object sequences where the verb is either continuous or
future.

(143) mbɔ̀rtá   katɔ̀tá ----> mbɔ̀rtá   kátɔ́tá
      katəta's age group [inalienable possession]
(144) ngɔ̀t pílex púnó ngɔ̀t ----> pílex púnó
      I am husking maize.

Igbo (Welmers 1973:138). Igbo contains a complex system of
syntactically determined tone sandhi rules. Welmers notes
that in some cases the sandhi between verb and object is the
same as the sandhi that occurs between genitive and head.
Further, both of these are different from the sandhi that
occurs between subject and verb. This fits the pattern for
phonological evidence described above.

Miscellaneous Evidence

This section contains one argument for VOB that does not fit
into any of the categories presented above.

Reciprocals in Chrau (Thomas 1971:72). There are two
reciprocal constructions in Chrau: those with what Thomas
calls joint or non-separated subjects (which are always
plural), and those with separated subjects. With a
non-separated subject and an intransitive verb, the
reciprocal construction consists of the plural subject
followed by the verb with a reciprocal prefix:

(145) vo'n   tăm-ôp
      we   recip-work
      We will work together.
(146) var   ndu   tăm-co'nh
      two   people recip-love
      Two people loved each other.

When the verb is transitive and there is an object NP,
the construction is the same with the object following the
verb:

(147) vo'n   tăm-dip   măt
      we   recip-look eyes
      We looked into each other's eyes.

With a separated subject and an intransitive verb, the
reciprocal construction consists of the first subject
followed by the verb with the reciprocal prefix, plus a
secondary "subject" marked with a particle /bay/. This
secondary subject may either precede or follow the verb:

(148) yau tămdwan   bay sipai
tiger recip-complete part rabbit
The tiger competed with the rabbit.

(149) něh tăm-dăh   bay ănh
3sg   recip-hunt part 1-sg
He went hunting with me.

(150) ănh bay něh tăm-gâl
1sg part 3sg recip-trade
I traded with him.

When the verb is transitive and there is an object NP, the secondary subject may precede the verb as in (151), or it may follow it. But if the secondary subject does follow the verb, it will ordinarily (and perhaps always) follow the entire verb-object complex:

(151) něh bay siklô   tăm-dip măt
3sg   part husband-her recip-look eyes
She and her husband looked into each others eyes

(152) něh tăm-pit   daq bay vatau
3sg recip-contest land part king
He contested the land with the king.

Here again is a case where it is more difficult to insert material between the object and transitive verb than between the subject and a transitive verb.

LIMITATIONS ON VOB

There are two limitations on the principle of VOB. The first limitation is the same as one placed on the TFP. The principle should not be interpreted as any sort of absolute language universal. Instead, it is to be interpreted as another of a number of independent functional principles which shape and constrain the grammars of natural languages. As one of a set of forces, the effect of the principle may be augmented or reduced or neutralized by the effect of other forces in some particular case.

The second limitation, discussed above, is that the principle embodies no claim about VP-constituency. The principle of VOB is not to be interpreted as a claim that there is a VP-constituent in either the underlying or surface structure of any language. It may be the case, however, that VOB may provide some explanation for why some language or group of languages has a VP-constituent as opposed, say, to a S-V constituent.

Chapter 5

THE ANIMATED FIRST PRINCIPLE

INTRODUCTION

This fifth chapter describes, motivates, and limits a third
functional principle that shapes the grammars of the
languages of the world: The Animated First Principle (AFP).
The basic claim embodied by this principle is a simple one.
In a transitive clause, all other things being equal, there
is a tendency for the most "animated": NP to precede other
NPs. An NP represents an "animated" entity to the extent it
matches the prototypical human agent.
     As with the other data chapters, there are several steps
which must be taken to motivate the AFP. The first section
describes more completely just what the AFP is intended to
capture, including describing precisely what the term
"animated" refers to. The second section presents the
argumentation used to motivate the AFP. Here, as with the
other chapters, it is necessary to demonstrate that
"animated" NPs tend to precede less animated NPs in
transitive clauses. The third section presents the data
through which the AFP is motivated. The data for this
principle are somewhat more restricted than for the other two
principles, and, consequently, this principle is somewhat
less well motivated. The final section presents the limits
on the AFP. It, like the other two principles, should not be
construed as an "absolute" linguistic universal, but rather
as one of a set of forces which interact to produce the
distribution of the basic constituent order types.

THE PRINCIPLE AND ITS INTERPRETATION

The principle of Animated First (AFP) is presented below in
(1):

     (1) The Animated First Principle: in simple basic
          transitive clauses, the NP which is most animated
          will precede NPs which are less animated.

102

The essential claim embodied by (1) is reasonably clear. In simple transitive clauses, the sort of clauses examined for both the TFP and VOB, the first NP will tend to be the one that is the most animated. In order to motivate this principle, it must be made clear how one is to determine which of two NPs is the more "animated."

The data which underpin the AFP are somewhat less extensive than for the other two principles. This is due primarily to a certain difficulty in finding cases in which the TFP was not a possible factor. However, there are a sufficient number of cases in which the order of elements in a simple transitive clause seems clearly to be determined by the relative animatedness of the NPs. These cases include absolute constraints on the ordering of elements in a transitive clause as well as strong preferences for an ordering consistent with the AFP.

"Animatedness" and the Animatedness Hierarchy

There are two components to the notion of "animatedness" used in this volume. The first component is primarily a pragmatic one. One NP will be more animated than another if, all other things being equal, the referent of the former NP is more animate (in the traditional sense) than the other. Thus, for English, the examples in (2) contrast more animate with less animate NPs:

(2) *More animate*   *Less Animate*
     woman   vase
     monkey   tortilla
     dog   rock
     spider   dust
     bacteria   grass

The primary difference between the two columns is that the members of the left-hand column are more capable of independent or dynamic activity than the members of the right-hand column. Inanimates, since they are not alive, are incapable of independent activity; full animates, like human beings, are fully capable of independent activity. Some animates, like bacteria, may be alive, but their potential for true independent activity is severely limited.

These examples can be transformed into a sort of hierarchy illustrating the relative animateness (not the animatedness) of these English NPs:

(3) woman > monkey > dog > spider > bacteria > grass>
     dust >rock> tortilla > vase

This specific hierarchy might be generalized as in (4):

103

(4)   *more animate > less animate*

and one common way to segment that hierarchy is shown in (5):

(5)   *human > other animate > inanimate*
      more animate   less animate

The grammars of different languages may break up the generalized hierarchy in different ways. For instance, English seems to make a simple split between animate and inanimate NPs after spider. So, for instance, the prototypical semantic agent in English is animate, and there is a significant difference in the meanings of (6) and (7) that is related to the difference in animateness between *woman* and *dust*:

(6)   The woman smothered the fire.
(7)   The dust smothered the fire.

That other languages are also sensitive to differences in animateness is not controversial. Still, it can be exemplified by noun classification in Bantu or Australian languages, or by pronominal systems as in Tibetan, for instance, and so on. What one does not expect to find is a language which lumps together non-contiguous chunks of the hierarchy.

The second aspect to the notion of animatedness is a semantic one. One NP will be more animated than another if it is higher on a hierarchy of semantic roles derived from Fillmore (1968:24-25, 33):

(8)   Hierarchy of case roles

      Agent > Instrumental > Benefactive/Dative > Patient

Fillmore's discussion was intended to describe his semantic cases in general as well as the assignment of semantic cases to underlying syntactic relations, especially *subject*. The underlying subject of an English sentence was argued to be the NP which was closest to the agent-end of the hierarchy.

The use here of the terms *agent*, *patient*, and so forth will follow the traditional pattern. The *agent* is the typically animate instigator of some event, the patient is the typically inanimate affected recipient of the action described in the verb, and so on. Following the traditional patterns is not to say that there are no problems with that pattern, but this pattern will suffice for the purposes of the present volume. However, excellent discussions of the problem of defining agent and its connection to animacy can be found in Cruse (1973) and DeLancey (1984). There is, however, one potential confusion to anticipate and eliminate. Semantic roles are not ultimately determinable independently of some clause, rather they are linked in some way to the predicate. For instance, the underlined phrases in (9) and (10) are *agents* in English.

(9) *John* hit Mary.
(10) Mary was hit *by John*.

This is true even if it were the case that it was some intentional act by Mary that led, as she planned, to her being hit by John.

At this point it is useful to combine the two semantic and pragmatic components into a single notion of *animatedness*, as well as combine the hierarchies in (3) and (8) into a single *animatedness* hierarchy. The reason for doing so is that while semantic roles and animacy are to a certain extent independent, they are also to a certain extent not independent.

Animacy and semantic role can be shown to be independent to a certain extent relatively easily. One need only consider cases of inanimate agents. Thus, the underlined NPs in (11) and (12) are clearly not animate, but they are the agents in the sentences.

(11) *The clorox* whitened my clothes.
(12) *Our new computer* finished those calculation in 132 seconds.

On the other hand, it can be argued that animacy and semantic role are not altogether independent. The essential link between the two is the fact that the prototypical agent is also animate (among other things). Thus, certain grammatical tests for 'agent' will never identify non-animates as agents, for they focus on properties that only animate beings have. For instance, only animates (and perhaps not even all of them) are capable of volitional action. Thus, two common tests for agent--purpose adverbial clauses and certain manner adverbials (Gruber 1967)--will not identify non-animates as agents:

(13) *The clorox carefully whitened my clothes.
(14) *The clorox whitened my clothes in order to make me happy.
(15) *Our new computer carefully finished those calculations in .32 seconds.
(16) *In order to meet the final deadline, our new computer finished those calculations in .32 seconds.

In addition, only agents will be the addressees of imperatives, since an imperative is an exhortion to do something. Further, the addressee of an imperative will typically be animate, as only animates have the potential for choosing to obey the imperative or not. This connection can be illustrated by the use of vocatives in imperatives. Vocatives can be addressed felicitously only to animates since only animates can respond:

(17)   Oh, Mary?
       What?
       Get lost!
(18) *Oh, rock?
       (no response)
(19) *oh, onion?
       (no response)

Vocative expressions may occur with any properly formed imperative, and there are no imperatives which may not take some vocative:

(20)   Oh John, give me another argument for Theme
       First.
(21)   Bart! Get the hell off that table.
(22) *Oh, rock, crash through that window.
(23) *Onion! Soften but do not brown in that butter.

The above examples serve to demonstrate that animacy and semantic role are not completely independent.

For the purposes here, one NP will be considered more animated than another if it is the case that it falls higher on an animatedness hierarchy. This hierarchy is presented in (24) below:

(24)   *The Animatedness Hierarchy*
       human > other animate > inanimate
       agent > benefactive/dative > patient
       more animated > less animated

This hierarchy combines the two components of animatedness discussed above. The most animated NP will be a human agent; the least animated NP will be an inanimate patient. In the middle will fall a range of cases including inanimate agents and animate patients. The latter two cases are the cases that illustrate the greatest possible conflict between animacy and semantic role. While the ultimate decision about which of these two is more animated requires more language-specific work, it seems to be the case that semantic role takes precedence over animacy. Thus, for the purposes here, *the wind* in (25) is more animated than *my brother*:

(25) *The wind* knocked *my brother* over.

It is worth discussing the connection between animacy and agent a bit more. This additional discussion should make clearer both why the two notions can be combined, and why in the specific hierarchy in (24) semantic role takes precedence over animacy when conflicts arise.

Cruse (1973) discusses in detail the problem of 'agentivity.' He provides a very clear description and analysis of much of the primary work on agentivity, including that of Fillmore, Halliday, Gruber, and Lyons.

In addition, however, he provides a very coherent (though tentative 1973:18) semantic analysis of the problem of his own. Cruse demonstrates that agentives cannot be identified merely by using *do*-clauses, and suggests that agentives may constitute a definable subset of doers. Four independent semantic features are involved in delimiting that set: volitive, effective, initiative, and agentive.

Though Cruse makes no claims in this regard, each feature he identifies one semantic aspect of the prototypical agent. The volitive feature involves a stated or implied act of will (1973:18). It is clear that only animates are capable of independent acts of will, and that not even all animates are so capable. Further, in a transitive clause an act of will generally be performed by the agent. The initiative feature involves the ability to begin an action "by giving a command" (1973:20). Again, it is clear that only animates can exercise an ability to command.

The effective feature involves the exertion of a force, which may be physical or metaphorical, through position or motion (1973:19). Here, too, most animates will be capable of changing position or of moving, but some non-animates, like the wind, are capable of motion. The agentive feature also involves the exertion of a force, but here the energy is internal. Clearly, humans and other large animates are ordinarily perceived as initiating actions through an internal energy source. Further, some non-animates, like cars or computers, also may be perceived as having an internal power source.

Stewart (1984) investigates the cognitive bases for the perception of animacy. She shows that the kinds of motion exhibited by objects, even inanimate objects like circles or triangles, affect their perception by subjects as animate. Objects which move in ways superficially inconsistent with simple Newtonian mechanics are taken to exhibit either volition or an internal source of energy, two classic components of agent. For instance, a moving object which stops and begins again is more likely to be perceived as animate than an object which simply continues its motion, as expected under the simple Newtonian principle of inertia.

107

Re-consideration of the animatedness hierarchy in (24) reveals that the prototypical agent--a human being--involves the union of all four of Cruse's semantic features. Thus, the underlined NP in (26) acts volitionally, at his own initiative, and using his own power source to effect the event:

(26) *John* prepared his cat's dinner.

Similarly, the prototypical patient involves none of these semantic features.

The cases in the middle of the hierarchy involve some subset of the four semantic features. The reason that *the wind* is more animated than my brother in (25) is that the wind has the semantic feature effective, and perhaps as well the agentive feature. In this case *my brother* has none of the four features. That is, with respect to the event being described in (25) my brother, though animate, exhibits none of Cruse's features. Thus, he is more like the prototypical patient than the prototypical agent; and he is less like the prototypical agent than is *the wind*.

Thus, animacy and semantic role may ultimately be related via these four semantic features (and perhaps others as well). The four features identify aspects of the prototypical agent, which is animate; thus, it is not surprising that the features focus in part on aspects of animacy. However, not all of these features are restricted to animates. The effective feature, in particular, is not limited to animates. Thus, the wind, a moving bullet, and a falling vase all would exhibit the effective feature, and might therefore be more animated in certain circumstances. Semantic role will take precedence over animacy alone in problematical middle cases when the given inanimate NP is behaving more like the prototypical agent, as determined by the four semantic features, than is the animate NP.

Having described animatedness and the animatedness hierarchy, it is useful to present some illustrative examples. In the cases listed immediately below, the underlined NPs represent the most animated NPs in those clauses (as determined through the animatedness hierarchy):

(27) *The mailman* crushed the beer can.
(28) *My sister* brushed the dog.
(29) *The barber* shaved my father.
(30) *The dog* ate the bone.
(31) *The dog* bit the cat.
(32) *The dog* bit my brother.
(33) *The wind* turned the weathervane.
(34) *The lightning* struck the dog.
(35) *The wind* blew my brother over.

The cases presented in (36) to (42) are more problematic:

(36) *The bacteria* infected the doctor.
(37) *The sun* baked the athlete to a golden brown.
(38) *This book* set me back 22 dollars.
(39) *The onions* made me cry.
(40) *Reading about pasta* interests me.
(41) *The puppy* soaked Lynn completely.
(42) *The story* led Eric to believe in ghosts.

These sentences illustrate some of the kinds of cases that would fall in the center of the hierarchy, and which are difficult to decide. Just how such cases should be resolved is not altogether clear. However, no cases of this problematic sort are included in the data.

Other Discussions of a Principle like the AFP

As with the other two principles, while the AFP does not represent a totally novel idea, there has not been a great deal of explicit discussion of this sort of principle.

Hawkinson and Hyman (1974) discuss what they call the Natural Topic Hierarchy. This hierarchy combines aspects of the AFP and the TFP into a single hierarchy. The order of elements in clauses is claimed to be predictable given this hierarchy.

Silverstein (1976) proposes a semantic hierarchy of animacy to help explain the syntactic facts of split ergativity. This hierarchy ranks NPs according to person and animacy:

(43) 1   2   3   human   animate   inanimate

While the hierarchy was not designed to deal with issues of constituent order, it does capture an important generalization about the prototypical perception of animacy, agency, and person in natural language.

Ransom (1977) discusses in very general terms the tendency for more animate NPs to precede less animate ones. She proposes a simplified general hierarchy, the Hierarchy, which is essentially the same as that in (5), to help explain constraints on the ordering of NPs and passive constructions in English, Navajo, and Japanese.

Schwartz (1974) claims that the three elements of a transitive clause should be interpreted as agent, predicate, and patient. Further, he notes that only three orders of elements are common: Agt Pred Pat, Pred Agt Pat, and Agt Pat Pred. He observes from this that there is "a prevailing tendency to announce the agent nominal before the patient"

(1974:625). Though this simplifies the problem of basic constituent order too much, it still recognizes the existence of a tendency for animated NPs to precede less animated ones.

The Form of Argumentation for the AFP

The evidence required to motivate the AFP must meet the following conditions. It must be demonstrated in a diverse set of languages that in general, in transitive clauses, the most animated NP (as determined by the animatedness hierarchy) tends to precede NPs which are less animated. Thus, for example, data in which there is obligatory movement of more animated NPs to the front of the sentence would support this generalization. In addition, data for which it can be demonstrated there is a preferred reading under which the first NP is the most animated will also support the AFP.

The evidence required to reject the AFP is also simply described. It must be shown in a diverse set of languages that, in general, in transitive clauses the most animated NP does not precede less animated NPs. This situation obtains either if less animated NPs tend to precede more animated NPs or if the distribution of more animated and less animated NPs is random.

The basic argument for the AFP parallels those used for the other two principles. All of the data presented below exhibit grammatical behavior in which more animated NPs precede less animated ones in transitive clauses. The data comes from diverse languages and in different forms. This similarity in behavior can be taken either as accidental or generally constrained. Since it is unlikely that such grammatical behavior is accidental, some principle like the AFP is needed if the general constraint on the behavior of animated NPs is to be captured.

THE DATA FOR THE AFP

This section contains five different language-specific arguments for the AFP. In each case it is demonstrated that in a transitive clause the more animated NPs tend to precede the less animated NPs. While language-specific data alone is not sufficient evidence for the AFP, the set of such arguments presented below together constitutes sufficient evidence to weakly motivate the AFP.

Unmarked Case Roles in Japanese has three postpositions which of the preceding NP: *ga*, *ni*, and *o*. *Ga* is used to signal that the preceding NP is the agent. *Ni* is used to signal that the preceding NP is a dative or benefactive. *O* is used to signal that the preceding NP is the patient. While the use of each of these postpositions is not obligatory, in more formal adult conversation any NP with one of the above semantic roles is marked with its respective postposition. When all of the NPs are marked the order of the NPs in the sentence can vary:

    (44) Kare ga Kanojo ni onnanoko o ageta
            3-sgm agt 3-sgf ben girl-pass-child pat give-past
            He have her the child.
    (45) Kare ga onnanoko o kanojo ni ageta
    (46) Kanojo ni kare ga onnanoko o ageta
    (47) Kanojo ni onnanoko o kare ga ageta
    (48) Onnanoko o kare ga kanojo ni ageta
    (49) Onnanoko o kanojo ni kare ga ageta

However, it is possible to delete the postpositions in Japanese sentences. In particular, Japanese parents may delete them in speaking to their children. The question that arises is how children interpret those sentences.

Sentences without postpositions are multiply ambiguous. However, in every case there does exist one unmarked, preferred interpretation in which the NPs are assigned semantic roles according to the animatedness hierarchy in order of their appearance. Thus, if the above sentences are presented without postpositions, the unmarked reading are different. However, the semantic structure remains constant: Agent first, Benefactive second, Patient last.

    (50) Kare kanojo onnanoko ageta
            he she child give-past
            He gave her the child.
            (Agt Ben Pat)
    (51) Kanojo kare onnanoko ageta
            She gave him the child.
            (Agt Ben Pat)
    (52) Onnanoko kanojo kare ageta
            The child gave him to her.
            (Agt Ben Pat)
    (53) Kanojo onnanoko kare ageta
            She gave him to thy child.
            (Agt Ben Pat)
    (54) Onnanoko kare kanojo ageta
            The child gave her to him.
            (Agt Ben Pat)
    (55) Kare onnanoko kanojo ageta

He gave her to the child.
(Agt Ben Pat)

In each case the unmarked interpretation involves the assignment of semantic roles to the NPs according to their position on the animatedness hierarchy.

Further, if one of the NPs is marked with a postposition, the preferred interpretation of the remaining NPs follows the animatedness hierarchy and the AFP (the position of the *marked* NP can, of course, vary):

(56) Kare ga kanojo onnanoko ageta
He gave her the child.
(Agt *Ben Pat*)

(57) Kanojo kare ga onnanoko ageta
He gave her the child.
(*Ben* Agt *Pat*)

(58) Kanojo onnanoko kare ga ageta
(*Ben Pat* Agt)

(59) Kare kanojo ni onnanoko ageta
(*Agt* Ben *Pat*)

(60) Kanojo ni kare onnanoko ageta
(Ben *Agt Pat*)

(61) Kare onnanoko kanojo ni ageta
(*Agt Pat* Ben)

(62) Kare kanojo onnanoko o ageta
(*Agt Ben* Pat)

(63) Kare onnanoko o kanojo ageta
(*Agt* Pat *Ben*)

(64) Onnanoko o kare kanojo ageta
(Pat *Agt Ben*)

Since the interpretation of sentences such as those above is clearly not random, some systematic principle must govern the typical interpretation. Clearly, some principle like the AFP controls those unmarked interpretations.

Marked Word Orders in K'ekchi (Pinkerton 1976b). K'ekchi is a VOS Mayan language. Like most verb-initial languages, K'ekchi permits the fronting of various constituents. As can be seen in the examples below, all orders are permitted:

(65) štiqkwasi li kwa   li išq   (VOS)
heated   the tortilla the woman

(66) štiqkwasi li išq li kwa   (VSO)

(67) li išq štiqkwasi li kwa   (SVO)

(68) li kwa štiqkwasi li išq   (OVS)

(69) li išq li kwa štiqkwasi   (SOV)

(70) li kwa li išq štiqkwasi   (OVS)

However, not all marked orders are permitted in every case. In cases where it is ambiguous which NP is the agent of the transitive verb, the first NP is always interpreted as agent. Thus, in (70) below, the only possible interpretation is the one given:

(71) li kašlan li c'i? škop   (SOV)
    the chicken the dog pecked
    The chicken pecked the dog.

This constraint, consistent with the AFP, precludes certain marked orders under special circumstances in K'ekchi. When the subject is animate or human and the object is inanimate, no confusion of semantic roles is possible, and, as (65-70) and (72-77) below show, all marked orders are possible:

(72) škwa? li kwa   li c'i?   (VOS)
    ate the tortilla the dog
(73) škwa? li c'i? li kwa   (VSO)
(74) li c'i? škwa? li kwa   (SVO)
(75) li kwa škwa? li c'i?   (OSV)
(76) li c'i? li kwa škwa?   (SOV)
(77) li kwa li c'i? skwa?   (OSV)

But when the subject is animate or human and the object is also animate or human, those marked orders are precluded in which the object precedes the subject. That is, those marked orders are precluded in which the first NP must be interpreted as patient in order to maintain the original interpretation in the set. For example, consider (78-83):

(78) ssak' li kwiinq li išq   (VOS-basic)
    hit   the man   the woman
    The woman hit the man.
(79) ssak' li išq li kwiinq   (VSO)
(80) li išq ssak' li kwiing   (SVO)
(81) ?li kwiinq ssak' li išq   (?OVS)
(82) li išq li kwiinq ssak'   (SOV)
(83) *li kwiinq li išq ssak'   (*OSV)

The same pattern would obtain if the subject was human (/kwiinq/-'man') and the object was animate (/c'i?/-'dog'), if the subject was animate (/kašlan/- 'chicken') and the object was animate (/c'i?/-'dog'), or if the subject was animate (/c'i?/-'dog') and the object was human (/kwiinq/-'man').

When the subject is inanimate and the object is animate or human, those marked orders are again precluded in which the first NP must be interpreted as patient in order to maintain the original interpretation in the set. Further,

113

the marked order VSO is also excluded, since ordinarily
agents are animate and the ordinary reading of such a VSO
sentence would be a VOS interpretation (with a different
meaning). Examples are presented in (84-89):

(84) špic' li kwiinq li kair   (VOS-basic)
      squash the man   the car
      The car squashed the man.
(85) *špic' li kair li kwiinq   (*VSO)
(86) li kair špic' li kwiinq   (SVO)
(87) *li kwiinq špic' li kair   (*OVS)
(88) li kair li kwiinq špic'   (SOV)
(89) *li kwiinq li kair špic'   (*OSV)

The same pattern holds exactly when the subject is
inanimate (/ceʔ/-'tree') and the object is animate
(/c'iʔ/-'dog').

The data from K'ekchi provide support for the AFP in
much the same way that the Japanese data does. Potential
ambiguities in the readings of transitive clauses are
resolved by reading the first NP as the agent--that is, as
the most animated NP. Thus, for a given semantic structure
certain marked orderings of the NPs are precluded. The AFP
provides a concise explanation of why those and only those
orders discussed above are precluded.

Benefactive-Patient Order in Sesotho

Sesotho (Morolong and Hyman 1977) is a Bantu language with
SVO as its basic constituent order. In bitransitive clauses
the basic order, like other Bantu languages, is S V IO O.

When there is a difference in animacy between the
benefactive and the patient, the order of elements
obligatorily follows that described by the animatedness
hierarchy. That is, the animate benefactive obligatorily
precedes the inanimate patient:

(90) Ke-phehétsé ngoaná lijó (Ben Pat)
      I-cooked   child food
      I cooked food for the child.
(91) *Ke-phehétsé lijó ngoaná (*Pat Ben)
(92) Ke-bítselítsé bana   mokété (Ben Pat)
      I-called   children feast
      I called the children to the feast.
(93) *Ke-bíitselítsé mokété baná (*Pat Ben)

However, when both NPs are equally animate, either order
is possible. But in such cases, the sentences are ambiguous:

(94) Ke-bítselítsé morena baná

```
            I-called       chief children
            I called the children to the chief.
               (Ben Pat)
                  OR
            I called the chief to the children.
               (Pat Ben)
    (95) Ke-bítselítsé baná       morena
            I-called       children chief
            I called the chief to the children.
               (Ben Pat)
                  OR
            I called the children to the chief.
               (Pat Ben)
```

While it is not stated which reading is the preferred
one, one would predict that the *Ben Pat* order is the unmarked
interpretation of such ambiguous sentences. The distribution
of NPs in bitransitive clauses thus constitutes additional
evidence for the AFP.

Subject-Object Inversion in Navajo

The basic constituent order of Navajo is SOV. We will be
concerned with constraints on alternative orderings of NPs
(Hale 1972, Frishberg 1972). The basic alternation is
illustrated in (96) and (97):

```
    (96) łįį'   dzaanééz yi-ztał
         horse mule       him-kicked
         The horse kicked the mule.
    (97) dzaanééz łįį'   bi-ztał
         mule       horse him-kicked
         The mule was kicked by the horse.
```

In (96) the subject (and agent) occurs first, followed
by the object and finally the verb with a marker /yi-/. In
(97) the order of phrases is reversed, and the marker on the
verb is /bi-/.
   Hale observes that there are certain cases in which the inversion
described above is not permitted. These are cases in which the animacy of
the subject is greater than that of the object. Thus, in (98) below,
subject-object inversion is blocked since the subject, /diné/, is more
animate than the object, /tsin/:

```
    (98) diné tsin naa'ayíítséél
         man  tree chopped-down-yi
         The man chopped down the tree.
    (99) *tsin diné naa'abíítséél
```

Hale also observes that there are cases in which
subject-object inversion is obligatory. These are cases in
which the animacy of the object is greater than that of the
subject. Thus, in (100) below, subject-object inversion is
obligatory since the object, /'ashkii/, is more animate than
the subject, /tó/:

    (100) 'ashkii tó   bi-isxį
           boy   water him-killed
           The water killed the boy.
    (101) *tó 'ashkii yi-isxį

It would appear, then, that the data from Navajo provide
additional support for the AFP. Subject-object inversion is
optional if the NPs are equal in animacy, blocked when the
subject is more animate, and obligatory when the object is
more animate. The basic constraint, then, seems to be that
the more animate of the two NPs must come first.

This is probably sufficient data to justify using Navajo
for the AFP. However, one might note that animatedness
involves more than animacy alone. The Navajo case would
provide even stronger support for the AFP if there existed
special cases or marginal cases which involved not just
animacy but also some of the additional semantic features
described above. There are such cases.

For instance, lightning and rain are each, respectively,
less animate (in the traditional sense) than either a horse
or a boy. Thus, one would expect the subject-object
inversions presented below:

    (102) łįį'   ii'ni'   bi-isxí
           horse   lightning him-killed
           The lightning killed the horse.
    (103) shiye'   níłtsá nábístłéé
           my   son rain   wet
           The rain wetted my son.

Based simply on animacy alone, one would not expect the
non-inverted forms to occur. But they do:

    (104) ii'ni'   łįį   yiisxį
    (105) níłtsá shiye' náyístłéé

In this sort of case lightning and rain are more
animated than horse or son because in this case the lightning
and rain involve at least the effective, and perhaps the
agentive feature, while the horse and the boy in this case
involve none of the features.

Thus, while the specific manner in which Navajo breaks
up the animatedness hierarchy is not completely understood,
it is clear that the ordering of NPs in Navajo involves

the factors of animacy and semantic role, and that the constraints on the ordering of NPs are well captured by the AFP.

The Order of Agent Chomeurs in Cebuano

The basic order of constituents in Cebuano is VSO. Cebuano, like other Philippine languages, has a set of promotion rules which advance objects, indirect objects, and certain non-terms to subject (Dryer 1978). The cycle-initial subject, of course, becomes a chomeur. This is illustrated below:

> (106)   nag-palit ang   babaye sa   saging
>   agt-buy   subj. woman non-subj. banana
>   The woman bought the bananas.
> (107)   gi-palit sa   babaye ang   saging
>   pat-buy non-subj. woman subj. bananas
>   focus
>   The bananas were bought by the woman.

In (106), the verb is initial, the subject is second, and the object is final. In (107), the verb is still initial, the former object has been promoted to subject, and the former subject has become a chomeur. The prefix on the verb in each case signals the semantic role of the surface subject.

Dryer observes that the unmarked order of constituents in the active is subject-indirect object-direct object-non-terms. And he further observes that it is common for promoted NPs to take the position of the cycle-initial term it replaces, and for the chomeur to take a position common of non-terms. In fact, there is a strong tendency for agent chomeurs to take the position of non-terms. Notice that if this were the case that the order of elements in a cycle-final sentence would match the order of grammatical relations in the Keenan-Comrie hierarchy (1977):

> (108)   Subject > Object > Indirect Object > various
>   non-terms

Now, while Relational Grammar explicitly does not claim that the order of cycle-final constituents *must* follow (108), it is the case that this order is frequent (though Dryer warns that additional data is required to demonstrate this fully). If a language orders its cycle-final constituents in some way different from (108), then such an ordering would be unusual in some way.

In Cebuano, sentences which have undergone one of the promotion rules order their cycle-final elements in the following manner (in the unmarked case):

(109)   agent chomeur > subject > object > indirect
         object > non-terms

This is illustrated in (110) and (111) below:

(110)   mi-hatag si   Maria sa   sabing kang Pedro
         agt-give sub Maria non- banana non- Pedro
                              sub   sub
         Maria gave the bananas to Pedro.
         (V S O IO)

(111)   gi-hatag   ni   Maria ang saging kang Pedro
         pat-given   non- Maria sub bananas non- Pedro
                     sub   sub
         The bananas were given to Pedro by Maria.
         (V Agt-Chomeur S IO)

(112)   gi-hatag-an   ni   Maria si   Pedro sa   saging
         loc-give-loc   non- Maria sub   Pedro non- bananas
                        sub   sub
         Pedro was given the bananas by Maria.
         (V Agt-Chomeur S O)

In (110), the basic order is illustrated. In (111), the
sentence has undergone one of the promotion rules (II-->I);
the order given is the unmarked order. In (112), the
sentence has undergone another of the promotion rules
(III-->I); the resulting order here also reflects the
unmarked case. In both non-basic sentences the first element
is the agent. This is unusual, but its unusualness comprises
additional data to underpin the AFP. That is, given that we
have a case in which the normally expected order of elements
does not occur, the variation in that order is predictable
via the AFP.

Klamath

It is reported in Banker (1964) that while all orderings of
constituents in a transitive clause are possible, when
sentences of the form N + N + V occur with no overt
morphological markings of case, the reading in which the
agent is first is statistically dominant (1964:341). Thus,
for example, the preferred reading of (113) is (114) not
(115):

(113)   sn'ewe'ts   hiswaqs   sle?a
         woman   man   saw
(114)   The woman saw the man.
(115)   The man saw the woman.

LIMITS ON THE AFP

Like the other two principles, the AFP should not be interpreted as an "absolute" language universal. It, too, is merely one of a set of forces which interact to produce the grammars of particular languages.

In addition, as was the case with the TFP, the most animated NP in a basic transitive clause (the agent) may be identified, for the purposes of this volume, with the subject of a basic constituent order. The primary justification for this is, again, Keenan (1976a) in which one of the properties of subject was agent.

However, as was also the case with the TFP, agent should not be identified with subject beyond this limited purpose. That is, subject can be considered with agent while considering basic constituent orders because in the unmarked case subject and agent do correlate strongly. However, in marked cases subject and agent do not always correlate, so assumption of equivalence of the two is incorrect.

Chapter 6

THE EXPLANATION AND CONCLUDING DISCUSSION

INTRODUCTION

This final chapter addresses two areas. The first section presents an explanation for the frequency distribution of constituent orders described in Chapter 2 in terms of the interaction of the three functional principles motivated in Chapters 3, 4, and 5. The second section presents some concluding discussion.

THE EXPLANATION

Requirements on the Explanation

If one reviews the frequency distribution of basic constituent orders presented in Table (1) below, there are several questions one would like to answer. First, one would like to explain why five constituent orders occur with some frequency (SOV, SVO, VSO, VOS, and OVS), but the other order (OSV) apparently does not. Second, one would like to know why two orders (SOV and SVO) clearly predominate the figures in Table (1) (over 85% of the sample), while verb initial languages form a respectable, but decidedly smaller, minority. Finally, it would be desirable to know why SOV languages outnumber SVO, why VSO and languages outnumber VOS, and why VOS and OVS languages outnumber OSV.

Minimum requirements for an explanation were originally set in Pullum (1977). Pullum states that the explanation must (i) identify all naturally occurring basic constituent orders, and (ii) must exclude all logically possible, but non-occurring, basic constituent orders. Since it seems certain that all six orders do occur, it seems better at this time to frame the minimum requirements in terms of frequency. Thus, the minimum requirements on the explanation can be recast in terms of frequency:

(1) Minimum requirements on an explanation of the distribution of basic constituent order types

    (a)   Identify those constituent orders which occur frequently.
    (b)   Identify those constituent orders which occur infrequently.

While the minimum requirements address the first question above, there are additional requirements which a more complete explanation of the basic constituent order typology should address. In particular, a more fully developed explanation should also explain the relative frequencies of the various constituent orders. It should explain why SOV and SVO languages outnumber verb-initial languages by more than 5 to 1. It should explain why VSO languages outnumber VOS languages by more than 4 to 1. These additional requirements are summarized in (2):

   (2)   Additional requirements on the explanation

     (a) Why do subject-initial languages outnumber verb-initial languages?
     (b) Why do object-initial languages occur so much less frequently than do subject-initial or verb-initial languages?
     (c) Why do VSO languages outnumber VOS?
     (d) Why do VOS and OVS languages outnumber OSV?
     (e) Why do SOV languages outnumber VSO?
     (f) Why do SVO languages outnumber VSO?
     (g) Why are VOS and OVS languages of approximately equal frequency?
     (h) Why are SOV and SVO languages of approximately equal frequency?

Though the minimum and additional requirements overlap to a certain extent, the basic difference between the two is that the minimum requirements are concerned with the basic identification of those orders which are more common and those which are less common, while the additional requirements are concerned with the more detailed question of their relative frequencies.

It will be seen immediately below that the explanation offered in this volume meets fully the minimum requirements described above. Further, it meets fully the additional requirements described above.

The Explanation and Concluding Discussion

The Explanation

Two perspectives will be taken on the explanation of the basic constituent order typology. The first perspective considers the frequency distribution of constituent orders with respect to verb position. The second perspective considers the distribution independent of verb position. For each perspective, the explanation offered is essentially the same. There is a language-general constraint that the ideal basic constituent order for a given verb position is one in which the three principles, TFP, and AFP, and VOB, are maximally realized.

The Realization of the Principles.

It is important to make clear what is intended by the term "realize," and under what circumstances each principle will count as realized in this explanation.

A principle is not realized if it is the case that the claim embodied by the principle does not hold for a given constituent order. Thus, if the hypothetical order VXYO existed, the principle of VOB would not be realized since the categories X and Y intercede between V and O.

A principle is realized if the claim embodied in the principle does hold for the given constituent order. Again, for the hypothetical order VOXY, the principle of VOB *does* hold, and is realized, since V and O occur together.

It was made clear earlier that for each of the principles TFP and AFP, the most thematic NP and the most animated NP were each identifiable with *subject* in basic sentences. This identification is an identification *only* of a strong correlation; it, again, is specifically not a claim that a subject *is* TI or that it *is* the most animated NP. Further, no claim is made that these will continue to correlate in *non-basic* sentences. But, *for the purpose here*, this correlation does hold and is useful for understanding the distribution of basic constituent orders. With this limitation in mind, one can consider when the principles count as *realized* and when they are not.

The TFP is realized if it is the case that the S precedes the O. The TFP is not be realized if the O precedes the S. The AFP is also realized if the S precedes the O. It is not realized if the O precedes the S. VOB is realized if it is the case that the V and O are juxtaposed; the order of the juxtaposition makes no difference. VOB is not realized if the S intervenes between the V and O. These realizations hold only for the purpose of examining the language-general distribution of basic constituent orders. No claim is being made here about the realization of any of these principles in particular languages.

122

The First Perspective: Considering Verb Position.

The three functional principles can be examined in
conjunction with verb position to produce the primary
explanation of the basic constituent order typology. Since
there are three logically possible positions for the verb to
take (initial, medial, and final), and since all three do
occur, the position of the verb will be taken as given and
the ordering possibilities with respect to each possible verb
position contrasted.

Verb final position (SOV vs. OSV). The verb final
constituent order possibilities are SOV and OSV. Given the
discussion of the TFP and the AFP and their mutual relation
to subject in basic sentences, it can be seen that with an
SOV order, both the TFP and the AFP are realized. Since in
basic sentences the syntactic subject tends to correlate with
both TI and the most animated NP (usually the agent), if the
subject is ordered before the object, both the TFP and the
AFP are realized. However, with an OSV order, neither the
TFP nor the AFP is realized, since the O precedes the S.
Further, with the SOV order, the principle of VOB is
realized; the V and O are in juxtaposition. However, for an
OSV possibility, the juxtaposition of O and V is precluded by
the S, and VOB is *not* realized.
   All of these facts are summarized in (3):

   (3) Summary of verb final realizations.

	TFP	AFP	VOB
SOV	YES	YES	YES
OSV	NO	NO	NO

With SOV order all of the principles are realized. But with
OSV order none of the principles are realized.

Verb medial position (SVO vs. OVS). The verb medial
constituent order possibilities are SVO and OVS. For an SVO
order, both the TFP and AFP again are realized: the S
precedes the O. However, with the OVS possibility neither
the TFP nor the AFP can be realized since the O precedes the
S.
   With the SVO possibility, VOB is realized. It is also
realized with the OVS possibility. These observations are
summarized in (4):

(4)   Summary of verb medial realizations.

	TFP	AFP	VOB
SVO	YES	YES	YES
OVS	NO	NO	YES

Discussion.   For the verb final and verb medial possibilities
the tremendous disparity in frequency between the
possibilities for each verb position seems to be related
directly to the realization of the three functional
principles.   In the verb final case, none of the principles
is realized for the OSV possibility, and there is at present
no absolutely clear case of an OSV language.   This is in
direct contrast to the maximum realization of the three
principles for SOV correlating with the highest frequency of
occurrence.

The same observations hold for the verb medial
possibilities.   With the OVS possibility, only one of the
three principles is realized, and there are only a few
reliably reported cases of OVS languages (Derbyshire 1977,
Derbyshire and Pullum 1981).   This represents about one
percent of the final sample.   With the SVO possibility all
three principles are realized, and the proportion of SVO
languages is equal to that for SOV.

Thus, the primary explanation for the frequency
distribution of basic constituent orders is captured in the
general principle stated in (5):

(5)   *The Principle of Maximal Realization (MRP):* The
      ideal basic constituent order for a given verb
      position is one in which the three principles, AFP,
      TFP, and VOB are maximized.

This principle can, and does, explain the primary
observations summarized above in (3) and (4).   In addition,
it can also explain the verb initial cases.

Verb initial position (VSO vs. VOS).   The verb initial
possibilities are VSO and VOS.   For the VSO possibility, only
two of the three principles are realized.   The TFP and the
AFP are realized because the S precedes the O.   However, VOB
cannot be realized, since the S intervenes between the O and
V.

124

For the VOS possibility, only one of the principles is realized--VOB. The AFP and the TFP are both blocked since the O precedes the S. These observations are summarized in (6):

(6) Summary of verb initial realizations.

	TFP	AFP	VOB
VSO	YES	YES	NO
VOS	NO	NO	YES

It is interesting and important to note that for the verb initial possibilities it is not logically possible for all three principles to be realized. If the AFP or the TFP is realized, the only position possible for the O is final position. The S intervenes between V and O and precludes the realization of VOB. On the other hand, if VOB is realized, the O and V will form a unit which results in the S going to final position. Thus, the O precedes the S and blocks the realization of the TFP and the AFP.

Therefore, for verb initial cases, the principles will be maximized if just *two* of the principles are realized. While there is a sizeable number of VOS languages, the predominating order for verb initial cases is the case in which two principles are realized--VSO.

It appears, then, that one can explain the relative frequencies of SVO to OSV, SVO to OVS, and VSO to VOS in terms of a tendency for the three grammatical principles to be maximized for a given verb position for the ideal basic constituent order. The MRP, therefore, provides an explanation which meets the minimum requirements described above. That is, the general principle explains which orders should occur frequently and which should not. This is summarized in (7):

(7) Meeting the minimum requirements.
    frequent   infrequent

SOV	>	OSV
SVO	>	OVS
VSO	>	VOS

A brief look at Table (1) shows that this is correct.

The Explanation and Concluding Discussion

Second Perspective: Considering Only Relative Frequencies

While the discussion above provides an explanation which
meets the minimum requirements set forth above, it is also
possible to meet the additional requirements which a complete
explanation of the distribution of basic constituent orders
should address. The additional requirements are restated in
(8):

(8) Additional requirements on the explanation

    (a) Why do subject-initial languages outnumber
        verb-initial languages?
    (b) Why do object-initial languages occur so much less
        frequently than do subject-initial or verb-initial
        languages?
    (c) Why do VSO languages outnumber VOS?
    (d) Why do VOS and OVS languages outnumber OSV?
    (e) Why do SOV languages outnumber VSO?
    (f) Why do SVO languages outnumber VSO?
    (g) Why are VOS and OVS languages of approximately
        equal frequency?
    (h) Why are SOV and SVO languages of approximately
        equal frequency?

The basic question that underlies all of the questions
in (8) is why one subgroup outnumbers the others. The basic
answer is seen in the orderings presented in (9):

(9) Number of principles realized for each order

$$\frac{3 = 3 > 2 > 1 = 1 > 0}{\text{SOV} = \text{SVO} > \text{VSO} > \text{VOS} = \text{OVS} > \text{OSV}}$$

The greater the number of principles that are realized, the
greater the frequency of the correlating constituent orders.
Several of the additional requirements can be met just
that easily. Question (a): Why do subject-initial languages
outnumber verb-initial languages (as well as all the others)?
The reason that subject-initial languages predominate in the
languages of the world is that subject-initial languages
permit the fullest realization of the three principles, while
verb-initial languages, as well as the other cases, permit
fewer principles to be realized. This establishes the
relative frequencies shown in (10):

(10) SOV   VSO
      SVO > VOS
               OVS
               OSV

Question (b): Why do object-initial languages occur so much less frequently than do subject-initial or verb-initial languages? Object-initial languages are so greatly outnumbered by subject-initial and verb-initial languages because object-initial and verb-initial languages permit relatively fewer principles to be realized (one or none). This establishes the further relative frequencies shown in (11):

(11) SOV   VSO   OVS
           >   >
      SVO   VOS   OSV

Question (c): Why do VSO languages outnumber VOS languages? The reason that VSO languages outnumber VOS languages is that VSO languages permit two of the principles to be realized, while VOS languages permit only one. This gives us (12):

(12) SOV   OVS
           > VSO > VOS >
      SVO   OSV

Question (d): Why do VOS and OVS languages outnumber OSV languages? The general principle, (5), also suggests that VOS and OVS languages outnumber OSV languages because these orders permit one principle to be realized, while the OSV possibility permits none:

(13) SOV > VSO > VOS > OVS > OSV
      SVO

And finally, though the answers to questions (e) and (f) are entailed by the answer to question (a), it is worthwhile to make the answers to these questions explicit. SOV languages outnumber VSO languages because SOV languages permit all three principles to be realized, as opposed to only two for VSO. SVO languages outnumber VSO languages because SVO languages also permit all three principles to be realized, as opposed to only two for VSO.
The remaining two questions are also easily answered. Question (g), why VOS languages equal OVS languages in frequency, is answered by observing that each order permits a single principle to be realized:

(14) SOV > VSO > VOS = OVS > OSV
      SVO

The remaining question, (h), why SOV equals SVO, can be addressed in the following manner. First, one must recall that the absolute frequencies are different--SOV 45.8%, SVO 41.5%. Under the explanation offered here the relative proportions of SOV and SVO languages should be the same. That is, since all three principles are realized for both SOV and SVO cases, their relative frequencies should be the same, too.

As it turns out, while the absolute frequencies are different, that difference is not a significant one statistically. An example can make this clearer. If one were to toss a coin 500 times, one would not expect exactly 250 heads and 250 tails, even though that would be the prediction of probability theory. With a fair coin one might actually observe 240 heads and 260 tails. Such variation from the expected number of heads and tails would not be statistically significant. On the other hand, if one tossed 400 heads and only 100 tails, the variation from the expected number of heads and tails would be significant statistically. In the first case, the variation would be due to chance; in the second case, the variation would be due to something other than chance.

The chi-square statistic can be used to determine whether such variation is due to chance or not. Thus, the chi-square test was used to determine whether or not the difference in proportion between SOV and SVO cases is statistically significant. The explanation offered above predicts that the difference should not be statistically significant; that is, that the variation between SOV and SVO cases is due to chance.

The null hypothesis for this test is that the variation between the proportions of SOV and SVO languages is not statistically significant. The degrees of freedom are one. The level of significance chosen is .05. Thus, the null hypothesis will be rejected if the chi-square sum is greater than 3.84.

A total of 349 languages was included in the final sample. Of these 183 were SOV and 166 were SVO. The explanation offered here predicts the proportions of SOV and SVO should be equal, or 50% of the total number of SOV and SVO languages collected. Thus, one expects that there would be 174.5 SOV languages and 174.5 SVO languages. These facts are reported in (15):

(15)   Contingency table for SOV vs. SVO cases.

	Observed	Expected
SOV	183	174.5
SVO	166	174.5

The chi-square computation for this contingency table is
.828, with one degree of freedom and a significance level of
.05. Thus, the null hypothesis cannot be rejected.
Therefore, the difference in proportion between the SOV and
SVO cases is not significant statistically, which is
precisely what is entailed by the explanation offered above:

(16) SOV = SVO > VSO > VOS = OVS > OSV

Therefore, the explanation offered in this volume addresses
this final additional requirement on any explanation of the
distribution of basic constituent orders.

This, then, concludes the explanation of the frequency
distribution of basic constituent orders. Two sets of
requirements on an explanation were proposed: a minimum set
and an additional set. The explanation presented here
addressed these requirements by proposing that the
distribution of basic constituent orders is explainable in
terms of the three independently motivated functional
principles (TFP, AFP, VOB) and a general principle (MRP) that
requires the maximum realization of the three principles.
This explanation succeeds fully in addressing all the minimum
requirements set for this problem. And, it addresses all of
the additional requirements on any explanation of the basic
constituent order typology.

CONCLUSIONS

This volume has attempted to provide an explanation to deal
with one specific problem in linguistic typology:

(17) What are the relative frequencies of the six basic
     constituent order types and how are those
     frequencies to be explained?

In order to do this it has provided a comprehensive
statistical analysis of the actual and relative frequencies
of the six basic order types, providing in addition the
actual data used to produce the analysis (Appendices A, B,
C). Three fundamental functional principles of linguistic
organization have been presented, hopefully with substantial
empirical motivation. And, these three principles have been
incorporated into a transparent explanation for the relative
frequencies of the basic constituent order types.

In reaching these goals there remain several issues that
warrant some final discussion. These include a discussion of
possible counterevidence to the principles offered above and,
more generally, a discussion of how the explanation offered
in this volume fits into the general goals and directions of
research in linguistic typology.

129

The Explanation and Concluding Discussion

Language-Specific Data as Counterevidence for the Principles

In the discussion of the argumentation for each principle
above, it was asserted that data from single languages could
not constitute sufficient counterevidence to refute a
language-general principle. The principal reason for this is
that under certain circumstances one principle may interact
with another in ways which may neutralize it. So, for
example, under the analysis presented here verb-initial
languages cannot in principle realize all three functional
principles. Either the TFP and AFP can be realized, yielding
VSO orders, or VOB can be realized, yielding VOS orders.
Examination of such languages may provide evidence that
appears to violate one or another of the three functional
principles. But such facts cannot constitute a valid
argument against a principle if (a) interactions are
permitted and (b) the logical possibility for full
realization of all principles is somehow blocked. This is
exactly the case for the TFP in the VOS language Ojibwa
(Tomlin and Rhodes 1979).

Observations about Verb-Initial Languages

Verb-initial languages cannot have all three principles
realized in basic sentences. In VOS languages, the object
precedes the subject, blocking the TFP and the AFP. In VSO
languages, the position of the subject precludes the
juxtaposition of verb and object, thus blocking VOB.
One way verb-initial languages resolve this problem is
to move constituents, most commonly the subject, to
pre-verbal position. Thus, while the three principles may be
blocked with respect to basic sentences, and therefore basic
constituent order, it is possible in non-basic sentences to
have all three principles realized.
But there is also strong evidence that at least in some
cases verb-initial languages do not resolve the conflict this
way, but permit the relevant principle to be 'violated'
systematically. In particular, it appears that some VOS
languages (and perhaps some OVS languages as well) do not
order thematic information first but last.
Tomlin and Rhodes (1979) argue strongly that in Ojibwa,
a VOS Algonquian language, thematic information is
consistently ordered *last*. This is shown in two ways. First,
symptomatic evidence in Ojibwa patterns exactly the opposite
of such evidence in other language types. For example,
indefinite NPs almost always *precede* the verb, they almost
never occur sentence finally. Since indefinite NPs correlate
with non-thematic information and explicitly *not* with
thematic information (see Chapter 3), and since the preposed
indefinite NPs are rule-produced, the Ojibwa data run exactly

130

counter to that observed for movement rules in Chapter 3. This kind of construction is, in fact, used to introduce new referents into a text, just as existentials, which tend to move indefinite NPs to the ends of sentences, are used in other languages.

In addition, definite NPs, which correlate with shared and with thematic information, tend to follow the verb and to gravitate to the end of the sentence. Further, unlike every other language examined in this study, Ojibwa does not have a topicalization strategy which fronts definite NPs. And this, coupled with the evidence about indefinite NPs, make it seem clear that the TFP is not realized in Ojibwa as it is in most other languages. In fact, it appears that the linear distribution of information in the Ojibwa texts examined is basically the reverse of that ordinarily found.

Second, there is direct evidence from the analysis of Ojibwa texts to show that thematic information comes later in Ojibwa. Using the method of establishing text goal hierarchies described above, Tomlin and Rhodes show that NPs independently identified as thematic consistently are placed at the ends of Ojibwa sentences and clauses. Parallel analysis of the English translations shows exactly the opposite pattern.

If the observations concerning Ojibwa are correct, observations which appear to be paralleled in a number of other languages (Mazatec-VOS, Malagasy-VOS, Oiampi-OVS), then it will be the case that at least one language, VOS, will be found not to have the TFP realized in it. Such an outcome is entailed by the approach taken here: both VOS and OVS languages (and possibly OSV as well) should fail to realize the TFP. No cases should be found of SOV, SVO, or VSO languages which do not.

In a similar vein, the approach taken here makes some predictions about the realization of the other principles in the less frequent word order types. Evidence for VOB in VSO and OSV languages should be difficult to obtain; evidence for the AFP should be difficult to obtain for VOS and OVS languages. It remains to be seen whether such outcomes actually obtain empirically.

Goals of Typological Research

On the surface at least the goals of typological research are straightforward. First, it is necessary to describe in concrete terms the nature of and extent of grammatical variation within the languages of the world. This in itself is no easy task, complicated as it is by the dual problem of structural categories which are too constraining, like subject, verb, and object, and semantic and pragmatic categories which are not constrained enough, like transitivity or agent or theme.

Second, it is necessary to explain the descriptions of typological variation one records. There are three constraints on typological explanation. One, it must account for the predominating patterns observed in the described data. In the present study this means, for instance, accounting for why subject-initial languages occur so much more frequently than the other orders. Two, one must account for the occurrence of rare and marked patterns. An explanation must permit the existence of marked patterns and provide a coherent and intuitively satisfying reason both for their existence and for their low frequency. And, three, an intuitively satisfying explanation must be framed in terms of underlying, causal principles which lead to the typological states observed.

Generalizations of structural regularities cannot meet these constraints. While they succeed in accounting for the predominating patterns observed, they fail both to provide insight into marked patterns and to provide any sort of causal motivation for the structural regularities observed. For example, the correct structural generalization that subjects tend to precede objects in the languages of the world does account for the principal observations. But it does not provide, nor can it in principle provide, any insight into why verb-initial orders are less frequent but more frequent than object-initial languages or into why these states of affairs should obtain at all.

Only functionally-grounded explanations can do this. The principal reason for this is that it is the process of discourse production and comprehension, engaged in by specific individuals, whose working grammars are shaped by constraints on human information processing abilities, that ultimately effects typological facts. It is the linguistic performance of individuals that leads to typological regularity.

If functionally-grounded explanations are required for typological explanation, then the discovery of principles of the sort proposed here becomes a crucial part of typological research. Such principles must be motivated by both cross-linguistic and psycholinguistic observations to ensure both their typological universality and their cognitive basis.

The Cognitive Basis for Functional Principles

While it has been beyond the scope of the present investigation, it is to be expected that one will be able to demonstrate that each of the functional principles proposed here should find its ultimate motivation in the processes and limitations of human information processing abilities.

It was argued above that thematic information represents the linguistic reflex of more fundamental processes of attention in human cognition. Under specific task and rhetorical circumstances certain aspects of the events or subject matter under scrutiny become either more salient or more important, and it these bits of information that attention is directed to. This has been shown convincingly in the area of visual information processing. For instance, Yarbus (1967) showed that eye movement patterns recorded for a given picture differ when subjects are given different general purposes for examining the picture. Under such task circumstances the locus of the fovea corresponds precisely to the locus of attention. More recent work on the visual processing of complex pictures confirms and expands Yarbus' original observations (Antes and Penland 1981, Friedman and Liebelt 1981, Loftus and Mackworth 1978). When a new task or purpose is placed before a subject, attention is reallocated, and the subject produces a new pattern of visual response.

Very much the same sort of thing seems to happen linguistically. It is no accident that discussions of theme invariably end up referring to 'focus' or 'point of view'. Such terms reflect awareness that under differing task and rhetorical conditions the speaker may either find his own attention shifted, or he may find it necessary to try to shift the attention of the hearer in some way or other. Linguistic studies by Chafe (1972, 1976, 1986) on the differential activation of information in memory, by Kuno (1972) on speaker empathy, and by Givón (1984 ed.) illustrate this phenomenon in language.

There are also several linguistic studies which examine the relation between attention and grammar more directly. As described above, Tomlin and Kellogg (1986) manipulate the general task orientation taken by subjects who must solve a mapping task by responding to oral instructions. Changes in attention allocation resulted in the facilitation of performance of the mapping task when the grammatical form of the instructions was consistent with that allocation and they resulted in inhibition of performance when the grammatical form of the instructions was inconsistent.

Tomlin (1986a) demonstrates that the syntactic alternation between nominal and pronominal NPs in English is directly a function of attention allocation. If attention is sustained on a referent during discourse production,

133

reference will be maintained with a pronominal form. If
attention is disrupted and returned to a referent during
discourse production, even for a very short time, as little
as a single clause, reference must be reestablished with a
nominal NP.

These studies show very clearly that the manipulation of
attention during discourse processing affects directly and
immediately the grammar of discourse production. Like the
Yarbus studies of attention during picture processing, they
show that changing attention allocation on the fly during
discourse processing results in changes in the linguistic
performance of subjects engaged in discourse production and
comprehension. If the evidence remains at the moment
inconclusive, it is certainly highly suggestive of a direct
and important connection between processes of attention
allocation and the use of grammar in discourse. That is, the
evidence is good that the TFP has substantial grounding in
cognitive constraints on information processing in discourse.

The situation is not as strong for either the AFP or
VOB, but it is not altogether missing either. For the AFP it
is necessary to demonstrate that there is some cognitive
basis for a preference to notice animated entities. There is
some limited psychological research which supports this.
Stewart (1984) investigates the relationship between object
motion and the perception of animacy. If geometric objects,
circles or triangles, are moved in particular ways, subjects
will describe them as animated and engaged in intentional and
controlled activity. Animacy, thus appears to represent a
very fundamental human concept, tied to agency (volition and
control) through such basic properties as the native and
source of motion in an object.

Research in linguistics also suggests a cognitive basis
for some principle like the AFP. DeLancey (1981, 1984) has
argued convincingly that the semantic concept of agent is
linked to more fundamental, and presumably universal, notions
of causation. Animacy as a component of agentivity
represents an artifact of the fact that only animates can
exhibit volition and control. These, in turn, are linked to
causation as special cases of ultimate and mediating causes
(1984: 182-184). In a similar vein, Langacker and his
students (Langacker 1979, Smith 1985, among others) have
argued that linguistic expression reflects iconically, at
least in unmarked construction, the conventional image of an
event described. Grammatical constructions can be analyzed
in terms of the source and flow of energy through an event
(Smith 1985) with the conventional flow of energy flowing
from the agent to a patient. Developmentally, children
interpret two argument propositions as agent before patient
before sorting out the semantics of marked structures like
passives (Ochs 1982).

134

While the evidence for the cognitive basis for the AFP is at this point not entirely convincing, it does seem very much the case that there is substantial reason to believe that additional research in this area will result in the grounding of the AFP in more general processes of cognition.

For VOB there exists at this time little, if any, serious evidence for its cognitive grounding. The hypotheses that seems most plausible at the present moment are two. First, the specific relationship of verb to object described above may reflect general semantic processes of predicate formation. There are clearly more events, actions, and states discernible and describable than there are lexical verbs to get the job done. Combining verbs with lexical complements clearly represents a principal means by which the range of predications possible in human language can be extended and elaborated. Consistent with such a point of view, Keenan (1984) observes that absolutives, which include subjects of intransitive clauses as well as objects of transitives, exhibit a number of semantic properties that show greater semantic dependency on the part of absolutives to verbs than is the case with ergatives, the subjects of transitive clauses. Absolutives show what Keenan terms 'existence dependency', wherein predicates can express the coming into existence of absolutives but not ordinarily ergatives (1984:200):

(18) A crowd gathered around John.
(19) He committed a crime/made a mistake.

Keenan observes, too, that the specific 'sense' of a predicate may differ depending on the nature of the associated absolutive (1984:201):

(20) John/The horse   :is still running.
     The car/the watch
     The faucet/His nose
     My Fair Lady
(21) John cut: his arm/foot.
                      his nails. his hair/his lawn.
                      the cake/the roast.
                      a path/a tunnel.
                      his whiskey with water.
                      production quotas/prices.

Such evidence is consistent with the specific motivation for VOB described above. Chafe (1986) has made a similar point in his comments about "unitary concepts" and certain VO constructions, such as noun incorporation.

The second, more general, hypothesis is that semantic concepts which are closely related to one another are realized syntactically through close proximity. Such a

135

hypothesis has been captured in several places in linguistics
as described in Chapter 4 (Bartsch and Vennemann 1972, Bazell
1953). However, there appears to be no psycholinguistic
literature to demonstrate that such a process is activated in
the linguistic performance of individuals during discourse
production or comprehension.

Alternative Principles Rejected

One of the remaining issues to be addressed in this volume is
why these three principles are the ones offered and not
others, and why there are just three principles and not, say,
two or six.
    First, there seem to be only a few alternative
candidates. These include a number of structural principles,
like Greenberg's observation that subjects tend to precede
objects, as well as two possible functional principles. In
general, none of the alternatives seem particularly
attractive, either in that they are not well motivated or are
not very specific or not applicable to the problem at hand.
    There appear to be three possible structural principles
one might consider:

(22) Possible structural principles
    1. Subjects tend to precede objects (Greenberg
        1963).
    2. Grammatical relations tend to linearize
        according to the Keenan-Comrie hierarchy
        (Pullum 1977).
    3. Subjects tend to occur at sentence peripheries
        (Dryer p.c.).

The first two principles are familiar ones and, while
incomplete explanations on their own, do describe well the
general typological situation. The third principle captures
the more detailed observation that in SOV languages adverbial
material tends to come between the subject and the remainder
of the constituents in the clause, SXOV (Dryer p.c.). In
addition, while exceptional, some VOS languages, like
Malagasy, keep their subjects on the periphery as well
(VOXS).
    There are three basic objections one can articulate
against these structural principles. The first objection is
theoretical. Under the functional approach adopted here
there seems to be no reason to postulate an independent set
of structure linearizing principles. Structure, either
grammatical relations or linear order, is assumed to realize
semantic or pragmatic functions of one sort or another. It
thus seems odd to postulate a principle of structure (order)

realizing structure (grammatical relations) unless the ideas of subject or grammatical relations represent some kind of shorthand for semantic or pragmatic functions.

The second objection is empirical. For these principles to be well motivated they should be motivated independently of the particular problem of dealing with basic constituent order frequencies. Greenberg's original observations cannot contribute to an explanation, for they represent simply a description of the facts obtaining. In this respect Pullum's proposal is satisfactory for the Keenan-Comrie hierarchy was motivated to deal with quite different syntactic issues (though as described above the overall explanation is not entirely well motivated).

The third objection is also theoretical. The three functional principles proposed here are strongly motivated, both in that there is substantial cross-linguistic data in support of each and in that there exists some evidence that each has, at least in principle, some psycholinguistic or cognitive grounding. The structural principles above have neither, except, again, to the extent that they represent alternative expressions of the three functional principles proposed here. What, after all, would be a cognitive motivation for having subjects before objects strictly from a *structural* point of view, unless it were to put thematic information or animated information in a needed location?

There appear to be only two functional principles to consider:

(23) Some alternative functional principles.
1. Heavy material comes later in the sentence (Mallinson and Blake 1981).
2. Old information precedes new information.

The first principle is one which is needed in functional explanations. It is clear that in many languages longer expressions are moved to the ends of sentences, presumably to make them easier to parse and interpret. However, this principle is not relevant to the consideration of the frequency of basic constituent order types, for the elements considered are all of the same basic weight and structure: simple nominal arguments and simple verbs. Thus, while needed to deal with the functional distribution of information in marked and unmarked sentence types in particular languages, this particular principle has little role to play in addressing the general question here.

The second principle represents an alternative widely used both in the literature and in informal discussion. However, this particular principle is either incorrect or too vague or too general. If 'old' information is taken to mean shared information, the principle is incorrect, for there is no direct connection between order and shared information,

only a correlation between thematic information and shared
information which gives the appearance that shared
information may have something to do with order. If, as is
often the case, 'old' information covers both shared and
thematic information, the principle is both too vague and too
general, for shared information and thematic information
represent distinct pragmatic categories, which tend to have
different and independent syntactic manifestations.

There thus appear to be no viable alternative candidates
to the three principles proposed above. Each of these has
been well motivated with cross-linguistic data from a wide
range of languages. Further, all three principles are
required, for each is independent of the others.

Functional Principles in Typological Research

There seem to be two paths that typological research must
take. In its initial stages, both for the sub-discipline as
a whole and for specific studies, attention must be devoted
to the systematic observation of structural regularities and
variation exhibited cross-linguistically. Explanations for
those structural regularities lead to the discovery of
functional principles relevant to understanding the
typological facts observed. This is the sort of study well
represented by the Stanford Universals group or by works like
Hawkins (1983) or Dryer's developing research into word order
(Dryer 1984, 1985). This is also the sort of study
represented by the present volume. Certain structural
observations, the relative frequencies of the six structural
constituent order types, led to an explanation grounded in
three well-motivated functional principles.

But in its second stage typological research turns the
order of inquiry around. It begins with the functional
principles and inquires how they are manifested structurally
in the languages of the world. Putting the question in this
manner frees one from certain hedges and limitations that the
former approach invites. For instance, in this volume the
TFP could be manifested only by the relative orderings of S
to O; all specific facts about the syntactic realization of
thematic information cross-linguistically were simplified to
fit into that framework. For this reason, it was necessary
to hedge that while the TFP represents a general constraint
on the ordering of information cross-linguistically, no claim
was made about the role of order *per se* in coding thematic
information in specific languages.

By turning the order of inquiry around a new sort of
opportunity arises. No structural presuppositions are made,
and the resulting typological observations can be more
fine-grained. For instance, by asking how thematic
information is manifested cross-linguistically, one can
observe that some languages, like Czech or Hungarian, use

order directly, but other languages, like English, code
thematic information via syntactic subject (Tomlin 1983) with
word order synchronically only a correlate of this. The kind
of typological taxonomy resulting from such inquiry has room
in it for cases which the present study was forced to
exclude. Dyirbal, for instance, is not represented in the
database because its word order facts simply cannot be
represented by S, O, and V. However, from the point of view
of its manifestation of thematic information the Dyirbal
absolutive as used in text looks remarkably similar to the
use of syntactic subject in English. Thus, on this one
functional dimension, it seems possible to characterize and
categorize languages which grosser structurally-oriented
typologies cannot.

The present volume, then, represents but a first step in
understanding cross-linguistically issues of functional
principles and basic word order. It has, within the
typological tradition begun by Greenberg and developed by
many others, systematically categorized the world's languages
within an established structural framework, determining with
some accuracy the relative frequencies of the six possible
orderings of subject, object, and verb. It has also offered
an explanation for those relative orderings grounded in three
independently motivated and cognitively grounded functional
principles; those orders are most frequent which are most
consistent with these functional principles, those orders are
least frequent which are least consistent with these
principles. As a first step in understanding the role of
functional explanation in typology, this, hopefully, is
sufficient, but the real challenge must come when the order
of inquiry is reversed and the discovery of how these three
principles are manifested cross-linguistically in particular
languages is begun.

REFERENCES

Antes, J.R. and Penland, J.G. 1981. Picture context effects
    on eye movement patterns. *Eye Movements: Cognition and
    Visual Perception*. 157-170. Eds. D.F. Fisher *et al*.
    Hillsdale, N.J.: Erlbaum

Awbery, G.M. 1976. *The Passive in Welsh*. Cambridge:
    Cambridge University Press

Bach, E. 1974. *Syntactic Theory*. New York: Holt, Rinehart
    and Winston

Bamgbose, Ayo. 1964. Verb-nominal collocations in Yoruba: a
    problem in syntactic analysis. *Journal of West African
    Languages* 1: 27-32

Banker, M.A.R. 1964. *Klamath Grammar*. University of
    California Publications in Linguistics 32. Los Angeles:
    University of California Press

Bartsch, R. and Vennemann, T. 1972. *Semantic Structures: A
    Study in the Relation Between Semantics and Syntax*.
    Frankfort and Main: Athenaum

Bates, E. and MacWhinney, B. 1979. A functionalist
    approach to the acquisition of grammar. *Developmental
    Pragmatics*. 167-211. Ed. E. Ochs and B. Schiefflin.
    New York: Academic Press

——————————————————————————. 1981. Functionalist
    approaches to grammar. *Language Acquisition: The State
    of the Art*. Eds. L. Gleitman and E. Wanner. New York:
    Cambridge University Press

Bates, E.; McNew, S.; MacWhinney, B.; Devescovi, A.; and
    Smith, S. 1982. Functional constraints on sentence
    processing: A cross-linguistic study. *Cognition* 11:
    245-299

140

Bazell, C.E. 1953. *Linguistic Form*. Istanbul: Istanbul Press

Bell, A. 1978. Language samples. *Universals of Human Language Volume 1*. 123-156. Ed. J. Greenberg. Stanford: Stanford University Press

Bese, L.; Dezso, L.; and Bulya, L. 1970. On the syntactic typology of the Uralic and Altaic languages. *Theoretical Problems of Typology and the Northern Eurasian Languages*. 113-128. Ed. L. Dezso and P. Hadju. Amsterdam: B.R. Govner

Blansitt, E. 1973. Bitransitive clauses. *Working Papers in Language Universals* 13: 1-26. Stanford: Language Universals Project, Stanford University

Bokamba, E.G. 1975. Observations on the immediate dominance constraint, topicalization, and relativization. *Studies in African Linguistics* 6: 1-22

Breckenridge, J. 1975. The post cyclicity of *es*-insertion in German. *Papers from the Eleventh Regional Meeting of the Chicago Linguistics Society*. 81-91. Eds. R. Grossman *et al*. Chicago: Chicago Linguistics Society

Byarushengo, E.R. and Tenenbaum, S. 1976. Agreement and word order: a case for pragmatics in Haya. *Proceedings of the Second Annual Meeting of the Berkeley Linguistics Society*. 89-99. Eds. H. Thompson *et al*. Berkeley: Berkeley Linguistics Society

Chafe, W. 1970. *Meaning and the Structure of Language*. Chicago: University of Chicago Press

_____. 1971. Directionality and paraphrase. *Language* 47: 1-26

_____. 1973. Language and memory. *Language* 49: 261-281

_____. 1974. Language and consciousness. *Language* 50: 111-133

_____. 1976. Givenness, contrastiveness, definiteness, subjects, topics, and points of view. *Subject and Topic*. 25-56. Ed. C.N. Li. New York: Academic Press

_____. 1986. Cognitive constraints on information flow. *Coherence and Grounding in Discourse*. Ed. R. Tomlin. Amsterdam: John Benjamins

Chung, S. 1976. On the subject of two passives in Indonesian. *Subject and Topic*. 57-98. Ed. C.N. Li. New York: Academic Press

Clancy, P. 1980. Referential choice in English and Japanese narrative discourse. *The Pear Stories: Cognitive, Cultural, and Linguistic Aspects of Narrative Production*. 127-201. Ed. W. Chafe. Norwood, N.J.: Ablex

Coate, H.H.J. and Oates, L. 1970. *A Grammar of Ngarinjn*. Canberra: Australian Institute of Aboriginal Studies

Comrie, B. 1973. The ergative: variations on a theme. *Lingua* 32: 239-253

_____. 1975. The antiergative: Finland's answer to Basque. *Papers from the Eleventh Regional Meeting of the Chicago Linguistics Society*. 112-121. Eds. R. Grossman *et al.* Chicago: Chicago Linguistics Society

Cruse, D.A. 1973. Some thoughts on agentivity. *Journal of Linguistics* 9: 11-23

Culicover, P. and Wexler, K. 1974. The invariance principle and universals of grammar. *Social Science Working Paper* 55. Irvine, Cal.: University of California

Daneš, F. 1970. One instance of Prague school methodology: functional analysis of utterance and text. *Theory and Method in Linguistics*. 132-146. Ed. P. Garvin. The Hague: Mouton

_____. 1974. FSP and the organization of the text. *Papers on Functional Sentence Perspective*. Ed. F. Daneš. The Hague: Mouton

DeLancey, S. 1981. An interpretation of split ergativity and related patterns. *Language* 57: 626-657

_____. 1984. Notes on agentivity and causation. *Studies in Language* 8: 181-213

Derbyshire, D.C. 1961. Hixkaryana (Carib) syntactic structure. *International Journal of American Linguistics* 27: 125-142, 226-236

_____. 1965. *Textos Hixkaryana*. Museu Paranese Emilio Goeldi, Publicacoes Avulsas, no. 3. Belem, Para.

_____. 1977. Word order universals and the existence of an OVS language. *Linguistic Inquiry* 8: 590-599

_____ and Pullum, G. 1981. Object-initial languages. *International Journal of American Linguistics* 47: 192-214

Diehl, L. 1975. Space case: some principles and their implications concerning linear order in natural language. *North Dakota Work Papers* 19: 93-150. Bismarck, N.D.: SIL

van Dijk, T. and Kintsch, W. 1983. *Strategies of Discourse Comprehension*. New York: Academic Press

Dik, S.C. 1978. *Functional Grammar*. Amsterdam: North-Holland

Dixon, R.M.W. 1977. *A Grammar of Yidiñ*. Cambridge: Cambridge University Press

Dryer, M. 1978. Some theoretical implications of grammatical relations in Cebuano. *University of Michigan Publications in Linguistics* 2.4: 1-43. Ann Arbor: Department of Linguistics, University of Michigan

_____. 1983. Word order in Tlingit. Unpublished paper. Department of Linguistics, University of Alberta

_____. 1984. A statistical study of word order universals. Final report for the Social Science and Humanities Research Council of Canada

_____. 1985. Universals of negative position. Paper presented at the Fourteenth Annual Linguistics Symposium, University of Wisconsin-Milwaukee, Wisconsin, March 1985

du Bois, J. 1980. The trace of identity in discourse. *The Pear Stories: Cognitive, Cultural, and Linguistic Aspects of Narrative Production*. 203-274. Ed. W. Chafe. Norwood, N.J.: Ablex

Fillmore, C. 1968. The case for case. *Universals in Linguistic Theory*. 1-90. Ed. E. Bach. New York: Holt, Rinehart and Winston

Foley, W. 1976. *Comparative Syntax in Austronesian*. Unpublished PhD dissertation. Department of Linguistics, University of California, Berkeley

143

_____ and Van Valin, R. 1977. On the organization of "subject" properties in universal grammar. *Berkeley Studies in Syntax and Semantics* 3: 293-320. Berkeley, Cal.: University of California

_____. 1984. *Functional Syntax and Universal Grammar*. Cambridge: Cambridge University Press

Fox, B. 1986. Anaphora in popular written English narratives. *Coherence and Grounding in Discourse*. Ed. R. Tomlin. Amsterdam: John Benjamins

Friedman, A. and Liebelt, L.S. 1981. On the time course of viewing pictures with a view towards remembering. *Eye Movements: Cognition and Visual Perception*. 137-156. Ed. D.F. Fisher *et al*. Hillsdale, N.J.: Erlbaum

Frishberg, N. 1972. Navajo object markers and the great chain of being. *Syntax and Semantics Volume* 1. 259-266. Ed. J. Kimball. New York: Seminar Press

Geytenbeek, B. and Geytenbeek, H. 1971. *Gidabal Grammar and Dictionary*. Canberra: Australian Institute of Aboriginal Studies

Givón, T. 1975. Serial verbs and syntactic change: Niger-Congo. *Word Order and Word Order Change*. 47-111. Ed. C.N. Li. Austin: University of Texas Press

_____. 1976. Topic, pronoun, and grammatical agreement. *Subject and Topic*. 149-188. Ed. C.N. Li. New York: Academic Press

_____. 1979. *On Understanding Grammar*. New York: Academic Press.

_____. 1981. Typology, functional domains, and passivization. Paper presented at the Linguistics Colloquium, University of Oregon, April 1981

_____ (ed). 1984. *Topic Continuity*. Amsterdam: John Benjamins

_____. 1985. *Syntax: A Functional-Typological Approach*. Volume 1. Amsterdam: John Benjamins

Glock, N. 1972. Clause and sentence in Saramaccan. *Journal of African Languages* 11: 45-61

Greenberg, J. 1963. Some universals of grammar with particular reference to the order of meaningful elements. *Universals of Language.* 58-90. Ed. J. Greenberg. Cambridge, Mass.: MIT Press

Gross, M. 1979. On the failure of generative grammar. *Language* 55: 859-885

Gruber, J. 1967. Look and see. *Language* 43: 937-947

Haga, C. 1976. On two movement rules in Norwegian. *University of Washington Working Papers* 2: 25-31

Hale, K. 1972. A note on subject-object inversion in Navajo. *Issues in Linguistics: Papers in Honor of Henry and Renee Kahane.* 300-309. Ed. B. Kachru *et al.* Champaign: University of Illinois Press

Halliday, M.A.K. 1967. Some aspects of the thematic organization of the English clause. Memorandum RM-5224-PR. Santa Monica, Cal.: Rand Corporation

_____. 1968. Notes on transitivity and theme in English, part 3. *Journal of Linguistics* 4: 179-214

Harrison, S. 1976. *Mokilese Reference Grammar.* Honolulu: The University Press of Hawaii

Hawkins, J.A. 1983. *Word Order Universals.* New York: Academic Press

Hawkinson, A. and Hyman, L. 1974. Hierarchies of natural topic in Shona. *Studies in African Linguistics* 5: 147-170

Hopper, P.J. and Thompson, S.A. 1980. Transitivity in grammar and discourse. *Language* 56: 251-299

Horton, A.E. 1949. *A Grammar of Luvale.* Johannesburg: Witwaterstrand Press

Hoskison, J.T. 1975. Focus and topic in Gude. *Proceedings of the Sixth Conference on African Linguistics. Ohio State Working Papers* 20: 227-233. Columbus, Ohio: Department of Linguistics

Hsieh, N.-I. 1976. Noun-modifier order as a consequence of VSO order. *Lingua* 42: 91-109

Hurford, J. 1977. The significance of linguistic generalizations. *Language* 53: 574-620

Hyman, L. 1975. On the change from SOV to SVO: evidence from Niger-Congo. *Word Order and Word Order Change*. 113-147. Ed. C.N. Li. Austin: University of Texas Press

Innes, G. 1966. *An Introduction to Grebo*. London: School of Oriental and African Studies

Johnson-Llaird, P.K. 1983. *Mental Models*. Cambridge, Mass.: Harvard University Press

Jones, L. 1977. *Theme in Expository Discourse*. Lake Bluff, Illinois: Jupiter Press

Jones, R.B. 1961. *Karen Linguistic Studies*. University of California Publications in Linguistics 25. Berkeley: University of California Press

Keenan, E.L. 1976a. Remarkable subjects in Malagasy. *Subject and Topic*. 247-302. Ed. C.N. Li. New York: Academic Press

_____. 1976b. Toward a universal definition of subject. *Subject and Topic*. 303-334. Ed. C.N. Li. New York: Academic Press

_____. 1984. Semantic correlates of the ergative/absolutive distinction. *Linguistics* 22: 197-224

_____ and Comrie, B. 1977. Noun phrase accessibility and universal grammar. *Linguistic Inquiry* 8: 63-99

Kenny, J. 1974. *A Numerical Taxonomy of Ethnic Units Using Murdock's 1967 World Sample*. Ann Arbor: University Microfilms

Kimenyi, A. 1976. Subjectivization rules in Kinyarwanda. *Proceedings of the Second Annual Meeting of the Berkeley Linguistics Society*. 258-268. Eds. H Thompson *et al*. Berkeley: Berkeley Linguistics Society

Kintsch, W. 1974. *The Representation of Meaning in Memory*. Hillsdale, N.J.: Erlbaum

_____ and van Dijk, T. 1978. Toward a model of text comprehension and production. *Psychological Review* 85: 363-394

Kroeber, A.L. 1909. Noun incorporation in American languages. *XVI Internationaler Amerikanisten-Kongress*. 569-576. Ed. F. Heger. Vienna and Leipzig: Hartleben

Krupa, V. 1982. Syntactic typology and linearization. *Language* 58: 639-645

Kuno, S. 1972. Functional sentence perspective: a case study from Japanese and English. *Linguistic Inquiry* 3: 269-320

Lang, A. 1975. *The Semantics of Classificatory Verbs in Enga (and other Papua New Guinea Languages)*. Pacific Linguistics Series B, no. 39. Canberra: Australian National University

Langacker, R.W. 1979. Grammar as image. *Linguistic Notes from La Jolla* 6: 88-126

Leben, W. 1975. A note on the base form of the Hausa verb. *Studies in African Linguistics* 6: 239-248

Lee, K. 1975. *Kusaiean Reference Grammar*. Honolulu: University of Hawaii Press

Lehmann, W. 1973. A structural principle of language and its implications. *Language* 49: 47-67

Li, C.N. (Ed.). 1976. *Subject and Topic*. New York: Academic Press

_____ and Thompson, S.A. 1976a. Strategies for signaling grammatical relations in Wappo. *Papers from the Thirteenth Regional Meeting of the Chicago Linguistics Society*. 450-467. Eds. W.A. Beach *et al*. Chicago: Chicago Linguistics Society

_____. 1976b. Subject and topic: a new typology of language. *Subject and Topic*. 457-490. Ed. C.N. Li. New York: Academic Press

_____. 1976c. On the issue of word order in a synchronic grammar: a case against movement transformations. *Lingua* 39: 169-181

Loftus, G.R. and Mackworth, N.H. 1978. Cognitive determinants of fixation location during picture viewing. *Journal of Experimental Psychology: Human Perception and Performance* 4: 565-572

Lord, C. 1977. How Igbo got from SOV serializing to SVO compounding. *Studies in African Linguistics Supplement* 7: 145-155

MacWhinney, B. 1982. Basic syntactic processes. *Language Acquisition: Syntax and Semantics.* 73-136. Ed. S. Kuczaj. Hillsdale, N.J.: Erlbaum

_____ and Bates, E. 1978. Sentential devices for conveying givenness and newness: a cross-cultural developmental study. *Journal of Verbal Learning and Verbal Behavior* 17: 539-558

Mallinson, G. and Blake, B.J. 1981. *Language Typology.* Amsterdam: North-Holland

Marascuilo, L.A. and McSweeney, M. 1977. *Nonparametric and Distribution-Free Methods for the Social Sciences.* Monterey, Cal.: Brooks/Cole Publishing

Mardirussian, G. 1975. Noun incorporation in universal grammar. *Papers from the Eleventh Regional Meeting of the Chicago Linguistics Society.* 383-389. Eds. R. Grossman *et al.* Chicago: Chicago Linguistics Society

Masica. C. 1976. *Defining a Linguistic Area: South Asia.* Chicago: University of Chicago Press

McCawley, J. 1972. An exhausting but not necessarily exhaustive list of idioms in English. Unpublished list

Merlan, F. 1976. Noun incorporation and discourse reference in Nahuatl. *International Journal of American Linguistics* 42: 177-191

Moerman, M. 1976. The preference for self-correction in a Tai conversational corpus. *Language* 54: 872:882

Morolong, M. and Hyman, L. 1977. Animacy, objects, and clitics in Sesotho. *Studies in African Linguistics* 8: 199-218

Mould, M. 1974. The syntax and semantics of the initial vowel in Luganda. *Third Annual Conference on African Linguistics.* 223-230. Ed. E. Voeltz. Bloomington: Indiana University

Munro, P. 1975. Subject copying, auxiliarization, and predicate raising: the Mojave evidence. *International Journal of American Linguistics* 42: 99-112

Murdock, G.P.   1966.   Cross-cultural sampling. *Ethnology* 5:
    97-114

_____.   1967.   *Ethnographic Atlas*.   Pittsburgh:
    University of Pittsburgh Press

_____.   1967-71.   Addenda and corrigenda to the
    ethnographic atlas.   *Ethnology* 6, 7, 8, 9

Newman, R.M.   1971.   Downstep in Ga'anda.   *Journal of African
    Languages* 10: 15-27

Nguyen, D.L.   1970.   Four syllable idiomatic expressions in
    Vietnamese.   Pacific Linguistic Series D, no. 16.
    Canberra: Australian National University

Ochs, E.   1982.   Ergativity and word order in Samoan child
    language.   *Language* 58:646-671

Perkins, R.D.   1980.   *The Evolution of Culture and Grammar*.
    Unpublished dissertation.   Department of Linguistics,
    SUNY, Buffalo

Perlmutter, D. and Postal, P.   1977.   Toward a universal
    characterization of passive.   Unpublished manuscript

Pettinari, C.   1983.   The function of a grammatical
    alternation in fourteen surgical reports.   *Applied
    Linguistics* 4: 55-76

Pinkerton, S.   1976.   Ergativity and word order. *Studies in
    K'ekchi*.   44-66.   Ed. S. Pinkerton. Austin: University
    of Texas

Postal, P.   1974.   *On Raising*.   Cambridge: MIT Press

Pullum, G.   1977.   Word order universals and grammatical
    relations.   *Grammatical Relations.   Syntax and Semantics
    Volume 8*.   249-277.   Ed. P. Cole and J. Sadock.   New
    York: Academic Press

Ransom, E.   1977.   Definiteness, animacy, and NP ordering.
    *Proceedings of the Third Annual Meeting of the Berkeley
    Linguistics Society*.   418-429.   Eds. K. Whistler *et al*.
    Berkeley: Berkeley Linguistics Society

Renck, G.L.   1975.   *A Grammar of Yagaria*.   Canberra:
    Australian National University

References

Rigsby, B. 1975. Nass-Gitksan: an analytical ergative syntax. *International Journal of American Linguistics* 41:4

Ross, J.R. 1967. *Constraints on Variables in Syntax.* Unpublished dissertation. Department of Linguistics, MIT

Ruhlen, M. 1975. *A Guide to the Languages of the World.* Stanford: Language Universals Project, Stanford University

Sanders, G. 1970. Constraints on constituent orders. *Papers in Linguistics* 2: 460-502

Sapir, E. 1911. The problem of noun incorporation. *American Anthropologist* 13: 250-283

Schachter, P. 1976. The subject in Philippine languages: topic, actor, actor-topic, or none of the above. *Subject and Topic.* 491-518. Ed. C.N. Li. New York: Academic Press

Schegloff, E.A.; Jefferson, G.: and Sacks, H. 1977. The preference for self-correction in the organization of repair in conversation. *Language* 53: 361-382

Schwartz, A. 1974. The VP-constituent of SVO languages. *Proceedings of the 11th International Congress of Linguistics.* 619-637. Ed. L. Heilmann. Bologna: Il Mulino

Sedlak, P. 1975. Direct/indirect object word order: a cross-linguistic analysis. *Working Papers in Language Universals* 18: 117-164. Stanford: Language Universals Project, Stanford University

Selkirk, E. 1972. *The Phrase Phonology of English and French.* Unpublished dissertation. Department of Linguistics, MIT

Silva, C.M. 1973. Stress shift in Lake Miwok. *You Take the High Node and I'll Take the Low Node: Papers from the Comparative Syntax Festival.* 65-70. Ed. C. Corum et al. Chicago: Chicago Linguistic Society

Silverstein, M. 1976. Hierarchy of features and ergativity. *Grammatical Categories in Australian Languages.* 112-171. Ed. R.M.W. Dixon. Canberra: Australian Institute of Aboriginal Studies

150

Smith, E.W. 1907. *A Handbook of the Ila Language*. Oxford: Oxford University Press

Smith, M.B. 1985. An analysis of German dummy subject constructions in cognitive grammar. Paper presented at the First Annual Pacific Linguistics Conference, University of Oregon,Eugene, Oregon, October 1985

Sneddon, J.N. 1975. *Tondano Grammar and Phonology*. Canberra: Australian National University

Spears, R. 1967. Tonal dissimilation in Maninka. *Journal of African Linguistics* 7: 88-100

Steele, S. 1975. On some factors that affect and effect word order. *Word Order and Word Order Change*. Ed. C.N. Li. Austin: University of Texas Press

Stewart, J. 1984. Object motion and the perception of animacy. Paper presented at the Psychonomic Society Meeting, San Antonio, Texas, November 1984

Tai, J. 1969. Coordinate reduction. Bloomington: Indiana University Linguistics Club.

Thomas, D. 1971. *Chrau Grammar*. Honolulu: University of Hawaii Press

Tomlin, R. 1974. Unpublished notes from a field methods course on Achenese. Department of Linguistics, University of Michigan

_____. 1976. A discourse constraint on some movement rules in English. Unpublished paper. Department of Linguistics, University of Michigan

_____. 1979. *An Explanation of the Distribution of Basic Constituent Orders*. Unpublished dissertation. Department of Linguistics, University of Michigan

_____. 1983. On the interaction of syntactic subject, thematic information, and agent in English. *Journal of Pragmatics* 7: 411-432

_____. 1985. Foreground-background information and the syntax of subordination. *Text* 5: 85-122

_____. 1986a. Linguistic reflections of cognitive events. *Coherence and Grounding in Discourse*. Ed. R. Tomlin. Amsterdam: John Benjamins

_____. 1986b. The identification of clause-level theme in text and discourse. Unpublished manuscript. Department of Linguistics, University of Oregon

_____ (ed). 1986. *Coherence and Grounding in Discourse.* Amsterdam: John Benjamins

_____ and Kellogg, W.A. 1986. Theme and attention orientation in procedural discourse. Unpublished paper. Department of Linguistics and the Cognitive Science Program, University of Oregon and IBM T.J. Watson Research Center

_____ and Rhodes, R. 1979. An introduction to information distribution in Ojibwa. *Papers from the Fifteenth Regional Meeting of the Chicago Linguistics Society.* 307-321. Eds. P. Clyne et al. Chicago: Chicago Linguistics Society

Tucker, A.N. and Bryan, M.A. 1966. *Linguistics Analyses. The Non-Bantu Languages of North-Eastern Africa. Handbook of African Languages, Part III.* Oxford: Oxford University Press

Ultan, R. 1969. Some general characteristics of interrogative systems. *Working Papers on Language Universals* 1: 41-63. Stanford: Language Universals Project, Stanford University

Vennemann, T. 1973. Explanation in syntax. *Syntax and Semantics II.* 1-50. Ed. J. Kimball. New York: Seminar Press

_____. 1974. Topics, subjects and word order; from SXV to SVX via TVX. *Historical Linguistics.* 339-376. Eds. J.M. Anderson and C. Jones. Amsterdam: North-Holland

Voegelin, C.F. and Voegelin, F.M. 1977. *Classification and Index of the World's Languages.* New York: Elsevier North-Holland

Watson, K. 1974. Identity deletion phenomena in Lango. *Third Annual Conference on African Linguistics.* 259-265. Ed. E. Voeltz. Bloomington: Indiana University Press

Weil, H. 1877 (1844). *De l'Ordre des Mots dans les Langues Anciennes Comparée aux Langues Modernes.* Trans. C. Super. Boston: Ginn & Co

Welmers, W. 1973. *African Language Structures*. Berkeley and Los Angeles: University of California Press

Wolfenden, E. 1971. *Hilagaynon Reference Grammar*. Honolulu: University of Hawaii Press

Woodbury, A. 1975. *Ergativity of Grammatical Processes: A Study of Greenlandic Eskimo*. Unpublished MA thesis. Department of Linguistics, University of Chicago

Yarbus, A.L. 1967. *Eye Movements and Vision*. trans. B. Haigh. New York: Plenum Press.

Appendix A

SOME LANGUAGES AND THEIR BASIC CONSTITUENT ORDERS

This appendix contains a list of 1063 languages and their basic constituent orders. The first column contains the name of the language. The second column contains the basic constituent order. The third column contains an areal code for the language (see Appendix C for a list which explains these codes). The fourth column contains the genetic affiliation of the language, determined through Voegelin and Voegelin (1977). The final column contains the references consulted in collecting or determining the basic constituent order. All of these references are listed separately at the end of this appendix.

LANGUAGE	ORDER	AREA	CLASSIFICATION	SOURCE
Abkhazian	SOV	MC	Caucasian: NW	Ruhlen 1975 Mallinson & Blake 1981 Hawkins 1983
Achenese	SVO	SE	Austronesian: Malayo-Polynesian: Hesperonesian: W Indonesian	Ibrahim (inf.)
Achi	SVO	MA	Penutian: Mayan: Quichean [extinct]	Blansitt 1973
Acholi	SVO	CA	Nilo-Saharan: Chari-Nile: E Sudanic: W Nilotic: Acholi	Heine 1975b Hawkins 1983 Greenberg 1963
Acoma	SOV	WNA	Isolate	Miller 1965
Adangme	SVO	WA	Niger-Kordofanian: Niger-Congo: Kwa: Ga-Adangme	Dakubu 1970
Adele	SVO	WA	Niger-Kordofanian: Niger-Congo: Kwa: C Togo: Na	Westermann & Bryan 1952
Adyukru	SVO	WA	Niger-Kordofanian: Niger-Congo: Kwa: Lagoon	Westermann & Bryan 1952
Adzera (Atzera)	SVO	NG	Austronesian: Oceanic: NE New Guinea (geo)	Ruhlen 1975 Capell 1971
Aghem	SVO	WA	Niger-Kordofanian: Niger-Congo: Benue-Congo: Bantoid: Nkom	Hawkins 1983

Aghu	SOV	NG	Indo-Pacific: Central New Guinea: C & S New Guinea: Awyu	Voorhoeve 1975a
Agta	VSO	SE	Austronesian: Malayo-Polynesian: Hesperonesian: NW Philippine Austronesian: Philippine: Cordilleran: Central Agta	Ultan 1969
Aguacatec	VSO	MA	Penutian: Mayan: Mamean	Quizar 1979
Agul	SVO	MC	Caucasian: N: NE: Lezghian	Ruhlen 1975
Ahom	SOV	I	Sino-Tibetan: Tibeto-Burman: Kam-Tai: SW Tai	Greenberg 1978 Grierson 1966 (1904)b
Aimol	SOV	SE	Sino-Tibetan: Tibeto-Burman: Naga-Kuki-Chin: Kuki	Grierson 1966 (1904)b
Ainu	SOV	E	Isolate	Ruhlen 1975 Hawkins 1983
Akha	SOV	SE	Sino-Tibetan: Tibeto-Burman: Burmese-Lolo: Lolo-Moso: S Lolo	Ruhlen 1975
Akhvakh	SOV	MC	Caucasian: NE: Avaro-Andi-Dido: Andi	Hawkins 1983
Akkadian	SOV	MC	Afro-Asiatic: Semitic: N Semitic [extinct]	Greenberg 1963
Alamblak	SOV	NG	Indo-Pacific: C New Guinea: Sepik: Sepik Hill	Whitehead 1982

LANGUAGE	ORDER	AREA	CLASSIFICATION	SOURCE
Alawa	SOV	A	Australian: Maran	Ruhlen 1975 Mallinson & Blake 1981
Albanian	SVO	EUR	Indo-European: Albanian	Ruhlen 1975 Steele 1978
Aleut	SVO	NNA	Eskimo-Aleut: Aleut	Ruhlen 1975
Ali	SVO	NG	Austronesian: Oceanic: NE New Guinea Austronesian	Capell 1971a
Altai	SOV	NNE	Altaic: Turkic: N Turkic	Ruhlen 1975 Hawkins 1983
Alutor	SOV	NNE	Chukchi-Kamchatkan [Paleosiberian]	Ruhlen 1975
Alyawarra	SOV	A	Australian: Pama-Nyungan: Arandic: Urtwa	Yallop 1977
Ame	SOV	A	Australian: Daly: Brinken-Wogaity: Brinken	Tryon 1974
Amele	SOV	NG	Indo-Pacific: C New Guinea: Bogia: Madang	Whitehead 1982
Amharic	SOV	NA	Afroasiatic: Semitic: S Semitic: Ethiopic	Heine 1975b Ruhlen 1975 Gragg 1972
Amo	SVO	WA	Niger-Kordofanian: Niger-Congo: Benue-Congo: Plateau Benue-Congo	Heine 1975b

Language	Word Order	Code	Classification	Reference
Amuesha	VSO	AND	Andean-Equatorial: Equatorial: Arawakan	Derbyshire 1982
Anal	SOV	SE	Sino-Tibetan: Tibeto-Burman: Naga-Kuki-Chin: Kuki	Grierson 1966 (1904)b
Andi	SOV	MC	Caucasian: NE: Avaro-Andi-Dido: Andi	Ruhlen 1975 Hawkins 1983
Andoa (Iquito)	SVO	AND	Andean-Equatorial: Andean: III: Zaporoan	Sedlak 1975 Ruhlen 1975
Andro	SOV	SE	Sino-Tibetan: Tibeto-Burman: Burmese-Lolo: Lolo-Moso	DeLancey (p.c.)
Aneityam	VOS	MEL	Austronesian: Oceanic: S New Hebrides	Capell 1976b
Angami (Tengtma)	SOV	SE	Sino-Tibetan: Tibeto-Burman: Naga-Kuki-Chin: Naga: E Naga	Grierson 1903
Angor (Bribriari)	SOV	NG	Indo-Pacific: Central New Guinea: N New Guinea: Murik	Ruhlen 1975 Whitehead 1982
Anguthimri	SOV	A	Australian: Pama-Nyungan: Pama-Maric: N Pama	Dryer 1984
Anyi	SVO	WA	Niger-Kordofanian: Niger-Congo: Kwa: Volta-Comoe: C Volta-Comoe	Heine 1975b
Ao	SOV	SE	Sino-Tibetan: Tibeto-Burman: Naga-Kuki-Chin: Naga: N Naga	Gowda 1975

159

LANGUAGE	ORDER	AREA	CLASSIFICATION	SOURCE
Apalai	OVS	T	Ge-Pano-Carib: Macro-Carib: Carib: N	Derbyshire & Pullum 1981
Arabic (Colloquial)	SVO	NA	Afroasiatic: Semitic: S Semitic: SW Semitic	Ruhlen 1975
Arabic (Literary)	VSO	MC	Afroasiatic: Semitic: S Semitic: SW Semitic	Ruhlen 1976 Dryer 1984
Aramaic (E)	VSO	A	Afroasiatic: Semitic: N Semitic: NW Semitic	Ruhlen 1975 Hawkins 1983
Aranda	SOV	A	Australian: Pama-Nyungan: Arandic	Ultan 1969 Hawkins 1983
Arapesh	SVO	NG	Indo-Pacific: Central New Guinea: N New Guinea: Torricelli: Arapesh	Greenberg 1963
Arawak	SVO	T	Andean-Equatorial: Equatorial: Maipuran: N Maipuran: Ta-Arawakan	Edwards 1979
Archi	SVO	MC	Caucasian: N: NE: Lezghian	Ruhlen 1975
Arecuna	OVS	T	Ge-Pano-Carib: Macro-Carib: Carib: N	Derbyshire & Pullum 1981
Armenian	SOV	MC	Indo-European: Armenian	Ruhlen 1975 Hawkins 1983

Arosi	SVO	A	Austronesian: Oceanic: E Oceanic: Arosi	Ruhlen 1975 Capell 1971b
Asmat	SOV	NG	Indo-Pacific: Central New Guinea: C & S New Guinea: Asmat	Ruhlen 1975 Voorhoeve 1975a
Au	SVO	NG	Indo-Pacific: N New Guinea: Torricelli: Palei: Wapei	Whitehead 1982
Auca	SOV	AND	Andean-Equatorial: Andean: Zaparoan	Dryer 1984
Auju	SOV	NG	Indo-Pacific: Central New Guinea: E New Guinea Highlands: Enga-Hule-Wiru: Mendi	Dryer 1984
Avar	SOV	MC	Caucasian: N: NE Avaro-Andi-Dido	Ruhlen 1975 Hawkins 1983 Mallinson & Blake 1981
Avukaya	SVO	CA	Nilo-Saharan: Chari-Nile: Central Sudanic: Moru-Ma'di	Heine 1975a, 1975b
Awa	SOV	NG	Indo-Pacific: Central New Guinea: E New Guinea Highlands: Gadsup-Auyana-Awa-Tairora: Gauwa	Steele 1975 Loving 1973
Awin	SOV	NG	Indo-Pacific: Central New Guinea: C & S New Guinea: Pare-Samo-Beami: Bosavi	Ruhlen 1975
Awiya	SOV	NA	Afroasiatic: Cushitic: Central Cushitic	Ruhlen 1975

161

LANGUAGE	ORDER	AREA	CLASSIFICATION	SOURCE
Awji	SOV	NG	Indo-Pacific: Central New Guinea: N New Guinea: N Papuan: Tami: Arso	Ruhlen 1975, Voorhoeve 1975a
Aymara	SOV	AND	Andean-Equatorial: Andean: Quechumaran	Porterie-Gutierrez 1976
Azerbaijani	SOV	MC	Altaic: Turkic: S Turkic	Ruhlen 1975, Householder 1965
Babatana	SVO	MEL	Austronesian: Oceanic: NW & C Solomons (geo): Choiseul	Capell 1976b
Bacairi	OVS	T	Ge-Pano-Carib: Macro-Carib: Carib: S	Derbyshire & Pullum 1981
Bagirmi	SVO	CA	Nilo-Saharan: Chari-Nile: Central Sudanic: Bagirmi	Heine 1975a, 1975b
Bahnar	SVO	SE	Austroasiatic: Mon-Khmer: Bahnaric: N Bahnaric	Sedlak 1975
Bai	SVO	CA	Niger-Kordofanian: Niger-Congo: Adamawa-Eastern: Eastern	Heine 1975a
Balanta (Ganja)	SVO	WA	Niger-Kordofanian: Niger Congo: W Atlantic: N W Atlantic	Heine 1975b, Ruhlen 1975
Balawaia	SOV	NG	Austronesian: Oceanic: Papua Austronesian	Dryer 1984

Language	Order	Region	Classification	Reference
Balti	SOV	EA	Sino-Tibetan: Tibeto-Burman: Tibetan	Culicover & Wexler 1974
Baluchi	SOV	I	Indo-European: Indo-Iranian: Iranian: W Iranian	Ruhlen 1975 Mallinson & Blake 1981
Bambara	SOV	WA	Niger-Kordofanian: Niger-Congo: Mande	Bird 1966 Hawkins 1983
Bamun	SVO	WA	Niger-Kordofanian: Niger-Congo: Benue-Congo: Bantoid	Westermann & Bryan 1952
Banda	SVO	CA	Niger-Kordofanian: Niger-Congo: Adamawa-Eastern: Banda	Heine 1975b
Bandem	SOV	WA	Niger-Kordofanian: Niger-Congo: Benue-Congo: Bantoid: Plateau Bantoid: Bandem	Hawkins 1983
Bankon (Bo)	SVO	WA	Niger-Kordofanian: Niger-Congo: Benue-Congo: Bantoid: Bantu: N W Bantu: Zone A: Basa	Heine 1975a, 1975b
Banoni	SVO	MEL	Austronesian: Oceanic: N W and Central Solomons (geo)	Capell 1971a
Bantik	VSO	SE	Austronesian: Hesperonesian: Bantik	Sneddon 1970
Barai	SOV	NG	Indo-Pacific: Central New Guinea: SE New Guinea: Ko	Dryer 1984 Whitehead 1982
Bari	SVO	CA	Nilo-Saharan: Chari-Nile: E Sudanic:	Greenberg 1966

163

LANGUAGE	ORDER	AREA	CLASSIFICATION	SOURCE
			Nilo-Hamitic: Bari	Heine 1975a Heine 1975b Spagnolo 1933 Steele 1978
Bariai	SOV	MEL	Austronesian: Oceanic: NE New Guinea Austronesian	Capell 1971a Capell 1976b
Bariba	SOV	WA	Niger-Kordofanian: Niger-Congo: Gur: Bargu	Heine 1975a, 1975b
Baruya	SOV	NG	Indo-Pacific: C & S New Guinea: Kukukuku	Whitehead 1982
Barya	SOV	NA	Nilo-Saharan: Chari-Nile: E Sudanic: Nara	Ruhlen 1975 Heine 1975a, 1975b
Bashkir	SOV	EUR	Altaic: Turkic: W Turkic	Ruhlen 1975 Hawkins 1983 Heath 1974
Basque	SOV	EUR	Isolate	Ruhlen 1975 Hawkins 1983 Mallinson & Blake 1981
Batak (Toba)	VOS	SE	Austronesian: Malayo-Polynesian: Hesperonesian: W Indonesian	Ruhlen 1975 Sihombing (inf)
Bats	SOV	MC	Caucasian: N: NE: Vejnax	Ruhlen 1975 Hawkins 1983

Language	Order	Code	Classification	References
Batwa	SVO	SA	Khoisan: S African Khoisan: Southern	Heine 1975a, 1975b
Baure	VOS	T	Andean-Equatorial: Equatorial: Arawakan: Maipuran: S: Maipuran	Derbyshire 1982 Keenan 1978 Hawkins 1983
Bedauye (Beja)	SOV	NA	Afroasiatic: Cushitic: Beja	Ruhlen 1975 Hawkins 1983 Hudson 1974
Bella Coola	VSO	NWNA	Salish: Bella Coola	Ruhlen 1975 Davis & Saunders 1978 Dryer 1984
Bembe	SVO	CA	Niger-Kordofanian: Niger-Congo: Benue-Congo: Bantoid: Bantu: Central W Bantu: Zone H: Kikongo	Ruhlen 1975
Benabena	SOV	NG	Indo-Pacific: Central New Guinea: E New Guinea Highlands: Gende-Siane-Gahuku-Kamano-Fore: Gahuku	Ruhlen 1975 Young 1971
Bengali	SOV	I	Indo-European: Indo-Iranian: Indic: E Indic	Ruhlen 1975 Hawkins 1983
Berta	SVO	NA	Nilo-Saharan: Chari-Nile: Berta	Ruhlen 1975 Dryer 1984

LANGUAGE	ORDER	AREA	CLASSIFICATION	SOURCE
				Tucker & Bryan 1966
Bezhita	SOV	MC	Caucasian: N: NE: Avaro-Andi-Dido: Dido	Ruhlen 1975
Biliau	SOV	NG	Austronesian: Oceanic: NE New Guinea / Austronesian	Lincoln 1978
Bilin	SOV	NA	Afroasiatic: Cushitic: Central Cushitic	Ruhlen 1975
Biloxi	SOV	ENA	Macro-Siouan: Siouan	Einaudi 1976
Bimin	SOV	NG	Indo-Pacific: Central New Guinea: Central & S New Guinea: OK: Mountain OK	Voorhoeve 1975a
Bimoba	SVO	WA	Niger-Kordofanian: Niger-Congo: Gur: Central Gur: More-Gurme	Blansitt 1973 / Jacobs 1966
Binandere	SOV	NG	Indo-Pacific: Central New Guinea: SE New Guinea: Binandere	Capell 1969
Bine	SOV	NG	Indo-Pacific: C & S New Guinea: Oriomo River	Whitehead 1982
Bini	SVO	WA	Niger-Kordofanian: Niger-Congo: Kwa: Edo: Central	Heine 1975b / Blansitt 1973
Birom	SVO	WA	Niger-Kordofanian: Niger-Congo: Benue-Congo: III / Plateau Benue-Congo:	Blansitt 1973 / Heine 1975b
Bisa	SOV	WA	Niger-Kordofanian: Niger-Congo: Mande	Prost 1968

Blackfoot	SVO	WNA	Macro-Algonquian: Algonquian	Ruhlen 1975, Dryer 1984
Boazi	SOV	NG	Indo-Pacific: C New Guinea: C & S New Guinea: Marind	Voorhoeve 1975a
Bobangi	SVO	CA	Niger-Kordofanian: Niger-Congo: Benue-Congo: Bantoid: NW Bantu: Zone C: Ngala	Whitehead 1899
Bongo	SVO	CA	Nilo-Saharan: Chari-Nile: Central Sudanic: Bongo	Heine 1975a, 1975b
Bontok	VSO	SE	Austronesian: Malayo-Polynesian: Hesperonesian: N W Philippine Austronesian: Cordilleran: Igorot	Seidenadel 1909
Bor	SVO	CA	Nilo-Saharan: Chari-Nile: E Sudanic: Nilotic: Dinka	Dryer 1984
Bororo	SVO	T	Ge-Pano-Carib: Macro-Ge-Bororo: Bororo	Huestis 1963
Boruca	SOV	CC	Macro-Chibchan: Chibchan: W Chibchan	Datz (p.c.)
Botlikh	SOV	MC	Caucasian: NE Caucasian: Avaro-Andi-Dido: Andi	Hawkins 1983
Botocudo	SOV	T	Ge-Pano-Carib: Macro-Ge: Botocudo	Loukotka 1955
Brahui	SOV	I	Dravidian: N	Hawkins 1983

LANGUAGE	ORDER	AREA	CLASSIFICATION	SOURCE
Brao	SVO	SE	Austroasiatic: Mon-Khmer: Bahnaric: W Bahnaric	Dryer 1984
Breton (Vannetais)	VSO	EUR	Indo-European: Celtic: Brythonic	Ruhlen 1975 Varin 1979 DeLancey (p.c.)
Bribri	SOV	MA	Macro-Chibchan: Chibchan: W Chibchan	de la Grasserie 1904
Brinken (Marithiel)	SOV	A	Australian: Daly: Brinken-Wogaity: Brinken	Tryon 1974
Buang	SVO	NG	Austronesian: Oceanic: NE New Guinea Austronesian	Kemp 1977
Budux	SOV	MC	Caucasian: N: NE: Lezghian	Ruhlen 1975 Hawkins 1983
Bukidnon	VSO	SE	Austronesian: Hesperonesian: NW Austronesian: Philippine: Sulic: Bukidnic	Dryer 1984 Hawkins 1983
Bulgarian	SVO	EUR	Indo-European: Slavic: S Slavic	Culivover & Wexler 1974 Downing 1977
Bulu	SVO	MEL	Austronesian: Oceanic: NE New Guinea Austronesian	Capell 1971a
Bulu	SVO	WA	Niger-Kordofanian: Niger-Congo: Benue-Congo: Bantoid: Bantu: NW Bantu: Zone A:	Heine 1975b

168

Bunak	SOV	SE	Indo-Pacific: Timor-Alor	Hawkins 1983
Bunum	VSO	SE	Austronesian: Malayo-Polynesian: Formosan Austronesian	Starosta 1973
Burera	SOV	A	Australian: Bureran	Ruhlen 1975
Burji	SOV	NA	Afroasiatic: Cushitic: E Cushitic: Highland E Cushitic	Heine 1975a
Burmese	SOV	SE	Sino-Tibetan: Tibeto-Burmese: Burmese-Lolo: Burmese	Steele 1978 Ruhlen 1975 Nguyen 1972
Burum	SOV	NG	Indo-Pacific: C New Guinea: Huon-Finisterre: Huon: C Huon	McElhanon 1967
Burushaski	SOV	I	Isolate	Ruhlen 1975 Lorimer 1939
Buryat	SOV	NNE	Altaic: Mongol	Ruhlen 1975 Ultan 1969
Bviri	SVO	CA	Niger-Kordofanian: Niger-Congo: Adamawa- Eastern: Eastern: V	Heine 1975a
Bwaidoga	SOV	NG	Austronesian: Oceanic: Papua Austronesian (geo)	Jenness & Ballantyne 1928

LANGUAGE	ORDER	AREA	CLASSIFICATION	SOURCE
Cabecar	SOV	CC	Macro-Chibchan: Chibchan: W Chibchan	Datz (p.c.)
Caddo	SOV	WNA	Macro-Siouan: Caddoan	Chafe 1976b
Cahuilla	SOV	CAL	Aztec-Tanoan: Uto-Aztecan: Takic: Cupan	Jacobs 1973
Caingang	SOV	T	Ge-Pano-Carib: Macro-Ge-Bororo: Macro-Ge: Ge: Caingang	Henry 1948
Cakchiquel	SOV	MA	Penutian: Mayan: Quichean	Ruhlen 1975 Townsend 1960 Craig (p.c.)
Cambodian (Khmer)	SVO	SE	Austroasiatic: Mon-Khmer: Khmer	Ruhlen 1975 Nguyen 1972
Candoshi	SOV	AND	Andean-Equatorial: Jivaroan	Anderson & Wise 1963
Cantonese	SVO	E	Sino-Tibetan: Chinese	Ruhlen 1975 Nguyen 1972
Capanahua	SOV	AND	Ge-Pano-Carib: Macro-Panoan: Pano-Tacana: Pano: C Pano	Loos 1970
Car	SVO	SE	Austroasiatic: Nicobarese	Ruhlen 1975
Carib, Island	VSO	CC	Andean-Equatorial: Equatorial: Arawakan: Maipuran: N Maipuran: Island Carib	Taylor 1958

Carib (Surinam)	SOV	CC	Ge-Pano-Carib: Macro-Carib: Carib: N	Derbyshire 1980
Carrier	SOV	NWNA	Na-Dene: Athapascan-Eyak: Athapascan: N Athapascan	Dryer 1979
Cashibo	SOV	AND	Ge-Pano-Carib: Macro-Panoan: Pano-Tacana: Pano: Central Pano	Dryer 1984
Cashinawa	SOV	T	Ge-Pano-Carib: Macro-Panoan: Pano-Tacana: Pano	Cromack 1968 Loos 1970
Catalan (Barcelona)	SVO	EUR	Indo-European: Italic: Romance: Ibero-Romance	Ruhlen 1975
Cayapa	SOV	AND	Macro-Chibchan: Paezan: Barbacoan: Cayapa-Colorado	Ruhlen 1975 Dryer 1984 Abrahamson 1962
Cayapo	SOV	T	Ge-Pano-Carib: Macro-Ge: Ge: Cayapo	Dryer 1984
Cebuano	VSO	SE	Austronesian: Malayo-Polynesian: Hesperonesian: NW Austronesian: Philippine: Sulic: Mesophilippine: Tagalic	Culicover & Wexler 1974 Dryer 1979 Hawkins 1983
Chacobo	SOV	T	Ge-Pano-Carib: Macro-Panoan: Pano-Tacana: Pano: SE (geo)	Loos 1970 Ruhlen 1975
Chama	SOV	AND	Ge-Pano-Carib: Macro-Panoan: Pano-Tacana:	Ruhlen 1975

171

LANGUAGE	ORDER	AREA	CLASSIFICATION	SOURCE
			Tacana: Tiatinagua	
Chambri	SOV	NG	Indo-Pacific: Central New Guinea: N New Guinea: Murik	Laycock & Z'graggen 1975
Chamir	SOV	NA	Afroasiatic: Cushitic: Central Cushitic	Greenberg 1963 / Hawkins 1983
Chamorro	SVO	MIC	Austronesian: Malayo-Polynesian: Hesperonesian: NW Austronesian: Chamorro	Cooreman 1985 / Topping 1973 / Hawkins 1983
Chatino (Yaitepec)	VSO	MA	Oto-Manguean: Zapotecan	Pride 1963 / Ruhlen 1975
Chechan	SOV	MC	Caucasian: N: NE: Vejnax	Ruhlen 1975 / Hawkins 1983
Chemehueve	SOV	WNA	Aztec-Tanoan: Uto-Aztecan: Numic: S Paiute	Press 1979
Chepang	SOV	I	Sino-Tibetan: Tibeto-Burman: Gyarung-Mishmi: E Pronominalized Himalayan	Baumann 1979
Cheremis (E)	SOV	EUR	Uralic: Finno-Ugric: Finno-Permic: Finno-Volgaic: Volgaic	Blansitt 1973 / Sebeok & Ingemann 1966
Chibcha	SOV	AND	Macro-Chibchan: Chibcha Proper: Chibchan: Eastern [extinct]	Greenberg 1963
Chimariko	SOV	CAI	Hokan	Dryer 1984

Language	Word Order	Region	Classification	References
Chimbu	SOV	NG	Indo-Pacific: Central New Guinea: E New Guinea Highlands: Hagen-Wahgi-Jimi-Chimbu: Chimbu	Ruhlen 1975 Bunn 1974
Chinantec	VSO	MA	Oto-Manguean: Chinantecan	Ruhlen 1975 Sedlak 1975 Hawkins 1983
Chinook	VSO	NWNA	Penutian: Chinookan [extinct]	Greenberg 1963 Steele 1978
Chipewyan	SOV	NNA	Na-Dene: Athapascan-Eyak: N Athapascan (geo)	Li 1946 Ruhlen 1975 Sedlak 1975
Chiru	SOV	SE	Sino-Tibetan: Tibeto-Burman: Naga-Kuki-Chin: Kuki	Grierson 1966 (1904)b
Chitimacha	SOV	ENA	Macro-Algonquian: Chitimacha	Swadesh 1946b Greenberg 1963
Choctaw	SOV	ENA	Macro-Algonquian: Muskogean	Todd 1975
Chol (Tumbala)	VOS	MA	Penutian: Mayan: Cholan	Ruhlen 1975
Chontal (Highland)	SVO	MA	Hokan: Tequislatecan	Turner 1968

LANGUAGE	ORDER	AREA	CLASSIFICATION	SOURCE
Chontol	VSO	MA	Penutian: Mayan: Cholan	Hawkins 1983
Chorti	SVO	MA	Penutian: Mayan: Chorti	Oakley 1965 Quizar 1979
Chrau	SVO	SE	Austroasiatic: Mon-Khmer: Bahnaric: South Bahnaric	Ruhlen 1975 Thomas 1971
Chuave	SOV	NG	Indo-Pacific: C New Guinea: E New Guinea Highlands: Hagen-Wahgi-Jimi-Chimbu: Chimbu	Givon 1979
Chuh (San Mateo)	VOS	MA	Penutian: Mayan: Chuh	Maxwell 1974
Chuh (San Sebastian)	VSO	MA	Penutian: Mayan: Chuh	Maxwell 1974
Chukchi	SVO	NNE	Chukchi-Kamchatkan [Paleosiberian]	Hawkins 1983
Chulym (Lower)	SOV	NNE	Altaic: Turkic: N Turkic	Ruhlen 1975
Chumash (Ineseno)	VOS	CAL	Hokan: Chumash	Applegate 1972
Chuvash	SOV	MC	Altaic: Turkic: Chuvash	Ruhlen 1975 Krueger 1961 Hawkins 1983
Circassian, E.	SOV	MC	Caucasian: NW	Ruhlen 1975

(Kabardian)

Language	Order	Region	Family	References
Circassian, W. (Adyge)	SOV	MC	Caucasian: NW	Ruhlen 1975 Hawkins 1983
Coahuilteco	SOV	WNA	Hokan	Troike 1967
Cocama	SVO	AND	Andean-Equatorial: Equatorial: Tupi: Tupi-Guarani: II	Blansitt 1973
Cocopa	SOV	WNA	Hokan: Yuman: Delta-California	Hawkins 1983
Coeur D'Alene	VOS	NWNA	Salish: Interior	Keenan 1978 Pullum 1981
Columbian	VSO	NWNA	Salish: Interior	Ingram 1975
Coptic	SVO	NA	Afroasiatic: Egyptian-Coptic	Heine 1975a Sedlak 1975
Cora	SOV	WNA	Aztec-Tanoan: Uto-Aztecan: Sonoran	Preuss 1932
Cree	SVO	NNA	Macro-Algonquian: Algonquian	Ruhlen 1975
Cua	SVO	SE	Austroasiatic: Mon-Khmer: N	Blansitt 1973 Burton 1969
Cuiva	SOV	T	Andean-Equatorial: Equatorial: Guahibo-Pamigua: Guahiban	Dryer 1984

LANGUAGE	ORDER	AREA	CLASSIFICATION	SOURCE
Culina	SOV	AND	Andean-Equatorial: Equatorial: Arawakan: Arauan	Derbyshire 1982
Cuna	SOV	CC	Macro-Chibchan: Chibcha Proper: Chibchan: Western	Greenberg 1963
Cupeno	SOV	CAL	Aztec-Tanoan: Uto-Aztecan: Takic: Cupan	Jacobs 1973
Czech	SVO	EUR	Indo-European: Slavic: W Slavic (geo)	Steele 1978 Ruhlen 1975
Dadog (Tadog)	SVO	EA	Nilo-Saharan: Chari-Nile: E Sudanic: Nilo-Hamitic: Nandi	Heine 1975b
Dafla	SOV	I	Sino-Tibetan: Tibeto-Burman: Gyarung-Mishmi: Non-Pronominalized Himalayan	Hamilton 1900
Daga	SOV	NG	Indo-Pacific: Central New Guinea: SE New Guinea: Daga	Hawkins 1983 Whitehead 1982 Murane 1974
Dagbani	SVO	WA	Niger-Kordofanian: Niger-Congo: Gur: C Gur: More-Gurma	Westermann & Bryan 1952 Wilson 1963
Dagur	SOV	EA	Ural-Altaic: Altaic: Mongol	Culicover & Wexler 1974 Hawkins 1983
Daju	SVO	CA	Nilo-Saharan: Chari-Nile: E Sudanic:	Ruhlen 1975

(Shatt)			E Sudanic: Daju	
Dalabon	SOV	A	Australian: Gunwingguan: Boun	Steele 1978
Dany, W.	SOV	NG	Indo-Pacific: Central New Guinea: W New Guinea Highlands: Greater Dani	Voorhoeve 1975a
Dargwa	SOV	MC	Caucasian: N: NE: Lak-Dargwa: Dargwa	Hawkins 1983
Dehu	SVO	MEL	Austronesian: Oceanic: Loyalty Islands	Blansitt 1973 Tryon 1968a
Delaware	VOS	ENA	Macro-Algonquian: Algonquian	Rhodes (p.c.)
Dera (Amgotro)	SOV	NG	Indo-Pacific: Central New Guinea: N New Guinea: N Papuan: Tami: Dera	Ruhlen 1975 Voorhoeve 1975a
Dhegiha	SOV	WNA	Macro-Siouan: Siouan	Dryer 1984
Didinga	VSO	CA	Nilo-Saharan: Chari-Nile: E Sudanic: E Sudanic: Beier-Didinga	Heine 1975a, 1975b Greenberg 1963
Dido	SVO	MC	Caucasian: N: NE: Avaro-Andi-Dido: Dido	Ruhlen 1975
Diegueno	SOV	CAL	Hokan: Yuman: Delta-Californian	Culicover & Wexler 1974 Givon 1979

LANGUAGE	ORDER	AREA	CLASSIFICATION	SOURCE
Dieri	SOV	A	Australian: Pama-Nyungan: Dieric: Karna	Ruhlen 1975 Dryer 1984
Digaru Mishmi	SOV	I	Sino-Tibetan: Gyarung Mishmi: Non-Pro-nominalized Himalayan	DeLancey (p.c.)
Dioi	SVO	SE	Sino-Tibetan: Tibeto-Burman: Kam-Tai: N Tai	DeLancey (p.c.)
Djadjala	SOV	A	Australian: Pama-Nyungan: Kulinic: Kulin	Ruhlen 1975
Djambarrpuynyu	SVO	A	Australian: Pama-Nyungan: Murngic	Buchanan 1978
Djapu	SOV	A	Australian: Pama-Nyungan: Murngic: Yulngu	Dryer 1984
Djingili	SOV	A	Australian: Tjingili-Wambayan	Chadwick 1975
Dobu	SOV	NG	Austronesian: Oceanic: Papua Austronesian	Hsieh 1976 Capell 1971a Lawton 1977
Dongola	SOV	NA	Nilo-Saharan: Chari-Nile: E Sudanic: Nubian	Tucker & Bryan 1966
Duala	SVO	WA	Niger-Kordofanian: Niger-Congo: Benue-Congo: Bantoid: Bantu: NW Bantu: Zone A: Duala	Epee 1975 Heine 1975a, 1975b
Duka	SVO	WA	Niger-Kordofanian: Niger-Congo: Benue-Congo: Plateau Benue-Congo: I	Dryer 1984

Duna	SOV	NG	Indo-Pacific: Central New Guinea: E New Guinea Highlands: Duna	Voorhoeve 1975a
Dyola	SVO	WA	Niger-Kordofanian: Niger-Congo: W Atlantic: N W Atlantic	Givon 1975a
Easter Island	VSO	POL	Austronesian: Oceanic: E Oceanic: Polynesian: Nuclear Polynesian: E Nuclear Polynesian: Easter Island	Chapin 1975
Efik (Calabar)	SVO	WA	Niger-Kordofanian: Niger-Congo: Benue-Congo: Cross River: Delta Cross	Heine 1975a / Ruhlen 1975 / Welmers 1968
Ekari	SOV	NG	Indo-Pacific: C New Guinea: W New Guinea Highlands: Wissell Lakes-Kemandoga	Boelaars 1950
Ekpeye	SVO	WA	Niger-Kordofanian: Niger-Congo: Kwa: Igbo	Hawkins 1983
Elamite	SOV	MC	Isolate [extinct]	Greenberg 1963
Empeo	SOV	SE	Sino-Tibetan: Tibeto-Burman: Naga-Kuki-Chin: Naga: W Naga	Greenberg 1963
Enga	SOV	NG	Indo-Pacific: Central New Guinea: E New Guinea Highlands: Enga-Hule-Wiru: Enga	Ruhlen 1975 / Lang 1975
Engenni	SVO	WA	Niger-Kordofanian: Niger-Congo: Kwa: Edo: Delta Edo	Dryer 1984

LANGUAGE	ORDER	AREA	CLASSIFICATION	SOURCE
English	SVO	EUR	Indo-European: Germanic: W Germanic: English	Hawkins 1983 Ruhlen 1975
Estonian	SVO	EUR	Uralic: Finno-Ugric: Finno-Permic: Finno-Volgaic: Finno-Lappic: Finnic	Ruhlen 1975 Hawkins 1983
Even	SOV	NNE	Altaic: Tungus: N Tungus	Ruhlen 1975 Hawkins 1983
Evenki	SOV	NNE	Altaic: Tungus: N Tungus	Ruhlen 1975 Hawkins 1983
Ewe	SVO	WA	Niger-Kordofanian: Niger-Congo: Kwa: Ewe	Heine 1975b Ruhlen 1975
Ewondo	SVO	WA	Niger-Kordofanian: Niger-Congo: Benue-Congo: Bantoid: Bantu: NW Bantu: Zone A: Yaunde-Fang	Heine 1975b Ruhlen 1975
Faiwol	SOV	NG	Indo-Pacific: Central New Guinea: Central & S New Guinea: OK: Mountain	Voorhoeve 1975a
Fasu	OSV	NG	Indo-Pacific: C New Guinea: E New Guinea Highlands: Fasu	Loeweke & May 1966
Fijian	VOS	POL	Austronesian: Oceanic: E Oceanic: Fijian	Arms 1974
Finnish	SVO	EUR	Uralic: Finno-Ugric: Finno-Permic: Finno-Volgaic: Finno-Lappic: Finnic	Ruhlen 1975 Tuominen (inf.)

Language	Order	Area	Classification	Reference
Foe	SOV	NG	Indo-Pacific: Central New Guinea: E New Guinea Highlands: Foi	Rule 1977
Fore (N)	SOV	NG	Indo-Pacific: Central New Guinea: E New Guinea Highlands: Gende-Siane-Gahuku-Kamano-Fore: Fore	Ruhlen 1975 Hawkins 1983
Foro	SOV	WA	Niger-Kordofanian: Niger-Congo: Gur: Senufo: Tagha-Dyimini	Westermann & Bryan 1952
Fox	VSO	WNA	Macro-Algonquian: Algonquian	Steele 1975
French	SVO	EUR	Indo-European: Italic: Romance: Gallo-Romance	Ruhlen 1975 Eckert (p.c.)
Frisian	SVO	EUR	Indo-European: Germanic	Keenan 1978
Friulian	SVO	EUR	Indo-European: Italic: Romance: Rhaeto-Romance	Ruhlen 1975
Fulani	SVO	WA	Niger-Kordofanian: Niger-Congo: W Atlantic: NW Atlantic	Stennes 1967 Ruhlen 1975
Fur	SOV	NA	Nilo-Saharan: Fur	Heine 1975a, 1975b Ruhlen 1975 Steele 1978
Futuna, W (Anima)	SVO	MIC	Austronesian: Oceanic: E Oceanic: Polynesian: Nuclear Polynesian: Samoic-	Capell 1976b

LANGUAGE	ORDER	AREA	CLASSIFICATION	SOURCE
			Outlier	
Gã	SVO	WA	Niger-Kordofanian: Niger-Congo: Kwa: Gã-Adangme	Ruhlen 1975, Hawkins 1983
Ga'anda	SVO	WA	Afroasiatic: Chadic: E Chadic: Tera	Ruhlen 1975
Gadsup	SOV	NG	Indo-Pacific: Central New Guinea: E New Guinea Highlands: Gadsup-Awyana-Awa-Tairora: Gauwa	Ruhlen 1975, Goddard 1967, Whitehead 1982
Gaelic, Scottish	VSO	EUR	Indo-European: Celtic: Goidelic	Ultan 1969
Gafat	SOV	NA	Afroasiatic: Semitic: S Semitic: Ethiopic [extinct]	Greenberg 1963
Gagauz	SVO	EUR	Altaic: Turkic: S Turkic	Ruhlen 1975
Gahuku	SOV	NG	Indo-Pacific: Central New Guinea: E New Guinea Highlands: Gende-Siane-Gahuku-Kamoano-Fore: Gahuku	Deibler 1973, Whitehead 1982
Galla	SOV	EA	Afroasiatic: Cushitic: E Cushitic: Lowland E Cushitic	Heine 1975a, 1975b, Ruhlen 1975, Gragg 1972
Garadjari	SOV	A	Australian: Pama-Nyungan: SW Pama-Nyungan: Marngu	Steele 1978

Language	Order	Code	Classification	References
Garawa	VSO	A	Australian: Garawan	Furby & Furby 1977
Garo	SOV	I	Sino-Tibetan: Tibeto-Burman: Bodo-Naga-Kachin: Bodo: Garo	Bonnerjea 1935, Ruhlen 1975, Hawkins 1983
Gbari (Kuta)	SVO	WA	Niger-Kordofanian: Niger-Congo: Kwa: Nupe-Gbari	Ruhlen 1975
Gbeya	SVO	CA	Nilo-Saharan: Chari-Nile: Central Sudanic: Kara	Steele 1978, Samarin 1966
Geez	VSO	NA	Afroasiatic: Semitic: S Semitic: Ethiopic	Ruhlen 1975, Gragg 1972
Gela	SVO	MEL	Austronesian: Oceanic: E Oceanic:	Capell 1971a
Geleba (Dasenech)	SOV	EA	Afroasiatic: Cushitic: E Cushitic: Lowland E Cushitic	Ruhlen 1975, Tucker & Bryan 1966
Georgian	SVO	MC	Caucasian: S Caucasian	Trask 1979
Gilbertese	VOS	MIC	Austronesian: Oceanic: Micronesian	Ruhlen 1975, Keenan and Hull 1973, Hawkins 1983
Gilyak	SOV	NNE	Isolate [Paleosiberian]	Ruhlen 1975, Hawkins 1983

LANGUAGE	ORDER	AREA	CLASSIFICATION	SOURCE
Ginux	SOV	MC	Caucasian: N: NE: Avaro-Andi-Dido: Dido	Ruhlen 1975
Gogodala	SOV	NG	Indo-Pacific: Central New Guinea: Central & S New Guinea	Voorhoeve 1975a
Gola	SVO	WA	Niger-Kordofanian: Niger-Congo: W Atlantic: N W Atlantic: Senegal-Portuguese Guinea	Westermann & Bryan 1952
Gondi	SOV	I	Dravidian: Central Dravidian	Dryer 1984 Subrahmanyam 1968
Gothic	SOV	EUR	Indo-European: Germanic: E	Hawkins 1983
Graged	SOV	NG	Austronesian: Oceanic: NE New Guinea Austronesian	Capell 1971a
Grebo	SVO	WA	Niger-Kordofanian: Niger-Congo: Kwa: Kru	Ultan 1979 Innes 1966 Sedlak 1975
Greek (Classical)	SVO	EUR	Indo-European: Greek	Ruhlen 1975 Hawkins 1983
Greek (Modern)	SVO	EUR	Indo-European: Greek	Ruhlen 1975 Hawkins 1983
Guan	SVO	WA	Niger-Kordofanian: Niger-Congo: Kwa: Volta-Comoe: E Volta-Comoe	Reinecke 1972 Greenberg 1963

184

Language	Order	Code	Classification	References
Guarani (Colloquial)	SVO	SSA	Andean-Equatorial: Equatorial: Tupi: Tupi-Guarani: I	Ruhlen 1975 Hawkins 1983 Rosbottom 1967
Guaymi	SOV	CC	Macro-Chibchan: Chibchan	Dryer 1984
Gude	VSO	WA	Afroasiatic: Chadic: E Chadic: Bata	Hoskison 1975 Heine 1975b
Guhu-Samane	SOV	NG	Indo-Pacific: Central New Guinea: SE New Guinea: Binandere	Dryer 1984
Gujarati	SOV	I	Indo-European: Indo-Iranian: Indic: Central Indic	Ruhlen 1975 Hawkins 1983
Gule	SVO	NA	Nilo-Saharan: Koman	Heine 1975a, 1975b
Gumbaingar	SOV	A	Australian: Pama-Nyungan: Kumbaingaric	Smythe 1949
Gunbalung	SVO	A	Australian: Gunwingguan: Gunwingguic	Blansitt 1973 Harris 1969
Gunwinggu	SOV	A	Australian: Gunwingguan: Gunwingguic	Ultan 1969 Steele 1978
Gurage	SOV	EA	Afroasiatic: Semitic: S Semitic: Ethiopic	Heine 1975a, 1975b
Gurung	SOV	I	Sino-Tibetan: Tibeto-Burman: Gyarung-	Glover 1974

LANGUAGE	ORDER	AREA	CLASSIFICATION	SOURCE
			Mishmi: Non-Pronominalized Himalayan	
Gusii	SVO	EA	Niger-Kordofanian: Niger-Congo: Benue-Congo: Bantoid: Bantu: NE Bantu: Zone E: Ragoli-Kuria	Ruhlen 1975
Guugu Yimidhirr	SOV	A	Australian: Pama-Nyungan: Pama-Maric: E Pama	Haviland 1979
Gyarung	SOV	I	Sino-Tibetan: Gyarung-Mishmi: Non-Pronomialized	DeLancey (p.c.)
Hadya	SOV	NA	Afroasiatic: Cushitic: E Cushitic: Highland E Cushitic	Heine 1975a
Hadzapi	VSO	EA	Khoisan: Hadzapi	Heine 1975a, 1975b
Haida	SOV	NWNA	Na-Dene: Haida	Swanton 1911 Hawkins 1983
Haitan Creole	SVO	CC	French-based creole	Ruhlen 1975
Hakka	SVO	E	Sino-Tibetan: Chinese	Dryer 1984
Halia (Hagus)	SVO	MEL	Austronesian: Oceanic: NW and Central Solomons (geo): Buka	Ruhlen 1975 Hawkins 1983

Language	Order	Code	Classification	Reference
Halkomelem	VSO	NWNA	Salish: Coast	Gerdts 1980
Ham	SOV	NG	Austronesian: Oceanic: NE New Guinea Austronesian	Capell 1971a
Harari	SOV	EA	Afroasiatic: Semitic: S Semitic: Ethiopic	Heine 1975a Greenberg 1963
Hare	SOV	NNA	Na-Dene: Athapascan-Eyak: Athapascan: N	Dryer 1979
Haroi	SVO	SE	Austronesian: Malayo-Polynesian: Hesperonesian: W Indonesian: Chamic	Goschnick 1977
Hausa (Kano)	SVO	WA	Afroasiatic: Chadic: W Chadic: Hausa-Gwandara	Heine 1975b Ruhlen 1975 Sedlak 1975 Jaggar 1978
Hawaiian	VSO	POL	Austronesian: Oceanic: E Oceanic: Polynesian: Nuclear Polynesian: E: Central	Ruhlen 1975 Hawkins 1983 Elbert & Pukui 1979
Hawu	VOS	SE	Austronesian: Malayo-Polynesian: Moluccan Austronesian: Fordatic	Capell 1976c Li & Lang 1979
Haya (Ziba)	SVO	CA	Niger-Kordofanian: Niger-Congo: Benue-Congo: Bantoid: Bantu: NW Bantu: Zone E: Haya-Jita	Byarushengo and Tenenbaum 1976
Hayu	SOV	I	Sino-Tibetan: Tibeto-Burman: Gyarung-Mishimi: Eastern	Michailovsky

187

LANGUAGE	ORDER	AREA	CLASSIFICATION	SOURCE
Hebrew	VSO	MC	Afroasiatic: Semitic: N Semitic: NW Semitic	Ruhlen 1975, Kopelovich (inf.)
Hianocoto	OVS	T	Ge-Pano-Carib: Macro-Carib: Carib: N	Derbyshire & Pullum 1981
Hidatsa	SOV	ENA	Macro-Siouan: Siouan	Ultan 1969, Matthews 1965
Higi (Nkafa)	SVO	WA	Afroasiatic: Chadic: E Chadic: Higi	Ruhlen 1975
Hilagaynon	VSO	SE	Austronesian: Malayo-Polynesian: Hesperonesian: NW Austronesian: Philippine: Sulic: Mesophilippine: Tagalic	Culicover & Wexler 1974, Wolfendon 1971, Hawkins 1983
Hindi-Urdu	SOV	I	Indo-European: Indo-Iranian: Indic: Central Indic	Hook (p.c.), Ruhlen 1975
Hiroi (Lamgang)	SOV	SE	Sino-Tibetan: Tibeto-Burman: Naga-Kuki-Chin: Kuki	Grierson 1966 (1904)
Hittite	SOV	MC	Indo-European: Anatolian	Givón 1979, Mallinson & Blake 1979
Hixkaryana	OVS	T	Ge-Pano-Carib: Macro-Carib: Carib	Derbyshire 1977
Hopi	SOV	WNA	Aztec-Tanoan: Uto-Aztecan	Ruhlen 1975

(Toreva)				Steele 1978
Hottentot (Korana)	SOV	SA	Khoisan: S African Khoisan: Central	Ruhlen 1975
Houailou	VOS	MEL	Austronesian: Oceanic: New Caledonia: S	Mallinson & Blake 1981
Hsemtung	SOV	SE	Sino-Tibetan: Tibeto-Burman: Naga-Kuki-Chin: Chin: C Chin	DeLancey (p.c.)
Huastec	VOS	MA	Penutian: Mayan: Huastecan	Pullum 1981 Quizar 1979
Huave	VOS	MA	Penutian: Mayan: Huave	Pullum 1981
Huichol	SOV	WNA	Aztec-Tanoan: Uto-Aztecan: Sonoran	Sedlak 1975 Ultan 1969
Hula	SOV	NG	Austronesian: Oceanic: Papua Austronesian	Capell 1971a
Huli	SOV	NG	Indo-Pacific: Central New Guinea: E New Guinea Highlands: Enga	Rule 1977
Hungarian	SVO	EUR	Uralic: Finno-Ugric: Ugric	Ruhlen 1975 Mallinson & Blake 1981 Hawkins 1983
Hurrian	SOV	MC	Hurrian	Trask 1979 Hawkins 1983

189

LANGUAGE	ORDER	AREA	CLASSIFICATION	SOURCE
Iai (Ouvea)	SVO	MEL	Austronesian: Oceanic: Loyalty Islands	Ruhlen 1975 Tryon 1968b Steele 1978
Iatmul	SOV	NG	Indo-Pacific: Central New Guinea: N New Guinea: Sepik: Middle Sepik: Ndu	Ruhlen 1975 Dryer 1984 Whitehead 1982
Ica	SOV	AND	Macro-Chibchan: Chibchan	Steele 1978
Idoma	SVO	WA	Niger-Kordofanian: Niger-Congo: Kwa: Idoma	George 1977
Idu	SOV	I	Sino-Tibetan: Tibeto-Burman: Gyarung-Mishmi: Non-Pronominalized Himalayan	DeLancey (p.c.)
Igbo (Umuahia)	SVO	WA	Niger-Kordofanian: Niger-Congo: Kwa: Igbo	Heine 1975b Ruhlen 1975
Iha	SOV	NG	Indo-Pacific: W New Guinea: IV = Iha	Voorhoeve 1975a
Ijo (Kalabiri)	SVO	WA	Niger-Kordofanian: Niger-Congo: Kwa: Ijo	Ruhlen 1975 Sedlak 1975
Ila	SVO	CA	Niger-Kordofanian: Niger-Congo: Benue-Congo: Bantoid: Bantu: Central E Bantu: Zone M: Lenje-Tonga	Smith 1907
Ilocano	VSO	SE	Austronesian: Malayo-Polynesian: Hesperonesian: NW Austronesian: Philippine: Cordilleran: Igorot	Culicover & Wexler 1974

Language	Order	Area	Classification	References
Ingassana (Tabi)	SVO	NA	Nilo-Saharan: Chari-Nile: Berta	Heine 1975a, 1975b Ruhlen 1975
Ingrian (Sojki)	SVO	EUR	Uralic: Finno-Ugric: Finno-Permic: Finno-Volgaic: Finno-Lappic: Finnic	Ruhlen 1975
Ingush	SOV	MC	Caucasian: N: NE: Vejnax	Ruhlen 1975 Hawkins 1983
Inupik	SVO	NNA	Eskimo-Aleut: Inuit	Ruhlen 1975
Iranxe	SOV	T	Andean-Equatorial: Equatorial: Arawakan: Maipuran: S Maipuran: Bolivian	Dryer 1984
Iraqw	SOV	EA	Afroasiatic: Cushitic: S Cushitic	Heine 1975a Ruhlen 1975 Hawkins 1983
Irish	VSO	EUR	Indo-European: Celtic: Goidelic	Ruhlen 1975 Mallinson & Blake 1981
Italian	SVO	EUR	Indo-European: Italic: Romance: Ibero-Romance	Ruhlen 1975 Sedlak 1975
Itonama	SVO	AND	Macro-Chibchan: Paezan: Itonama	Ruhlen 1975 Dryer 1984 Camp & Liccardi 1967

LANGUAGE	ORDER	AREA	CLASSIFICATION	SOURCE
Ivatan	VSO	SE	Austronesian: Malayo-Polynesian: Hesperonesian: NW Austronesian: Philippine: Ivatan	Culicover & Wexler 1974
Ixil	VSO	MA	Penutian: Mayan: Mamean	Elliott 1961 Ruhlen 1975 Dryer 1984
Izi	SVO	CA	Niger-Kordofanian: Niger-Congo: Kwa: Igbo	Dik 1978
Jacaltec	VSO	MA	Penutian: Mayan: Kanjobalan	Ruhlen 1975 Day 1973 Steele 1978 Craig 1977
Jahai	SVO	SE	Austroasiatic: Malacca: Semang	Schebesta 1926-28
Jalanga	SOV	A	Australian: Pama-Nyungan: Jalanga	Ruhlen 1975
Jamaican Creole	SVO	CC	English based creole	Ultan 1969 Sedlak 1975
Jamamadi	OSV	AND	Andean-Equatorial: Equatorial: Arawakan: Arauan	Derbyshire 1982
Janjero	SOV	EA	Afroasiatic: Omotic: W Omotic: Janjero-Keford-Ometa-Gimira	Heine 1975a
Japanese	SOV	E	Altaic: Japanese	Steele 1978

				Ruhlen 1975
Jaquai	SOV	NG	Indo-Pacific: C & S New Guinea: Marind	Boelaars 1950
Jarawa	SVO	WA	Niger-Kordofanian: Niger-Congo: Benue-Congo: Bantoid: Jarawan Bantu	Heine 1975a, 1975b
Javanese	SVO	SE	Austronesian: Malayo-Polynesian: Hesperonesian: W Indonesian	Keenan 1978
Jei	SOV	NG	Indo-Pacific: C & S New Guinea: Frederik Hendrik Island & SE W Irian	Boelaars 1950
Jelmek	SOV	NG	Indo-Pacific: C & S New Guinea: Frederik Hendrik Island & SE W Irian	Boelaars 1950
Jibaro	SOV	AND	Andean-Equatorial: Jivaroan	Beuchat & Rivet 1909
Jiwadja	SOV	A	Australian: Iwaidjan: Iwaijic	Hsieh 1976 Steele 1978
Juat	SOV	A	Australian: Pama-Nyungan: SW Pama-Nyungan	Ruhlen 1975

LANGUAGE	ORDER	AREA	CLASSIFICATION	SOURCE
Kachari	SOV	SE	Sino-Tibetan: Tibeto-Burman: Bodo-Naga-Chin: Bodo	Endle 1944
Kachin	SOV	SE	Sino-Tibetan: Tibeto-Burman: Bodo-Naga-Kachin: Kachin	Grierson 1903, Hawkins 1983, Hertz (n.d.)
Kadu	SOV	SE	Sino-Tibetan: Tibeto-Burman: Burmese-Lolo: Lolo-Moso	DeLancey (p.c.)
Kaffa	SOV	NA	Afroasiatic: Omotic: W Omotic: Janjero-Keford-Ometa-Gimira	Heine 1975a, 1975b
Kahuga	SVO	WA	Niger-Kordofanian: Niger-Congo: Benue-Congo: Plateau Benue-Congo: I: b: C	Westermann & Bryan 1952
Kairiru	SVO	NG	Austronesian: Oceanic: NE New Guinea: Austronesian	Capell 1971a
Kalabra	SVO	NG	Indo-Pacific: Western New Guinea: II	Voorhoeve 1975b
Kaliai	SVO	NG	Austronesian: Oceanic: NE New Guinea: Austronesian	Ruhlen 1975, Hsieh 1976, Hawkins 1983
Kalispel	VSO	NWNA	Salish: Interior	Vogt 1940
Kalkutung	SOV	A	Australian: Pama-Nyungan: Kalkutung	Ruhlen 1975, Blake 1969

Language	Order	Area	Classification	Reference
Kam	SVO	E	Sino-Tibetan: Tibeto-Burman: Kam-Tai: Kam-Sui	DeLancey (p.c.)
Kamba	SVO	EA	Niger-Kordofanian: Niger-Congo: Benue-Congo: Bantoid: Bantu: NE Bantu: Zone E: Kikuyu-Kamba	Blansitt 1973
Kambatta (Alaba)	SOV	NA	Afroasiatic: Cushitic: E Cushitic: Highland E Cushitic	Heine 1975a
Kambot	SOV	NG	Indo-Pacific: Central New Guinea: N New Guinea: Bogia: Ramu	Laycock & Z'ggraggen 1975
Kamchadal (Napan)	SOV	NNE	Chukchi-Kamchatkan [Paleosiberian]	Ruhlen 1975 Hawkins 1983
Kamdang	SVO	NA	Niger-Kordofanian: Kordofanian: Tumtum	Tucker & Bryan 1966
Kamilaroi	SOV	A	Australian: Pama-Nyungan: Wiradjuric	Greenberg 1963
Kamoro	SOV	NG	Indo-Pacific: Central New Guinea: Central & S New Guinea: Asmat	Voorhoeve 1975a
Kanakhoe	SOV	SA	Khoisan: S African Khoisan: Tshukwe: VI	Heine 1975b
Kanauri	SOV	I	Sino-Tibetan: Gyarung-Mishmi: W Pronominalized Himalayan	DeLancey (p.c.)
Kanembu	SOV	CA	Nilo-Saharan: Saharan	Heine 1975a
Kanite	SOV	NG	Indo-Pacific: C New Guinea: E New Guinea	McCarthy 1965

LANGUAGE	ORDER	AREA	CLASSIFICATION	SOURCE
Kanjobal	VSO	MA	Highlands: Gende-Siane-Gahuku-Kamano-Fore: Kamano Penutian: Mayan: Kanjobalan	Quizar 1979
Kannada	SOV	I	Dravidian: South	Ruhlen 1975 Hawkins 1983 Ullrich 1968
Kanum	SOV	NG	Indo-Pacific: C & S New Guinea: Frederik Hendrik Island & SE W Irian	Boelaars 1950
Kanuri	SOV	WA	Nilo-Saharan: Saharan	Heine 1975a, 1975b Ruhlen 1975
Kaolib	SVO	NA	Niger-Kordofanian: Kordofanian: Kaolib	Heine 1975a, 1975b
Kapau	SOV	NG	Indo-Pacific: Central New Guinea: Central and South New Guinea: Kukukuku	Steele 1978 Ruhlen 1975 Oates and Oates 1968 Sedlak 1975
Kapingamarengi	VSO	MIC	Austronesian: Oceanic: E Oceanic: Polynesian: Nuclear Polynesian: Samoic Outlier	Elbert 1948 Chung 1976, 1978 Dik 1978
Kara	SVO	CA	Nilo-Saharan: C Sudanic: Kara	Heine 1975b

Karaboro	SOV	WA	Niger-Kordofanian: Niger-Congo: Gur: Senufo	Heine 1975b
Karachay	SOV	MC	Altaic: Turkic: W Turkic	Ruhlen 1975
Karaim (Trakaj)	SOV	EUR	Altaic: Turkic: W Turkic	Ruhlen 1975
Karakalpak	SOV	MC	Altaic: Turkic: C Turkic	Wurm 1951 Ruhlen 1975 Dryer 1984
Karata	SOV	MC	Caucasian: NE Caucasian: Avaro-Andi-Dido: Andi	Hawkins 1983
Karen	SVO	SE	Sino-Tibetan: Tibeto-Burman: Karen	Jones 1961 Janzen 1976
Karok	SOV	CAL	Hokan	Steele 1978
Karon-Dori	SVO	NG	Indo-Pacific: Western New Guinea: II	Voorhoeve 1975b
Kasem	SVO	WA	Niger-Kordofanian: Niger-Congo: Gur: C Gur: Grusi: N Grusi	Hewer 1976
Katcha	SVO	NA	Niger-Kordofanian: Kordofanian: Tumtum	Heine 1975a, 1975b Ruhlen 1975
Kate	SOV	NG	Indo-Pacific: Central New Guinea: Huon-	Greenberg 1963

197

LANGUAGE	ORDER	AREA	CLASSIFICATION	SOURCE
			Finisterre: Huon: Eastern	
Kati, Northern	SOV	NG	Indo-Pacific: Central New Guinea: Central & S New Guinea: OK: Lowland	Capell 1971a Renck 1977a Voorhoeve 1975a
Kati, Southern	SOV	NG	Indo-Pacific: Central New Guinea: Central & S New Guinea: OK: Lowland	Voorhoeve 1975a
Katla	SVO	NA	Niger-Kordofanian: Kordofanian: Katla	Heine 1975a Ruhlen 1975 Heine 1975b
Kaugel	SOV	NG	Indo-Pacific: C New Guinea: E New Guinea Highlands: Hagen-Wahgi-Jimi-Chimbu	Whitehead 1982
Kaun (!kaun)	SVO	SA	Khoisan: S African Khoisan: S	Ruhlen 1975
Kavalan	VOS	SE	Austronesian: Malayo-Polynesian: Formosan Austronesian	Li 1978
Kazakh	SOV	MC	Altaic: Turkic: Central Turkic	Ruhlen 1975 Hawkins 1983
Keigana	SOV	NG	Indo-Pacific: Central New Guinea: E New Guinea Highlands: Gende-Siane-Gahuku-Kamano-Fore: Kamano	Ruhlen 1975
K'ekchi	VOS	MA	Penutian: Mayan: K'ekchi	Pinkerton 1976
Keliko	SVO	CA	Nilo-Saharan: Chari-Nile: Central Sudanic:	Heine 1975a

Kerek	SOV	NNE	Chukchi-Kamchatkan [Paleosiberian]	Ruhlen 1975
Ket	SOV	NNE	Yeneseian [Paleosiberian]	Ruhlen 1975 Hawkins 1983
Kewa (Muli)	SOV	NG	Indo-Pacific: Central New Guinea: E New Guinea Highlands: Enga-Hule-Wire: Mendi	Ruhlen 1975 Franklin 1967 Sedlak 1975 Whitehead 1982
Khakas	SOV	NNE	Altaic: Turkic: N Turkic	Ruhlen 1975 Hawkins 1983
Khalka	SOV	E	Altaic: Mongol	Steele 1975 Hawkins 1983
Khamti	SOV	SE	Sino-Tibetan: Tibeto-Burman: Kam-Tai: Tai: SW	Greenberg 1963
Kharia	SOV	I	Austroasiatic: Munda: South	Steele 1978 Ruhlen 1975
Khasi	SVO	I	Austroasiatic: Mon-Khmer: Khasi	Ruhlen 1975 Mallinson & Blake 1981
Khmu	SVO	SE	Austroasiatic: Mon-Khmer: Khmuic	Mallinson & Blake 1981
Kia	SVO	MEL	Austronesian: Oceanic: NW & C Solomons	Capell 1976b

LANGUAGE	ORDER	AREA	CLASSIFICATION	SOURCE
			Austronesian (geo): New Georgia	
Kikongo	SVO	CA	Niger-Kordofanian: Niger-Congo: Benue-Congo: Bantoid: Bantu: Central W Bantu: Zone H: Kikongo	Ruhlen 1975 Bokamba 1976 de Clerq 1907
Kikuyu	SVO	EA	Niger-Kordofanian: Niger-Congo: Benue-Congo: Bantoid: Bantu: NE Bantu: Zone E: Kikuyu-Kamba	Blansitt 1973
Kimaghama	SOV	NG	Indo-Pacific: Central New Guinea: Central & S New Guinea: Fred. Hendrik Is. & SE W Irian	Voorhoeve 1975a
Kimeru	SVO	EA	Niger-Kordofanian: Niger-Congo: Benue-Congo: Bantoid: Bantu: NE Bantu: Zone E: Kikuyu-Kamba	Hodges 1976
Kinyarwanda	SVO	EA	Niger-Kordofanian: Niger-Congo: Benue-Congo: Bantoid: Bantu: NE Bantu: Zone D: Ruanda-Rundi	Kimenyi 1976
Kiowa	SOV	WNA	Uto-Aztecan: Aztec-Tanoan: Tanoan	Dryer 1984
Kipea	VSO	T	Andean-Equatorial: Equatorial: Cariri	Adam 1897
Kiranti	SOV	I	Sino-Tibetan: Tibeto-Burman: Gyarung-Mishmi: E Pronominalized Himalayan	DeLancey (p.c.)
Kire	SOV	NG	Indo-Pacific: C New Guinea: C & S New Guinea: Kiwai	Stanhope 1972

Kiriwina	SOV	NG	Austronesian: Oceanic: Papua Austronesian	Capell 191c Crowley 1978
Kis	SOV	NG	Austronesian: Oceanic: NE New Guinea Austronesian	Capell 1976a
Kitabal	SOV	A	Australian: Pama-Nyungan: Bandjalandic	Ruhlen 1975
Kitja	SOV	A	Australian: Djeragan: Gidjic	Ruhlen 1975
Kive	SOV	NG	Indo-Pacific: Central New Guinea: Central & S New Guinea: Kiwai	Stanhope 1972
Klamath	SOV	NWNA	Macro-Penutian: Penutian	Dryer 1984
Kobon	SOV	NG	Indo-Pacific: Central New Guinea: E New Guinea Highlands: Hagen-Wahgi-Jimi-Chimbu: Karam	Dryer 1984
Koiali,(Mtn.)	SOV	NG	Indo-Pacific: Central New Guinea: SE New Guinea: Koiari	Garland and Garland 1975
Koita	SOV	NG	Indo-Pacific: Central New Guinea: SE New Guinea: Koiari	Dutton 1975
Koko-Jelandji	SOV	A	Australian: Pama-Nyungan: Pama-Maric: E Pama	Ruhlen 1975
Kolami (Wardha)	SOV	I	Dravidian: Central	Steele 1978 Emeneau 1955

201

LANGUAGE	ORDER	AREA	CLASSIFICATION	SOURCE
Koma	SVO	NA	Nilo-Saharan: Koman	Ruhlen 1975
Komering	SVO	SE	Austronesian: Hesperonesian: W Indonesian	Ruhlen 1975 Tucker & Bryan 1966 Dryer 1984 Sindapati 1970
Komi (Zyrian)	SOV	EUR	Uralic: Finno-Ugric: Finno-Permic: Permic	Ruhlen 1975
Konda	SOV	I	Dravidian: Central	Krishnamurti 1969
Koneraw	SOV	NG	Indo-Pacific: Central New Guinea: Central & S New Guinea: Fred. Hendrik Is. & SE W Irian	Voorhoeve 1975a
Konkow	SOV	CAL	Penutian: Maidu	Ultan 1969
Korana	SOV	SA	Khoisan: S African Khoisan: Nama-Ora	Heine 1975b
Korape	SOV	NG	Indo-Pacific: C New Guinea: SE New Guinea: Binandere	Whitehead 1982
Korean	SOV	E	Altaic: Korean	Ruhlen 1975 Ramstedt 1939 Park (inf.) Hawkins 1983
Koryak	SVO	NNE	Chukchi-Kamchatkan [Paleosiberian]	Hawkins 1983

Language	Order	Region	Classification	References
Kota	SOV	I	Dravidian: South	Ruhlen 1975
Kove	SVO	NG	Austronesian: Oceanic: NE New Guinea Austronesian	Chowning 1973 Capell 1971c
Koya (Gommu	SOV	I	Dravidian: Central	Ruhlen 1975 Tyler 1969 Steele 1978
Kpelle	SOV	WA	Niger-Kordofanian: Niger-Congo: Mande: SW Mande	Welmers 1964 Hsieh 1976 Hawkins 1983
Kposo	SVO	WA	Niger-Kordofanian: Niger-Congo: Kwa: C Togo: Ka	Westermann & Bryan 1952
Kraho	SOV	T	Ge-Pano-Carib: Macro-Ge-Bororo: Macro-Ge: Ge: Timbira	Shell 1952
Kredj	SVO	CA	Nilo-Saharan: Chari-Nile: Central Sudanic: Kresh	Greenberg 1963
Krio	SVO	WA	English-based creole	Givón 1979
Krongo	SVO	NA	Niger-Kordofanian: Kordofanian: Tumtum	Heine 1975a, 1975b Hawkins 1983
Kru	SVO	WA	Niger-Kordofanian: Niger-Congo: Kwa: Kru	Ruhlen 1975 Heine 1975b

203

LANGUAGE	ORDER	AREA	CLASSIFICATION	SOURCE
Kryts	SOV	MC	Caucasian: N: NE: Lezghian	Hawkins 1983
Kuanua	SVO	NG	Austronesian: Oceanic: E Oceanic: Bismarck Archipelago	Ruhlen 1975 Hawkins 1983 Capell 1971
Kulere	SVO	WA	Niger-Kordofanian: Niger-Congo: Gur: Senufo	Heine 1975a
Kumauni	SOV	I	Indo-European: Indo-Iranian: Indic: N Indic	Ruhlen 1975
Kumyk	SOV	MC	Altaic: Turkic: W Turkic	Ruhlen 1975
Kunama	SOV	NA	Nilo-Saharan: Chari-Nile: Kunama	Heine 1975a, 1975b Ruhlen 1975
Kundu	SVO	WA	Niger-Kordofanian: Niger-Congo: Benue-Congo: Bantoid: Bantu: NW Bantu: Zone A: Lundu-Balong	Heine 1975b
Kung (!xu)	SVO	SA	Khoisan: S African Khoisan: Kung	Heine 1975a, 1975b
Kunimaipa	SOV	NG	Indo-Pacific: Central New Guinea: SE New Guinea: Goilala	Dryer 1984 Whitehead 1982
Kunjen	SOV	A	Australian: Pama-Nyungan: Pama-Maric: V Pama	Ruhlen 1975

Language				
Kurdish	SOV	MC	Indo-European: Indo-Iranian: Iranian: W Iranian	Ruhlen 1975
Kurku	SOV	I	Austroasiatic: Munda: Kurku	Ultan 1969
Kurukh	SOV	I	Dravidian: N	Ruhlen 1975
Kusaiean	SVO	MIC	Austronesian: Oceanic: Micronesian	Lee 1975
Kusundu	SOV	I	Sino-Tibetan: Tibeto-Burman: Gyarung-Mishmi: E Pronominalized Himalayan	Reinhard & Toba 1970
Kutenai	VOS	NWNA	Isolate	Dryer 1984
Kuvi	SOV	I	Dravidian: Central	Dryer 1984
Kwakiutl	VSO	NWNA	Wakashan: Kwakiutlan	Greenberg 1963
Kwoma	SOV	NG	Indo-Pacific: N New Guinea: Sepik	Kooyers 1975
Lafofa	SOV	NA	Niger-Kordofanian: Kordofanian: Talodi	Heine 1975
Lahu (Black)	SOV	SE	Sino-Tibetan: Tibeto-Burman: Burmese-Lolo: Lolo-Mosu: ungrouped	Steele 1978 / Ruhlen 1975
Lai	SOV	I	Sino-Tibetan: Tibeto-Burman: Naga-Kuki-Chin: Chin: C Chin	DeLancey (p.c.)
Lak	SOV	MC	Caucasian: NE Caucasian: Lak-Bargwa	Hawkins 1983

LANGUAGE	ORDER	AREA	CLASSIFICATION	SOURCE
Lakalai (Nakanai)	SVO	MEL	Austronesian: Oceanic: NE New Guinea Austronesian	Chowning 1973 Capell 1971c
Lakota (Dakota)	SOV	ENA	Macro-Siouan: Siouan	Beuchel 1939 Rood 1973
Lala	SVO	WA	Niger-Kordofanian: Niger-Congo: Adamawa-Eastern: Adamawa: VII	Westermann & Bryan 1952
Lamba	SVO	CA	Niger-Kordofanian: Niger-Congo: Benue-Congo: Bantoid: Bantu: C E Bantu: Zone M: Bisa-Lamba	Doke 1922
Lango	SVO	CA	Nilo-Saharan: Chari-Nile: E Sudanic: Nilotic	Tucker & Bryan 1966
Languda	SVO	WA	Niger-Kordofanian: Niger-Congo: Adamawa-Eastern: Adamawa: I	Newman 1976
Lao	SVO	SE	Sino-Tibetan: Tibeto-Burman: Kam-Tai: Tai: SW	Ruhlen 1975 Nguyen 1972
Lapp (Kola)	SVO	EUR	Uralic: Finno-Ugric: Finno-Permic: Finno-Volgaic: Finno-Lappic: Lappic	Hsieh 1976 Ruhlen 1975
Lashi	SOV	SE	Sino-Tibetan: Tibeto-Burman: Bodo-Naga-Chin: Kachin	DeLancey (p.c.)
Latin	SOV	EUR	Indo-European: Italic: Latin-Faliscan	Ruhlen 1975

Language				
Lau	SVO	MEL	Austronesian: Oceanic: E Oceanic	Simon (p.c.)
Latvian	SVO	EUR	Indo-European: Baltic: E Baltic	Blansitt 1973
Lavakaleve	SOV	MEL	Indo-Pacific: Central Melanesian: Central Solomons	Todd 1975
Lelemi	SVO	WA	Niger-Kordofanian: Niger-Congo: Kwa: Central Togo: Na	Höftmann 1971
Lenakel	SVO	MEL	Austronesian: Oceanic: S New Hebrides	Lynch 1974
Lenca	SOV	MA	Macro-Chibchan: Chibcha Proper	Greenberg 1963
Lendu	SOV	CA	Nilo-Saharan: Chari-Nile: Central Sudanic: Lendu	Heine 1975a
Lezghian	SOV	MC	Caucasian: N: NE: Lezghian	Hawkins 1983
Lhasa (Central Tibetan)	SOV	E	Sino-Tibetan: Tibeto-Burman: Tibetan	Ruhlen 1975 DeLancey (p.c.)
Lhota	SOV	SE	Sino-Tibetan: Tibeto-Burman: Naga-Kuki-Chin: Naga: N Naga	Grierson 1903
Lisu	SOV	E	Sino-Tibetan: Tibeto-Burman: Burmese-Lolo: Lolo-Moso: ungrouped	Roup 1971 Hawkins 1983

LANGUAGE	ORDER	AREA	CLASSIFICATION	SOURCE
Lithuanian	SVO	EUR	Indo-European: Baltic: E Baltic	Lisauskas (inf.) Ruhlen 1975 Sedlak 1975
Livonian	SVO	EUR	Uralic: Finno-Ugric: Finno-Permic: Finno-Volgaic: Finno-Lappic: Finnic	Ruhlen 1975
Logbara	SVO	CA	Nilo-Saharan: Chari-Nile: Central Sudanic: Moru-Ma'di	Heine 1975a Ruhlen 1975
Loga	SVO	CA	Nilo-Saharan: Chari-Nile: Central Sudanic: Moru-Ma'di	Heine 1975a
Lomongo	SVO	CA	Niger-Kordofanian: Niger-Congo: Benue-Congo: Bantoid: Bantu: NW Bantu: Zone C: Lomongo: Nkundo	Hulstaert 1966
Lotuko	VSO	CA	Nilo-Saharan: Chari-Nile: E Sudanic: Nilo-Hamitic: Lotuho	Greenberg 1963
Luanguia	VSO	MIC	Austronesian: Oceanic: E Oceanic: Polynesian: Nuclear: Samoic-Outlier	Ruhlen 1975
Luganda	SVO	CA	Niger-Kordofanian: Niger-Congo: Benue-Congo: Bantoid: Bantu: NE Bantu: Zone E: Nyoro-Ganda	Ruhlen 1975 Hawkins 1983
Luiseno	SVO	CAL	Aztec-Tanoan: Uto-Aztecan: Takic	Steele 1978

208

				Ruhlen 1975
Luo	SVO	E	Nilo-Saharan: Chari-Nile: E Sudanic: Nilotic: Luo	Heine 1975b Dalgish 1977 Blansitt 1973 Givón 1976a
Lunda	SVO	CA	Niger-Kordofanian: Niger-Congo: Benue-Congo: Bantoid: Bantu: Central W Bantu: Zone L: Lunda	Steele 1975
Lushei	SOV	SE	Tibeto-Burman: Naga-Kuki-Chin: Chin: Central Chin	Greenberg 1963 Hillard 1977
Luvale	SVO	CA	Niger-Kordofanian: Niger-Congo: Benue-Congo: Bantoid: Bantu: SW Bantu: Zone K: Chokwe-Luchazi	Horton 1949
Maba	SOV	NA	Nilo-Saharan: Maban	Heine 1975a, 1975b Ruhlen 1975
Maccassarese	SVO	SE	Austronesian: Malayo-Polynesian: C & S Celebes: S Celebes	Hawkins 1983
Machiguenga	VOS	AND	Andean-Equatorial: Arawakan: Maipuran: Pre-Andine Maipuran: Montana	Snell & Wise 1963
Madi	SVO	CA	Nilo-Saharan: Chari-Nile: Central Sudanic:	Heine 1965b

LANGUAGE	ORDER	AREA	CLASSIFICATION	SOURCE
			Moru-Ma'di	
Madik	SVO	NG	Indo-Pacific: Western New Guinea: II	Voorhoeve 1975b
Mae	VSO	MEL	Austronesian: Oceanic: E Oceanic: Polynesian: Nuclear: Samoic-Outlier	Ruhlen 1975
Magari	SOV	I	Sino-Tibetan: Tibeto-Burman: Gyarung-Mishmi: Eastern	Dryer 1984
Magi	SOV	NG	Indo-Pacific: Central New Guinea: Southeast New Guinea: Mailu	Thomson 1975
Magori	SOV	NG	Indo-Pacific: Central New Guinea: SE New Guinea: Mailu	Dutton 1976
Maidu (NE)	SOV	CAL	Penutian: Maidu	Ruhlen 1975
Maisin	SOV	NG	Indo-Pacific: Central New Guinea: SE New Guinea: Daga	Capell 1976c
Maithili	SOV	I	Indo-European: Indo-Iranian: Indic: E Indic	Sedlak 1975 Jha 1958
Makasei	SOV	SE	Indo-Pacific: Timor-Alor	Greenberg 1963
Makleu	SOV	NG	Indo-Pacific: C & S New Guinea: Frederik Hendrik Island & SE W Irian	Boelaars 1950
Makushi	OVS	T	Ge-Pano-Carib: Macro-Carib: Carib: N	Derbyshire & Pullum 1981

Language	Word order	Area	Classification	References
Malagasy	VOS	SA	Austronesian: Malayo-Polynesian: Hesperonesian: W Indonesian	Ruhlen 1975 Keenan and Hull 1973
Malay	SVO	SE	Austronesian: Malayo-Polynesian: Hesperonesian: W Indonesian	Ruhlen 1975 Hawkins 1973 Keenan and Hull 1973 Greenberg 1963
Malayalam	SOV	I	Dravidian: S	Ruhlen 1975 Prabolhachandran 1973
Malinka	SOV	WA	Niger-Kordofanian: Niger-Congo: Mande: NW Mande: N	Rowlands 1959 Ruhlen 1975
Malto	SOV	I	Dravidian: N	Das 1973
Mam	VSO	MA	Penutian: Mayan: Mamean	Quizar 1979
Mambila	SVO	WA	Niger-Kordofanian: Niger-Congo: Benue-Congo: Bantoid: Mambila-Wute	Heine 1975b
Mambuyag	SVO	A	Australian: Pama-Nyungan: Mabuiagic	Dryer (p.c.) Roberts 1977
Mamvu	SVO	CA	Nilo-Saharan: Chari-Nile: C Sudanic: Mangbetu-Efe	Heine 1975a Heine 1975b Sedlak 1975
Manam	SOV	NG	Austronesian: Oceanic: NE New Guinea	Capell 1971c

LANGUAGE	ORDER	AREA	CLASSIFICATION	SOURCE
			Austronesian	Gregerson 1976
Manchati	SOV	I	Sino-Tibetan: Gyarung-Mishmi: W Pronominalized Himalayan	DeLancey (p.c.)
Manchu	SOV	NNE	Altaic: Tungus: S Tungus	Hawkins 1983
Mandan	SVO	WNA	Macro-Siouan: Siouan	Kennard 1936
Mandarin	SVO	E	Sino-Tibetan: Chinese	Ruhlen 1975 Steele 1978
Mangbetu	SVO	CA	Nilo-Saharan: Chari-Nile: Central Sudanic: Mangbetu	Heine 1975a, 1975b Ruhlen 1975
Manggari	VOS	SE	Austronesian: Malayo-Polynesian: E Indonesian: Bima-Sumba	Capell 1976a
Mankaya	SVO	WA	Niger-Kordofanian: Niger-Congo: W Atlantic	Heine 1975b
Manmanua	VOS	SE	Austronesian: Malayo-Polynesian: Hesperonesian: NW Austronesian: Philippine: Sulic: Meso-Philippine: Tagalic: Manmanua	Steele 1978
Mansaka	VSO	SE	Austronesian: Malayo-Polynesian: Hesperonesian: NW Austronesian: Philippine: Sulic: Mesophilippine: Mansakic	Hawkins 1983
Mantion	SVO	NG	Indo-Pacific: Western New Guinea: I	Voorhoeve 1975c

Language	Order	Code	Classification	References
Maori	VSO	POL	Austronesian: Oceanic: E Oceanic: Polynesian: Nuclear: E: Central	Ruhlen 1975, Hawkins 1983
Mapuche (Araucanian)	SVO	AND	Penutian: Araucanian	Blansitt 1973
Maramanindji	SOV	A	Australian: Daly: Brinken-Wogaity: Brinken	Tryon 1974
Maranunggu	SOV	A	Australian: Daly: Brinken-Wogaity: Wogaity	Ruhlen 1975, Tryon 1972, Steele 1978
Mararit	SOV	CA	Nilo-Saharan: Chari-Nile: E Sudanic: E Sudanic: Tama	Heine 1975a, 1975b
Marathi	SOV	I	Indo-European: Indo-Iranian: Indic: Marathi	Ruhlen 1975, Hook (p.c.)
Marengar	SVO	A	Australian: Daly: Brinken-Wogaity: Wogaity	Tryon 1974
Margany	SOV	A	Australian: Pama-Nyungan: Pama-Maric: Mari	Dryer 1984
Margi	SVO	WA	Afroasiatic: Chadic: E Chadic: Bura	Ruhlen 1975, Dryer 1984, Hoffman 1953
Marind-Anim	SOV	NG	Indo-Pacific: Central New Guinea: Central and South New Guinea: Marind	Greenberg 1963, Voorhoeve 1975a

LANGUAGE	ORDER	AREA	CLASSIFICATION	SOURCE
Marshallese	SVO	MIC	Austronesian: Oceanic: Micronesian	Hawkins 1983
Masai	VSO	EA	Nilo-Saharan: Chari-Nile: E Sudanic: Nilo-Hamitic: Masai	Heine 1975a, 1975b Ruhlen 1975
Masakin	SOV	NA	Niger-Kordofanian: Kordofanian: Talodic	Heine 1975a
Mataco	SVO	SSA	Ge-Pano-Carib: Macro-Panoan: Mataco: Mataco	Hunt 1940
Matagalpa	SOV	CC	Macro-Chibchan: Chibcha Proper: Misumalpan	Greenberg 1963
Matukar	SOV	NG	Austronesian: Oceanic: NE New Guinea Austronesian	Capell 1971b
Maung	SVO	A	Australian: Iwaidjan	Ruhlen 1975 Hsieh 1976 Hawkins 1983
Mauwake	SOV	NG	Indo-Pacific: C New Guinea: Bogia: Adelbert Range: Pihom	Whitehead 1982
Maya (Mopan)	SVO	MA	Penutian: Mayan: Maya	Ruhlen 1975
Mazahua	VSO	MA	Oto-Manguean: Otomian: Central	Blansitt 1973
Mazatec	VOS	MA	Oto-Manguean: Popolocan	Ruhlen 1975
Mba	SVO	CA	Niger-Kordofanian: Niger-Congo: Adamawa-	Ruhlen 1975

Language	Word Order	Code	Classification	References
Mbaka-Limba	SVO	CA	Niger-Kordofanian: Niger-Congo: Adamawa-Eastern: Eastern: I	Tucker & Bryan 1966 Dryer 1984 Eastern: VI
Mbugu	SVO	EA	Afroasiatic: Cushitic: S Cushitic	Heine 1975a
Mbum	SVO	CA	Niger-Kordofanian: Niger-Congo: Adamawa-Eastern: Adamawa: VI	Heine 1975a, 1975b
Meax	SVO	NG	Indo-Pacific: Western New Guinea: I	Voorhoeve 1975c
Megiar	SOV	NG	Austronesian: Oceanic: NE New Guinea	Capell 1971c
Meithei (Manipuri)	SOV	SE	Sino-Tibetan: Tibeto-Burman: Naga-Kuki-Chin: Meithei	Grierson 1966 (1904)
Mekeo	SOV	NG	Austronesian: Oceanic: Papua Austronesian	Capell 1971c
Mende	SOV	WA	Niger-Kordofanian: Niger-Congo: Mande	Aginsky 1935 Blansitt 1973 Spears 1967
Mengen	SVO	MEL	Austronesian: Oceanic: Bismark Archipelago	Chowning 1978
Menya	SOV	NG	Indo-Pacific: C & S New Guinea: Kukukuku	Whitehead 1982

215

LANGUAGE	ORDER	AREA	CLASSIFICATION	SOURCE
Mianmin	SOV	NG	Indo-Pacific: Central New Guinea: Central & S New Guinea: OK: Mountain	Voorhoeve 1975a
Miao	SVO	SE	Sino-Tibetan: Miao-Yao: Miao	Chang and Kworay 1972
Midob	SOV	NA	Nilo-Saharan: Chari-Nile: E Sudanic: E Sudanic: Nubian	Tucker & Bryan 1966
Miju Mishmi	SOV	I	Sino-Tibetan: Tibeto-Burman: Gyarung-Mishmi: W Pronominalized Himalayan	DeLancey (p.c.)
Mikir	SOV	SE	Sino-Tibetan: Tibeto-Burman: Naga-Kuki-Chin: Naga: E Naga	Grussner 1978 DeLancey (p.c.)
Min, N.	SVO	E	Sino-Tibetan: Chinese	DeLancey (p.c.)
Min, S.	SVO	E	Sino-Tibetan: Chinese	DeLancey (p.c.)
Minangkabau	SVO	SE	Austronesian: Malayo-Polynesian: Hespero-nesian: W Indonesian	Keenan & Comrie 1979
Mindiri	SVO	NG	Austronesian: Oceanic: NE New Guinea Austronesian	Capell 1971c
Miwok, Bodega	SVO	CAL	Penutian: Miwok-Costanoan: Miwok	Callaghan 1970
Miwok, Lake	SOV	CAL	Penutian: Miwok-Costonoan: Miwok: W	Silva 1973
Miwok, Sierra	SVO	CAL	Penutian: Miwok-Costanoan: Miwok	Blansitt 1973

Language	Order	Code	Classification	Reference
Mixtec	VSO	MA	Oto-Manguean: Mixtecan	Ruhlen 1975 Hawkins 1983
Mnong Rolom	SVO	SE	Austroasiatic: Mon-Khmer: Bahnaric: S	Blansitt 1973
Moi	SVO	NG	Indo-Pacific: Western New Guinea: II	Voorhoeve 1975b
Mojave	SOV	WNA	Hokan: Yuman: Upriver	Steele 1975 Steele 1978 Hawkins 1983
Mokilese	SVO	MIC	Austronesian: Oceanic: E Oceanic: Micronesian: Nuclear: E: Central	Harrison 1976
Mombum	SOV	NG	Indo-Pacific: C New Guinea: C & S New Guinea: Frederick Hendrik Island & SE W Irian	Boelaars 1950 Voorhoeve 1975a
Mongour	SOV	E	Altaic: Mongol	Hawkins 1983
Moni	SOV	NG	Indo-Pacific: Central New Guinea: W New Guinea Highlands: Wissel Lakes-Kemandoga	Voorhoeve 1975a
Mono	SVO	MEL	Austronesian: Oceanic: NW & C Solomons Austronesian (geo): Buka	Capell 1976b
Monpa	SOV	I	Sino-Tibetan: Tibeto-Burman: Gyarung-Mishmi: E Pronominalized Himalayan	DeLancey (p.c.)
Monumbo	SOV	NG	Indo-Pacific: Central New Guinea: Bogia:	Sedlak 1975

LANGUAGE	ORDER	AREA	CLASSIFICATION	SOURCE
			Monumbo	
Mor	SVO	NG	Indo-Pacific: W New Guinea: I	Laycock 1978
Moraid	SVO	NG	Indo-Pacific: Western New Guinea: II	Voorhoeve 1975b
Moraori	SOV	NG	Indo-Pacific: C & S New Guinea: Frederik Hendrik Island & SE W Irian	Boelaars 1950
Mordvin	SOV	EUR	Uralic: Finno-Ugric: Finno-Permic: Finno-Volgaic: Volgaic	Ruhlen 1975
Moru (Amadi)	SVO	CA	Nilo-Saharan: Chari-Nile: Central Sudanic: Moru-Ma'di	Heine 1975a Ruhlen 1975
Mosquito	SOV	CC	Macro-Chibchan: Misumalpan	Dryer 1984
Mossi	SVO	WA	Niger-Kordofanian: Niger-Congo: Gur: Central Gur: More-Gurma	Blansitt 1973
Motu	SOV	NG	Austronesian: Oceanic: Papua Austronesian	Capell 1971a Hsieh 1976 Hawkins 1983
Movima	VSO	T	Andean-Equatorial: Macro-Tucanoan: Movima	Ruhlen 1975 Judy 1965 Judy & Judy 1967
Moxo (Ignaciano)	VOS	T	Andean-Equatorial: Equatorial: Arawakan: S Maipuran	Ruhlen 1975

Language	Order	Region	Classification	References
Mullukmulluk	SOV	A	Australian: Daly: Mulluk: Mullukmulluk	Birk 1976 Tryon 1974
Mundari	SOV	I	Austroasiatic: Munda	Blansitt 1973 Sinha 1975
Munduruku	SOV	T	Andean-Equatorial: Equatorial: Tupi	Dryer 1984
Mura (Piraha)	SOV	T	Macro-Chibchan: Paezan: Mura	Ruhlen 1975
Murle	VSO	CA	Nilo-Saharan: Chari-Nile: E Sudanic: E Sudanic: Beier-Didinga	Ruhlen 1975
Murut (Timugan)	VSO	SE	Austronesian: Malayo-Polynesian: Hesperonesian: NW Austronesian: Murutic	Prentice 1971
Musgu	SVO	CA	Afroasiatic: Chadic: E Chadic: Matakam-Mandara	Meyer-Bahlberg 1972
Mwera	SVO	SA	Niger-Kordofanian: Niger-Congo: Benue-Congo: Bantoid: Bantu: SE Bantu: Zone P: Yao	Harries 1950
Nabak	SOV	NG	Indo-Pacific: C New Guinea: Huon-Finisterre: Huon: S Huon	Whitehead 1982
Nama	SOV	SA	Khoisan: S African Khoisan: Nama-Ora	Heine 1975b Hawkins 1983

220

LANGUAGE	ORDER	AREA	CLASSIFICATION	SOURCE
Nandi	VSO	EA	Nilo-Saharan: Chari-Nile: E Sudanic: Nilo-Hamitic: Nandi	Ruhlen 1975, Givón 1976b
Narak	SOV	NG	Indo-Pacific: C New Guinea: E New Guinea Highlands: Hagen-Wahgi-Jimi-Chimbu: Jimi	Whitehead 1982
Naron	SOV	SA	Khoisan: S African Khoisan: Tshukwe	Heine 1975b
Nasioi	SOV	MEL	Indo-Pacific: Bougainville: E Bougainville: Nasioi	Ruhlen 1975
Navajo	SOV	WNA	Na-Dene: Athapascan-Eyak: Apachean	Ruhlen 1975, Edgerton 1963, Steele 1978
Ndogo	SVO	EA	Niger-Kordofanian: Niger-Congo: Benue-Congo: Bantoid: Bantu: NE Bantu: Zone D: Ruanda-Rundi	Heine 1975a
Ndom	SOV	NG	Indo-Pacific: Central New Guinea: Central & S New Guinea: Frederik Hendrik Is. & SE W Irian	Voorhoeve 1975a
Ndunga	SVO	EA	Niger-Kordofanian: Niger-Congo: Adamawa-Eastern: Eastern: VI	Tucker & Bryan 1966
Negidal (Nizovsk)	SOV	NNE	Altaic: Tungus: N Tungus	Ruhlen 1975
Nenema	SOV	MEL	Austronesian: Oceanic: New Caledonia: N	Ruhlen 1975

Language	Order	Region	Classification	Reference
Nengone	SVO	MEL	Austronesian: Oceanic: Loyalty Islands	Tryon 1967
Nepali	SOV	I	Indo-European: Indo-Iranian: Indic: N Indic	Bandhu 1973 Ruhlen 1975
Netherlandic-German (includes Dutch, German, Afrikaans, Yiddish, etc. as dialects)	SVO	EUR	Indo-European: Germanic: W Germanic	Ruhlen 1975
Newari	SOV	I	Sino-Tibetan: Tibeto-Burman: Gyarung-Mishmi: Non-Pronominalized Himalayan	Greenberg 1963 DeLancey (p.c.)
Newole	SOV	WA	Niger-Kordofanian: Niger-Congo: Kwa: Kru	Heine 1975a
Nez Perce	VSO	NWNA	Penutian: Sahaptin-Nez Perce	Dryer 1984
Ngarndji	SOV	A	Australian: Tjingili-Wambayan	Ruhlen 1975
Ngawun	SVO	A	Australian: Pama-Nyungan: Mayapic	Dryer 1984
Ngbandi	SVO	CA	Niger-Kordofanian: Niger-Congo: Adamawa-Eastern: Eastern: II	Heine 1975a Ruhlen 1975
Ngengomerai	SOV	A	Australian: Pama-Nyungan: Wiradjuric	Dryer 1984
Ngiyambaa	SOV	A	Australian: Pama-Nyungan: Wiradjuric	Dryer 1984
Ngizim	SVO	WA	Afroasiatic: Chadic: W Chadic: Ngizim	Keenan and Hull

LANGUAGE	ORDER	AREA	CLASSIFICATION	SOURCE 1973
Ninggirum	SOV	NG	Indo-Pacific: Central New Guinea: Central & S New Guinea: OK: Lowland	Voorhoeve 1975a
Nissan (Nehan)	SVO	MEL	Austronesian: Oceanic: Bismarck Archipelago	Todd 1978b
Nitinat	VSO	NWNA	Wakashan: Nootkan	Perlmutter & Postal 1977
Niuean	VSO	POL	Austronesian: Oceanic: E Oceanic: Polynesian: Tongic	Ruhlen 1975 Seiter 1980 Dryer 1984
Nkom	SVO	WA	Niger-Kordofanian: Niger-Congo: Benue-Congo: Bantoid: Nkom	Heine 1975b
Nkosi	SVO	WA	Niger-Kordofanian: Niger-Congo: Benue-Congo: Bantoid: Bantu: NW Bantu: Zone A: Lundu-Balong	Heine 1975a
Nogai	SOV	MC	Altaic: Turkic: Central Turkic	Ruhlen 1975
Nootka	VSO	NWNA	Wakashan: Nootkan	Rose and Carlson 1984
Noni	SVO	WA	Niger-Kordofanian: Niger-Congo: Benue-Congo: Bantoid: Plateau Bantoid: Mambila-Wute: Misaje	Hawkins 1983
Nora	SOV	SE	Sino-Tibetan: Tibeto-Burman: Bodo-Naga-Chin:	Grierson 1966

Kachin: Nung

Nubian	SOV	NA	Nilo-Saharan: Chari-Nile: E Sudanic: E Sudanic: Nubian	Heine 1975a Ruhlen 1975 Hawkins 1983
Nuer (W)	VSO	CA	Nilo-Saharan: Chari-Nile: E Sudanic: Nilotic: Nuer	Heine 1975b Ruhlen 1975
Nukuoro	VSO	MIC	Austronesian: Oceanic: E Oceanic: Polynesian: Nuclear Polynesian: Samoic-Outlier	Ruhlen 1975
Numbami	SVO	NG	Austronesian: Oceanic: NE New Guinea Austronesian	Pawley 1978
Nung	SVO	SE	Sino-Tibetan: Tibeto-Burman: Kam-Tai: Tai: C	Ruhlen 1975 Dryer 1984
Nunggubuyu	SOV	A	Australian: Nunggubuyan	Ruhlen 1975
Nupe (Bida)	SVO	WA	Niger-Kordofanian: Niger-Congo: Kwa: Nupe-Gbari	Ruhlen 1975 Smith 1970 Hawkins 1983
Nyaheun	SVO	NG	Austroasiatic: Mon-Khmer: Bahnaric: W Bahnaric	Davis 1973
Nyali	SVO	EA	Niger-Kordofanian: Niger-Congo: Benue-Congo: Bantoid: Bantu: NE Bantu: Zone D: Bira-Huku	Heine 1975b

223

LANGUAGE	ORDER	AREA	CLASSIFICATION	SOURCE
Nyang	SVO	WA	Niger-Kordofanian: Niger-Congo: Benue-Congo: Bantoid: Mamfe Bantu	Heine 1975a, 1975b
Nyangiya	SVO	CA	Nilo-Saharan: Chari-Nile: E Sudanic: E Sudanic: Teuso	Heine 1975a, 1975b
Nyimang	SOV	CA	Nilo-Saharan: Chari-Nile: E Sudanic: E Sudanic: Nyimang	Ruhlen 1975 Heine 1975a
Nyulnyul (Bardi)	SOV	A	Australian: Nyulnyulan	Ruhlen 1975
Nzakara	SVO	CA	Niger-Kordofanian: Niger-Congo: Adamawa-Eastern: Eastern III	Tucker & Bryan 1966
Oiampi	SOV	T	Andean-Equatorial: Equatorial: Tupi: Tupi-Guarani: I	Jensen 1980
Oirat (Kalmyk)	SOV	NNE	Altaic: Mongol	Ruhlen 1975 Hawkins 1983
Ojibwa	VOS	ENA	Macro-Algonquian: Algonquian	Rhodes (p.c.)
Oksapmin	SOV	NG	Indo-Pacific: C New Guinea: C & S New Guinea	Lawrence 1971
Olcha	SOV	NNE	Altaic: Tungus: S Tungus	Ruhlen 1975
Old Church Slavonic	VSO	EUR	Indo-European: Slavic: S	Hawkins 1983

Language			Classification	Reference
Ontgong Java	VOS	MIC	Austronesian: Oceanic: E Oceanic: Polynesian: Nuclear Polynesian: Samoic-Outlier	Hobbins 1928-30
Oriya	SOV	I	Indo-European: Indo-Iranian: Indic: E Indic	Ruhlen 1975
Oroch	SOV	NNE	Altaic: Tungus: S Tungus	Ruhlen 1975
Orokaiva (Isivita)	SOV	NG	Indo-Pacific: Central New Guinea: SE New Guinea: Binandere	Ruhlen 1975 Healey, Isorembo, and Chittleborough 1969 Sedlak 1975
Ossetic (Iron)	SOV	MC	Indo-European: Indo-Iranian: Iranian: E Iranian: N Iranian (geo)	Ruhlen 1975 Hawkins 1983
Ostyak (E,W)	SOV	EUR	Uralic: Finno-Ugric: Ugric	Ruhlen 1975
Otomi	VOS	MA	Oto-Manguean: Otomian: Central	Hess 1968 Dryer 1984 Hawkins 1983
Pacoh	SVO	SE	Austroasiatic: Mon-Khmer: Katuic	Watson 1966
Paipai	SOV	WNA	Hokan: Yuman: Pai	Hawkins 1983
Palauan	SVO	MIC	Austronesian: Malayo-Polynesian: NW Austronesian: Palau	Josephs 1975

LANGUAGE	ORDER	AREA	CLASSIFICATION	SOURCE
Palaung	SVO	SE	Austroasiatic: Mon-Khmer: Palaung-Wa	Dryer 1984
Pale	SVO	SE	Sino-Tibetan: Tibeto-Burman: Karen	Janzen 1976
Palikur	SVO	T	Andean-Equatorial: Equatorial: Arawakan: Maipuran: E Maipuran	Derbyshire 1982
Pambia	SVO	CA	Niger-Kordofanian: Niger-Congo: Adamawa-Eastern: Eastern: III	Tucker & Bryan 1966
Pame	SVO	MA	Oto-Manguean: Otomian: N Otomian	Dryer 1984
Pampangan	VSO	SE	Austronesian: Malayo-Polynesian: Hesperonesian: NW Austronesian: Philippine: Sulic: Mesophilippine: Pampangan	Mirikitani 1972 Ruhlen 1975 Steele 1978
Panare	OVS	T	Ge-Pano-Carib: Macro-Carib: Carib: N	Derbyshire & Pullum 1981
Pangasinan	VOS	SE	Austronesian: Hesperonesian: NW Austronesian: Philippine: Cordilleran: Kalinga	Benton 1971
Panjabi	SOV	I	Indo-European: Indo-Iranian: Indic: Central Indic	Gill & Gleason 1969 Ultan 1969
Pao-An	SOV	E	Altaic: Mongol	Hawkins 1983

Language	Order	Code	Classification	Reference
Papiamento	SVO	CC	Portuguese-based creole	Greenberg 1963
Pare (Pa)	SOV	NG	Indo-Pacific: Central New Guinea: Central & S New Guinea: Pare-Samo-Beami-Bosavi	Voorhoeve 1975a
Parji (Bastar)	SOV	I	Dravidian: Central	Ruhlen 1975
Pashto	SOV	I	Indo-European: Iranian: E Iranian: Pashto	Dryer 1984 Ruhlen 1975
Passamaquoddy (Malecite)	SVO	ENA	Macro-Algonquian: Algonquian	Teeter 1971 Steele 1978
Paumari	SVO	AND	Andean-Equatorial: Equatorial: Arawakan: Arauan	Derbyshire 1982
Pawaian	SOV	NG	Indo-Pacific: C New Guinea: E New Guinea Highlands: Pawaia	Trety 1969
Pazah	VOS	SE	Austronesian: Malayo-Polynesian: Formosan Austronesian	Li 1978
Pengo	SOV	I	Dravidian: Central	Ruhlen 1975 Hawkins 1983
Persian	SOV	MC	Indo-European: Indo-Iranian: Iranian: W Iranian	Ruhlen 1975 Hawkins 1983
Pima	VSO	WNA	Aztec-Tanoan: Uto-Aztecan: Sonoran	Hawkins 1983

LANGUAGE	ORDER	AREA	CLASSIFICATION	SOURCE
(Papago)				
Piro	SOV	WNA	Aztec-Tanoan: Tanoan [extinct]	Keenan 1978
Piro	SOV	AND	Andean-Equatorial: Equatorial: Arawakan: Maipuran	Matteson 1965 Derbyshire 1982
Pisa	SOV	NG	Indo-Pacific: Central New Guinea: Central & S New Guinea: Awyu	Voorhoeve 1975a
Pitjatjatjara	SOV	A	Australian: Pama-Nyungan: SW Pama-Nyungan: Wati	Ruhlen 1975 Dryer 1984 Blake 1979
Pittapitta	SOV	A	Australian: Pama-Nyungan: Pittapittic	Ruhlen 1975 Dryer 1984
Piva	SVO	MEL	Austronesian: Oceanic: NW & C Solomons Austronesian (geo): Buka	Lincoln 1976
Po-ai	SVO	E	Sino-Tibetan: Tibeto-Burman: Kam-Tai: N Tai	DeLancey (p.c.)
Pocoman	VOS	MA	Penutian: Mayan: Quichean	Quizar 1979
Pocomchi	VOS	MA	Penutian: Mayan: Quichen	Ruhlen 1975
Pokau	SOV	NG	Austronesian: Oceanic: Papua Austronesian (geo)	Lanyon-Orgill 1943-46
Pokot	VSO	EA	Nilo-Saharan: Chari-Nile: E Sudanic: Nandi	Heine 1975b

Language	Order	Area	Classification	References
Polish	SVO	EUR	Indo-European: Slavic: W Slavic (geo)	Ruhlen 1975 Mallinson & Blake 1981
Podopa	SOV	NG	Indo-Pacific: C New Guinea: E New Guinea Highlands: Mikaru	Whitehead 1982
Pomo (East)	SOV	CAL	Hokan: Pomo	McLendon 1975
Pomo (Kashaya)	SOV	CAL	Hokan: Pomo	Steele 1975
Pomo (SE)	SOV	CAL	Hokan: Pomo	Mochinsky 1974
Pongwe	SVO	WA	Niger-Kordofanian: Niger-Congo: Benue-Congo: Bantoid: Bantu: NW Bantu: Zone B: Nyene	Heine 1975b
Ponosakan	VSO	SE	Austronesian: Malayo-Polynesian: N Celebes (geo): Minhasa	Sneddon 1970
Popoloca	SVO	MA	Oto-Manguean: Popolocan: Popoloca	Williams & Longacre 1967
Portugese	SVO	EUR	Indo-European: Italic: Romance: Ibero-Romance	Ruhlen 1975 Hawkins 1983
Provençal	SVO	EUR	Indo-European: Italic: Romance: Gallo-Romance	Ruhlen 1975
Pukapuka	VSO	POL	Austronesian: Oceanic: E Oceanic: Samoic Outlier	Steele 1978
Puluwat	SVO	MIC	Austronesian: Oceanic: Micronesian	Elbert 1974

229

LANGUAGE	ORDER	AREA	CLASSIFICATION	SOURCE
Pungupungu	SOV	A	Australian: Daly: Brinken-Wogaity: Wogaity	Tryon 1974
Purum	SOV	SE	Sino-Tibetan: Tibeto-Burman: Naga-Kuki-Chin: Kuki	Grierson 1966 (1904)
Qemant	SOV	NA	Afroasiatic: Cushitic: Central Cushitic	Heine 1975a Appleyard 1975
Quechua	SOV	AND	Andean-Equatorial: Andean: II: Quechumaran	Ruhlen 1975 Hawkins 1983 Levinsohn 1976 Spenset et. al. 1967
Quiche	SVO	MA	Penutian: Mayan: Quichean	Blansitt 1973
Quileute	VSO	NWNA	Chimakuan	Greenberg 1963
Ralte	SOV	SE	Sino-Tibetan: Tibeto-Burman: Naga-Kuki-Chin: Chin: N Chin	Grierson 1966 (1904)
Rangkas	SOV	I	Sino-Tibetan: Tibeto-Burman: Gyarung-Mishmi: W Pronominalized Himalayan	DeLancey (p.c.)
Rangkhol (Hrangkhol)	SOV	SE	Sino-Tibetan: Tibeto-Burman: Naga-Kuki-Chin: Kuki	Grierson 1966 (1904)
Rarotongan	VSO	POL	Austronesian: Oceanic: E Oceanic: Polynesian: Nuclear: E: Central	Ruhlen 1975

Language	Order	Region	Classification	Reference
Rashad	SOV	NA	Niger-Kordofanian: Kordofanian: Tegali	Tucker & Bryan 1966
Rawa	SOV	NG	Indo-Pacific: Central New Guinea: Huon-Finisterre: Finisterre: W Finisterre: Gusap-Mot	Ruhlen 1975 Claassen and McElhanon 1970
Remo	SOV	I	Austroasiatic: Munda: South	Blansitt 1973
Rendille	SOV	EA	Afroasiatic: Cushitic: E Cushitic: Lowland E Cushitic	Heine 1975a Comen 1978
Rengma	SOV	SE	Sino-Tibetan: Tibeto-Burman: Naga-Kuki-Chin: Naga: E Naga	DeLancey (p.c.)
Reshe	SVO	WA	Niger-Kordofanian: Niger-Congo: Benue-Congo: Plateau Benue-Congo: I	Heine 1975a
Riantana	SOV	NG	Indo-Pacific: Central New Guinea: Central & S New Guinea: Fred. Hendrik Is. & SE W Irian	Voorhoeve 1975a
Rikbaktsa	SOV	T	Andean-Equatorial: Equatorial: Tupi: Tupi-Guarani: I	Dryer 1984
Romany (Baltic)	SVO	EUR	Indo-European: Indo-Iranian: Indic: Romany	Ruhlen 1975
Rong	SOV	I	Sino-Tibetan: Tibeto-Burman: Bodo-Naga-Chin: Naga	Dryer 1984 Mainwaring 1876
Ronga	SVO	SA	Niger-Kordofanian: Niger-Congo: Benue-Congo:	Blansitt 1973

231

LANGUAGE	ORDER	AREA	CLASSIFICATION	SOURCE
			Bantoid: Bantu: SE Bantu: Zone S: Tswa-Ronga	
Rotokas	SOV	MEL	Indo-Pacific: Bougainville: W Bougainville	Lincoln 1976
Rotuman	SVO	MEL	Austronesian: Oceanic: E Oceanic: Rotuman	Ultan 1969 Hawkins 1983
Roviana	VSO	MEL	Austronesian: Oceanic: NW and Central Solomons (geo): New Georgia	Keenan and Hull 1973 Todd 1978a
Rumanian	SVO	EUR	Indo-European: Italic: Romance: E Romance	Ruhlen 1975 Hawkins 1983
Runyankore	SVO	EA	Niger-Kordofanian: Niger-Congo: Benue-Congo: Bantoid: Bantu: NE Bantu: Zone E: Nyoro-Ganda	Morris and Kirwan 1957
Russian	SVO	EUR	Indo-European: Slavic: E Slavic (geo)	Ruhlen 1975 Sedlak 1975 Korn (inf)
Rutul	SVO	MC	Caucasian: N: NE: Lezghian	Ruhlen 1975 Hawkins 1983
Rvwang	SOV	SE	Sino-Tibetan: Tibeto-Burman: Bodo-Naga-Chin: Kachin: Rawang	Barnard 1934 Morse 1965
Ryukyuan	SOV	E	Altaic: Japanese	Ruhlen 1975

232

				Hawkins 1983
Sa'a	SVO	MEL	Austronesian: Oceanic: E Oceanic	Simon (p.c.) Ivaus 1911
Sahaptin	VSO	NWNA	Penutian: Sahaptin-Nez-Perce	Steele 1978
Saho	SOV	NA	Afroasiatic: Cushitic: Lowland E Cushitic	Tucker & Bryan 1966
Sakao	SVO	MEL	Austronesian: Oceanic: NW New Hebrides: Santo	Dryer 1984
Salish, Puget	VSO	NWNA	Salish: Coast	Steele 1978 Ransom 1945
Samo	SOV	NG	Indo-Pacific: C & S New Guinea: Pare-Samo-Beami-Bosavi	Shaw 1973
Samo	SOV	NG	Indo-Pacific: Left May	Voorhoeve 1975a
Samoan	VSO	POL	Austronesian: Oceanic: E Oceanic: Polynesian: Nuclear: Samoic-Outlier	Ruhlen 1975
Sandawe	SOV	EA	Khoisan: Sandawe	Heine 1975a, 1975b Greenberg 1963
Sanglechi (Ishkashmi)	SOV	MC	Indo-European: Indo-Iranian: Iranian: E Iranian: Pamir (geo)	Ruhlen 1975
Sango	SVO	CA	Niger-Kordofanian: Niger-Congo: Adamawa-	Samarin 1963

233

LANGUAGE	ORDER	AREA	CLASSIFICATION	SOURCE
			Eastern: Eastern: II	Ruhlen 1975
Santeli	SOV	I	Austroasiatic: Munda: E	Masica 1976
Sanuma	SOV	T	Macro-Chibchan: Waican: Waica: Sanima	Borgmann 1974 Hodgkinson 1981
Sara (Majingai)	SVO	CA	Nilo-Saharan: Chari-Nile: Central Sudanic:	Heine 1975a, 1975b Ruhlen 1975
Saramaccan	SVO	T	English-based creole	Glock 1972
Sarcee	SOV	NNA	Na-Dene: Athapascan-Eyak: Athapascan: N	Dryer (p.c.) Hofer 1974
Sayula	SVO	MA	Penutian: Mixe-Zoque	Ruhlen 1975
Scandinavian, Continental (includes Danish, Norwegian, Swedish)	SVO	EUR	Indo-European: Germanic: N Germanic	Ruhlen 1975
Scandinavian, Insular (includes Icelandic)	SVO	EUR	Indo-European: Germanic: N Germanic	Ruhlen 1975
Seediq	VOS	SE	Austronesian: Malayo-Polynesian: Formosan Austronesian	Starosta 1973

Language	Order	Region	Classification	Reference
Selepet	SOV	NG	Indo-Pacific: C New Guinea: Huon-Finisterre: Huon: W	Hawkins 1983 Whitehead 1982
Selkup	SOV	NNE	Uralic: Samoyedic	Ruhlen 1975
Seme	SOV	WA	Niger-Kordofanian: Niger-Congo: Gur: Seme	Heine 1975a, 1975b
Sentani	SOV	NG	Indo-Pacific: Central New Guinea: N New Guinea: N Papuan: Sentani	Ruhlen 1975 Voorhoeve 1975a
Serbo-Croatian	SVO	EUR	Indo-European: Slavic: S Slavic (geo)	Ruhlen 1975
Sere	SVO	CA	Niger-Kordofanian: Niger-Congo: Adamawa-Eastern: Eastern: V	Heine 1975a
Seri	SOV	WNA	Hokan	Langdon 1979
Sesotho	SVO	SA	Niger-Kordofanian: Niger-Congo: Benue-Congo: Bantoid: Bantu: Zone S: Sotho-Tswana	Morolong & Hyman 1977
Sgaw	SVO	SE	Sino-Tibetan: Tibeto-Burman: Karen	DeLancey (p.c.)
Shan	SVO	SE	Sino-Tibetan: Tibeto-Burman: Kam Tai: SW Tai: NW	Mallinson & Blake 1981
Sharanahua (Shawanawa)	SOV	T	Ge-Pano-Carib: Macro-Panoan: Pano-Tacana: Pano: C Pano	Kemp 1977
Shasta	SOV	CAL	Hokan	Langdon 1979

LANGUAGE	ORDER	AREA	CLASSIFICATION	SOURCE
Shatt	SVO	CA	Nilo-Saharan: Chari-Nile: E Sudanic: E Sudanic: Daju	Tucker & Bryan 1966
Shilha (Agadir)	VSO	NA	Afroasiatic: Berber: Shilha	Ruhlen 1975
Shilluk	SVO	NA	Nilo-Saharan: Chari-Nile: E Sudanic: Shilluk	Greenberg 1963 Heine 1975b
Shina	SOV	I	Indo-European: Indo-Iranian: Indic: Dardic: Sina	Keenan 1978
Sho (Aso)	SOV	SE	Sino-Tibetan: Tibeto-Burman: Naga-Kuki-Chin: Chin: S Chin	Grierson 1966 (1904)
Shona (Zezuru)	SVO	SA	Niger-Kordofanian: Niger-Congo: Benue-Congo: Bantoid: Bantu: SE Bantu: Zone P: Matumbi	Ruhlen 1975 Keenan and Hull 1973 Hawkins 1983
Shor	SOV	NNE	Altaic: Turkic: N Turkic	Ruhlen 1975
Shoshone	SOV	WNA	Aztec-Tanoan: Uto-Aztecan: Numic	Crapo 1976
Shugni	SOV	MC	Indo-European: Indo-Iranian: Iranian: E Iranian: Shugni	Ruhlen 1975
Siane	SOV	NG	Indo-Pacific: Central New Guinea: E New Guinea Highlands: Gende-Siane-Gahuku-	Salisbury 1956

Kamano-Fore: Siane

Language	Order	Area	Classification	References
Sidamo	SOV	NA	Afroasiatic: Cushitic: E Cushitic: Highland E Cushitic	Heine 1975a / Ruhlen 1975 / Hawkins 1983
Sierra Miwok	SVO	CAL	Penutian: Miwok-Costanoan: Miwok	Blansitt 1973
Sierra Populuca	VSO	MA	Penutian: Mixe-Zoque	Blansitt 1973
Simi	SOV	SE	Sino-Tibetan: Tibeto-Burman: Naga-Kuki-Chin: Naga: E Naga	Culicover & Wexler 1974 / Grierson 1967 (1904)
Sindhi	SOV	I	Indo-European: Indo-Iranian: Indic: NW Indic	Ruhlen 1975
Sinhalese	SOV	I	Indo-European: Indo-Iranian: Indic: Singhalese-Maldivian	Ruhlen 1975
Sipaia	SOV	T	Andean-Equatorial: Equatorial: Tupi: Yuruna	Nimrendaju 1924
Siriono	SVO	T	Andean-Equatorial: Tupi: Tupi-Guarani: II	Firestone 1965 / Ruhlen 1975
Siroi	SOV	NG	Indo-Pacific: Ganglau	Wells 1979 / Whitehead 1982
Sissano	SVO	NG	Austronesian: Oceanic: NE New Guinea Austronesian	Laycock 1973 / Capell 1971b

237

LANGUAGE	ORDER	AREA	CLASSIFICATION	SOURCE
Sizang	SOV	I	Sino-Tibetan: Tibeto-Burman: Naga-Kuki-Chin: Chin: N Chin	DeLancey (p.c.)
Sko	SOV	NG	Indo-Pacific: Central New Guinea: N New Guinea: N Papuan: Tami: Sko	Ruhlen 1975
Slovenian	SVO	EUR	Indo-European: Slavic: S Slavic	Downing 1977
Snohomish	VSO	NWNA	Salish: Coast	Steele 1975 Ransom 1945
Somali	SOV	EA	Afroasiatic: Cushitic: E Cushitic: Lowland E Cushitic	Heine 1975a Sedlak 1975 Steele 1978
Songhai	SVO	NA	Nilo-Saharan: Songhai	Greenberg 1963 Kendall 1971
Sora	SOV	I	Austroasiatic: Munda: South	Mallinson & Blake 1981
Spanish	SVO	EUR	Indo-European: Italic: Romance: Ibero-Romance	Ruhlen 1975 Hawkins 1983
Squamish	VSO	NWNA	Salish: Coast	Ultan 1969 Steele 1978
Sre	SVO	SE	Austroasiatic: Mon-Khmer: Bahnaric: S Bahnaric	Manley 1972

Stieng	SVO	SE	Austroasiatic: Mon-Khmer: S Bahnaric	Dryer 1984
Subtiaba	SVO	CC	Hokan: Tlapanecan [extinct]	Greenberg 1963
Suena	SOV	NG	Indo-Pacific: Central New Guinea: SE New Guinea: Binandere	Ruhlen 1975
Sumerian	SOV	MC	Isolate [extinct]	Greenberg 1963
Sundanese	SVO	SE	Austronesian: Malayo-Polynesian: Hesperonesian: W Indonesian	Robins 1968
Sungor	SOV	CA	Nilo-Saharan: Chari-Nile: E Sudanic: E Sudanic: Tama	Heine 1975a, 1975b
Sunwar	SOV	I	Sino-Tibetan: Tibeto-Burman: Gyarung-Mishmi: W Pronominalized Himalayan	DeLancey (p.c.)
Susu	SOV	WA	Niger-Kordofanian: Niger-Congo: Mande: N Mande	Dryer 1984
Svan	SOV	MC	Caucasian: S Caucasian	Hawkins 1983
Swahili (Kiswahili)	SVO	EA	Niger-Kordofanian: Niger-Congo: Benue-Congo: Bantoid: Bantu: Central E Bantu: Zone G: Swahili	Polomé 1967 Ruhlen 1975 Bokamba 1976 Sedlak 1975
Swazi	SVO	SA	Niger-Kordofanian: Niger-Congo: Benue-Congo: Bantoid: Bantu: SE Bantu: Zone S: Nguni	Steele 1975 Sedlak 1975

LANGUAGE	ORDER	AREA	CLASSIFICATION	SOURCE
Swit	SOV	NG	Austronesian: Oceanic: NE New Guinea Austronesian	Capell 1971
Syiahga-Yenimu	SOV	NG	Indo-Pacific: Central New Guinea: Central & S New Guinea: Awyu	Voorhoeve 1975a
Tabasaran	SOV	MC	Caucasian: N: Lezghian	Hawkins 1983
Tacana	SOV	AND	Ge-Pano-Carib: Macro-Panoan: Pano-Tacana: Tacana	Ottaviano & Ottaviano 1967
Taensa	VSO	ENA	Macro-Algonquian: Natchez	Haumonte et al. 1887
Tagabili	VSO	SE	Austronesian: Malayo-Polynesian: Hesperonesian: NW Austronesian: Philippine: Bilic	Greenberg 1963
Tagalog	VSO	SE	Austronesian: Malayo-Polynesian: Hesperonesian: NW Austronesian: Philippine: Sulic: Mesophilippine: Tagalic: Tagalog	Naylor (inf.) Ruhlen 1975
Tagbu	SVO	CA	Niger-Kordofanian: Niger-Congo: Adamawa-Eastern: Eastern: V	Heine 1975a
Tagoi	SOV	NA	Niger-Kordofanian: Kordofanian: Tegali	Heine 1975a, 1975b
Tahitian	VSO	POL	Austronesian: Oceanic: E Oceanic: Polynesian:	Dryer 1984

			Nuclear Polynesian: E Polynesian	Hawkins 1983
Tai (Black)	SVO	SE	Sino-Tibetan: Tibeto-Burman: Kam-Tai: Tai: SW	Ruhlen 1975
Tairora	SOV	NG	Indo-Pacific: Central New Guinea: E New Highlands: Gadsup-Auyana-Awa-Tairora: Tairora	Dryer 1984
Takelma	SOV	NWNA	Penutian: Takelma	Dryer 1984
Talodi	SVO	NA	Niger-Kordofanian: Kordofanian: Talodi	Heine 1975a, 1975b
Talysh	SOV	MC	Indo-European: Indo-Iranian: Iranian: W Iranian	Ruhlen 1975
Tama	SOV	CA	Nilo-Saharan: Chari-Nile: E Sudanic: E Sudanic: Tama	Ruhlen 1975 / Dryer 1984 / Tucker & Bryan 1966
Tamang	SOV	I	Sino-Tibetan: Tibeto-Burman: Gyarung-Mishmi: Non-Pronominalized Himalayan	Keenan 1978
Tamazight	VSO	NA	Afroasiatic: Berber: Tamazight-Riff-Kayble Group	Ruhlen 1975
Tami	SOV	NG	Austronesian: Oceanic: NE New Guinea: Austronesian	Capell 1971b
Tamil	SOV	I	Dravidian: S	Ruhlen 1975 / Hawkins 1983

LANGUAGE	ORDER	AREA	CLASSIFICATION	SOURCE
Tangsa	SOV	I	Sino-Tibetan: Tibeto-Burman: Bodo-Naga-Chin: Naga	DeLancey (p.c.)
Tangsarr	SOV	SE	Sino-Tibetan: Tibeto-Burman: Bodo-Naga-Chin: Kachin: Rawang	DeLancey (p.c.)
Taraoan Mishmi	SOV	SE	Sino-Tibetan: Tibeto-Burman: Naga-Kuki-Chin: Kuki: C Kuki	DeLancey (p.c.)
Tarascan	SVO	MA	Isolate	Foster 1971 Steele 1978
Tat	SOV	MC	Indo-European: Indo-Iranian: Iranian: W Iranian	Ruhlen 1975
Tatar	SOV	EUR	Altaic: Turkic: W Turkic	Ruhlen 1975 Hawkins 1983 Poppe 1961
Teda	SOV	NA	Nilo-Saharan: Saharan	Greenberg 1963
Telefol	SOV	NG	Indo-Pacific: Central New Guinea: Central and South New Guinea: OK: Mountain	Ruhlen 1975 Healey 1965 Sedlak 1975 Voorhoeve 1975a
Telugu	SOV	I	Dravidian: Central	Ruhlen 1975 Hawkins 1983

Language	Order	Region	Classification	References
Temein	SVO	NA	Nilo-Saharan: Chari-Nile: E Sudanic: E Sudanic: Temein	Heine 1975a, 1975b Ruhlen 1975
Temiar	SVO	SE	Austroasiatic: Malacca: Sakai	Benjamin 1976
Temne	SVO	WA	Niger-Kordofanian: Niger-Congo: W Atlantic: Mel	Heine 1975b Hutchinson 1969 Yillah 1975
Tenetehara	VSO	T	Andean-Equatorial: Equatorial: Tupi: Tupi-Guarani: I	Ruhlen 1975 Dryer 1984
Teop	SOV	MEL	Austronesian: Oceanic: NW and Central Solomons	Capell 1971b
Tepeth	VSO	CA	Nilo-Saharan: Chari-Nile: E Sudanic: E Sudanic: Teuso	Heine 1975a, 1975b Ruhlen 1975
Tera (Wuyo)	SVO	WA	Afroasiatic: Chadic: E Chadic: Tera	Ruhlen 1975 Dryer 1984
Tereno	VOS	T	Andean-Equatorial: Equatorial: Arawakan: Maipuran: S Maipuran: Parana	Derbyshire 1982
Terraba	SOV	CC	Macro-Chibchan: Chibchan: W Chibchan	Datz (p.c.)
Teso	VSO	CA	Nilo-Saharan: Chari-Nile: E Sudanic: Nilo-Hamitic: Teso	Heine 1975b Keenan 1978

LANGUAGE	ORDER	AREA	CLASSIFICATION	SOURCE
Tetelcingo	SVO	WNA	Aztec-Tanoan: Uto-Aztecan: Aztecan	Ultan 1969
Teuso	VSO	CA	Nilo-Saharan: Chari-Nile: E Sudanic: Teuso	Heine 1975b
Tewa	SOV	WNA	Aztec-Tanoan: Tanoan	Kroskrity 1978
Thado	SOV	SE	Sino-Tibetan: Tibeto-Burman: Naga-Kuki-Chin: Chin: N Chin	Grierson 1966 (1904)
Thai (Bangkok)	SVO	SE	Sino-Tibetan: Tibeto-Burman: Kam-Tai: SW	Grima (p.c.) Ruhlen 1975 Nguyen 1972
Thao	VOS	SE	Austronesian: Malayo-Polynesian: Formosan Austronesian	Li 1978
Tho	SVO	SE	Sino-Tibetan: Tibeto-Burman: Kam-Tai: C Tai	Day 1966
Thulung	SOV	I	Sino-Tibetan: Tibeto-Burman: Gyarung-Mishmi: Eastern	Allen 1975
Tiddim	SOV	I	Sino-Tibetan: Tibeto-Burman: Naga-Kuki-Chin: Chin: N Chin	DeLancey (p.c.)
Tifal	SOV	NG	Indo-Pacific: Central New Guinea: Central & S New Guinea: OK: Mountain	Voorhoeve 1975a
Tigak	SVO	MEL	Austronesian: Oceanic: Bismarck Archipelago	Dryer 1984

Tigre (Mensa)	SOV	NA	Afroasiatic: Semitic: S Semitic: Ethiopic	Heine 1975a Ruhlen 1975
Tigrinya	SOV	NA	Afroasiatic: Semitic: S Semitic: Ethiopic	Gragg 1972 Heine 1975a
Tillamook	VSO	NWNA	Salish: Tillamook	Ruhlen 1975
Tima	SVO	NA	Niger-Kordofanian: Kordofanian: Katla	Tucker & Bryan 1966
Timbe	SOV	NG	Indo-Pacific: C New Guinea: Huon-Finisterre: Huon: W Huon	Whitehead 1982
Timputs	SOV	MEL	Austronesian: Oceanic: NW and Central Solomons (geo)	Capell 1971b
Tindi	SOV	MC	Caucasian: NE Caucasian: Avaro-Andi-Dido: Andi	Hawkins 1983
T'in	SVO	SE	Austroasiatic: Mon-Khmer: Khmuic	Filbeck 1973
Tiv	SVO	WA	Niger-Kordofanian: Niger-Congo: Benue-Congo: Bantoid: Tiv-Batu	Heine 1975b
Tiwi	SVO	A	Australian: Tiwi	Osborne 1974
Tlingit	SOV	NWNA	Na-Dene	Keenan 1978 Hawkins 1983
Tocharian	SOV	E	Indo-European: Tocharian	Hawkins 1983

LANGUAGE	ORDER	AREA	CLASSIFICATION	SOURCE
Toaripi	SOV	NG	Indo-Pacific: C New Guinea: SE New Guinea: Toaripi	Brown 1973
Tobati	SOV	NG	Austronesian: S Halmahera-W New Guinea	Capell 1976a
Tojolabal	VOS	MA	Penutian: Mayan: Tzeltalan	Furbee-Losee 1976
Tombulu	VSO	SE	Austronesian: Malayo-Polynesian: N Celebes (geo): Minhasa	Sneddon 1970
Tondano	VSO	SE	Austronesian: Malayo-Polynesian: N Celebes (geo): Minhasa	Sneddon 1970
Tongan	VSO	POL	Austronesian: Oceanic: E Oceanic: Polynesian: Tongic	Ultan 1969 Steele 1978 Hawkins 1983
Tongoa (Nguna)	SVO	MEL	Austronesian: Oceanic: E Oceanic: Efate-Epi	Ruhlen 1975 Capell 1971c
Tonkawa	SOV	WNA	Macro-Algonquian	Hoijer 1931 Troike 1967
Tonsawang	VSO	SE	Austronesian: Malayo-Polynesian: N Celebes (geo): Minhasa	Sneddon 1970
Tonsea	VSO	SE	Austronesian: Malayo-Polynesian: N Celebes (geo): Minhasa	Sneddon 1970

Tontemboan	VSO	SE	Austronesian: Malayo-Polynesian: N Celebes (geo)	Sneddon 1970
Toposa	VSO	CA	Nilo-Saharan: Chari-Nile: E Sudanic: E Nilotic: Teso	Givón 1976a
Torau	SOV	MEL	Austronesian: Oceanic: NW and Central Solomons (geo)	Capell 1971c
Totonac	SVO	MA	Penutian: Totonacan	Dryer 1984
To'ava'ita	SVO	MEL	Austronesian: Oceanic: E Oceanic	Simon (p.c.)
Trique	VSO	MA	Oto-Manguean: Mixtecan	Longacre 1966 Steele 1978
Trukese	SVO	MIC	Austronesian: Oceanic: Micronesian	Dannis (inf.)
Tsang	SOV	I	Sino-Tibetan: Tibeto-Burman: Bodo-Naga-Chin: Naga	Hawkins 1983
Tsaxur	SVO	MC	Caucasian: N: NE: Lezghian	Ruhlen 1975

LANGUAGE	ORDER	AREA	CLASSIFICATION	SOURCE
Tschama	SOV	AND	Ge-Pano-Carib: Macro-Panoan: Pano-Tacana: Pano	Tessmann 1929 Loos 1970
Tsimshian	VSO	NWNA	Penutian: Tsimshian	Ruhlen 1975 Rigsby 1975
Tswana	SVO	SA	Niger-Kordofanian: Niger-Congo: Benue-Congo: Bantoid: Bantu: SE Bantu: Zone S: Sotha-Tswana	Cole and Mokaila 1962 Sedlak 1975
Tuamotuan	VSO	POL	Austronesian: Oceanic: E Oceanic: Polynesian: Nuclear: E: Central	Ruhlen 1975
Tuareg	VSO	NA	Afroasiatic: Berber	Keenan 1978
Tubu	SOV	NA	Nilo-Saharan	Heine 1975a, 1975b
Tulu	SOV	I	Dravidian: C	Kolver 1969
Tumleo	SVO	NG	Austronesian: Oceanic: NE New Guinea Austronesian	Capell 1971b
Tung-Hsiang	SOV	E	Altaic: Mongol	Hawkins 1983
Tunica	SOV	ENA	Macro-Algonquian: Tunica (extinct)	Ruhlen 1975 Hawkins 1983
Turkana	VSO	CA	Nilo-Saharan: Chari-Nile: E Sudanic:	Greenberg 1963

Language	Word Order	Region	Classification	References
			Nilo-Hamitic: Teso	Heine 1975b
Turkish	SOV	MC	Altaic: Turkic: S Turkic	Oszoy (inf.) / Ruhlen 1975 / Sedlak 1975
Turkmen	SOV	MC	Altaic: Turkic: S Turkic	Ruhlen 1975 / Hawkins 1983
Tuscarora	SVO	ENA	Macro-Siouan: Iroquoian	Williams 1973 / Steele 1978
Tuva	SOV	NNE	Altaic: Turkic: N Turkic	Ruhlen 1975
Tuscarora	SVO	ENA	Macro-Siouan: Iroquoian	Williams 1973 / Steele 1978
Twi	SVO	WA	Niger-Kordofanian: Niger-Congo: Kwa: Volta-Comoe: Central Volta-Comoe	Greenberg 1963 / Heine 1975b
Tyebari	SOV	WA	Niger-Kordofanian: Niger-Congo: Gur: Senufo	Laughren 1976
Tyeraity	SOV	A	Australian: Daly: Mulluk: Mullukmulluk	Tryon 1974
Tzeltal	VOS	MA	Penutian: Mayan: Tzeltalan	Ruhlen 1975 / Hawkins 1983
Tzotzil	VSO	MA	Penutian: Mayan: Tzeltalan	Cowan 1969
Tzutuzil	SVO	MA	Penutian: Mayan: Quichean	Carlin 1970

LANGUAGE	ORDER	AREA	CLASSIFICATION	SOURCE
Ubyx	SOV	MC	Caucasian: NW	Hawkins 1983
Udi	SVO	MC	Caucasian: NE Caucasian: Lezghian	Hawkins 1983
Udihe	SOV	NNE	Altaic: Tungus: S Tungus	Ruhlen 1975 Hawkins 1983
Uduk	SVO	NA	Nilo-Saharan: Koman	Tucker & Bryan 1966
Uighur	SOV	EUR	Altaic: Turkic: E Turkic	Ruhlen 1975 Hawkins 1983
Ukrainian	SVO	EUR	Indo-European: Slavic: E Slavic (geo)	Ruhlen 1975
Ulau-Suain	SVO	NG	Austronesian: Oceanic: New Guinea Austronesian	Capell 1976a
Ulithian	SVO	MIC	Austronesian: Oceanic: Micronesian	Steele 1978 Ruhlen 1975
Uradhi	SOV	A	Australian: Pama-Nyungan: Pama-Maric: N Pama	Dryer 1984
Umbundu	SVO	SA	Niger-Kordofanian: Niger-Congo: Benue-Congo: Bantoid: Bantu: SW Bantu: Zone R: Umbundu	Downing 1977
Urartian	SOV	MC	Hurrian: Urartian	Greenberg 1963
Urhobo	SVO	WA	Niger-Kordofanian: Niger-Congo: Kwa: Edo: S	Keenan and Hull 1973

250

Uri	SOV	NG	Indo-Pacific: Central New Guinea: Huon-Finisterre: Finisterre: E	Ruhlen 1975
Usarufa	SOV	NG	Indo-Pacific: Central New Guinea: E New Guinea Highlands: Gadsup-Auyana-Awa-Tairora: Gauwa	Bee 1973 Whitehead 1982
Uzbek	SOV	MC	Altaic: Turkic: E Turkic:	Sjoberg 1963 Ruhlen 1975 Sedlak 1975
Vagala	SVO	WA	Niger-Kordofanian: Niger-Congo: Gur: C Gur	Pike 1966
Vai	SOV	WA	Niger-Kordofanian: Niger-Congo: Mande: NW Mande	Dryer 1984
Vanimo	SOV	NG	Indo-Pacific: C New Guinea: N Papuan: Tami: Sko	Whitehead 1982
Varise	SVO	MEL	Austronesian: Oceanic: NW & C Solomons Austronesian (geo): Choiseul	Capell 1976b
Veda	SOV	I	Indo-European: Indo-Iranian: Indic: Singhalese-Maldivian	Culicover & Wexler 1974
Vespian	SOV	EUR	Uralic: Finno-Ugric: Finno-Permic: Finno-Volgaic: Finno-Lappic: Finnic	Ruhlen 1975
Vietnamese	SVO	SE	Austroasiatic: Mon-Khmer: Viet-Muong	Steele 1978 Nguyen 1972

LANGUAGE	ORDER	AREA	CLASSIFICATION	SOURCE
Vitu	SVO	MEL	Austronesian: Oceanic: NE New Guinea Austronesian	Capell 1971a
Vogul	SOV	EUR	Uralic: Finno-Ugric: Ugric	Ruhlen 1975 Kalman 1965 Hawkins 1983
Votyak	SOV	EUR	Uralic: Finno-Ugric: Finno-Permic: Permic	Ruhlen 1975
Vute	SVO	WA	Niger-Kordofanian: Niger-Congo: Benue-Congo: Bantoid: Mambila-Wute	Heine 1975b
Wab	SOV	NG	Indo-Pacific	Lincoln 1978
Waffa (Kusing)	SOV	NG	Indo-Pacific: Central New Guinea: E New Guinea Highlands: Tairora	Ruhlen 1975
Wageman	SOV	A	Australian: Gunwingguan: Yangmanic	Ruhlen 1975 Dryer 1984
Waica	SOV	T	Macro-Chibchan: Chibcha Proper: Waican	Ruhlen 1975
Waiwai	SOV	T	Ge-Pano-Carib: Macro-Carib: Carib: N	Derbyshire 1980
Wakhi	SOV	MC	Indo-European: Indo-Iranian: Iranian: E Iranian: Wakhi	Ruhlen 1975 Dryer 1984 Lorimer 1958

Walamo (Gofa)	SOV	EA	Afroasiatic: Omotic: W Omotic: Janjero-Keford-Ometa-Gimira	Ruhlen 1975 Mallinson & Blake 1981
Walbiri	SOV	A	Australian: Pama-Nyungan: SW Pama-Nyungan: Ngarga	Steele 1978 Hawkins 1983 Reece 1970
Wambon	SOV	NG	Indo-Pacific: Central New Guinea: Central & S New Guinea: Awyu	Voorhoeve 1975a
Wapishana	SVO	T	Andean-Equatorial: Equatorial: Arawakan: Maipuran: Wapishanan	Tracy 1974
Wappo	SOV	CAL	Yukian	Li and Thompson 1976a
Wara	SOV	WA	Niger-Kordofanian: Niger-Congo: Gur: Senufo	Givón 1979
Warao	SOV	T	Macro-Chibchan: Paezan: Warao	de Goeje 1930 Ruhlen 1975
Warat (Komor)	SOV	A	Australian: Daly: Mulluk: Daly:	Tryon 1974
Waris	SOV	NG	Indo-Pacific: C New Guinea: N Papuan: Tami: Waris	Whitehead 1982
Washo	SOV	CAL	Hokan: Washo	Steele 1975
Waskia	SOV	NG	Indo-Pacific: Central New Guinea: Bogia:	Dryer 1984

LANGUAGE	ORDER	AREA	CLASSIFICATION	SOURCE
			Adelbert Range: Isumrud	Hawkins 1983
Waura	SVO	T	Andean-Equatorial: Equatorial: Arawakan: Maipuran: E Maipuran: Xingu	Derbyshire 1982
Wedau	SOV	NG	Austronesian: Oceanic: Papuan Austronesian	Capell 1976c Hawkins 1983 Clarke 1977
Welsh	VSO	EUR	Indo-European: Celtic: Brythonic	Ruhlen 1975 Awbery 1976
Wembi	SOV	NG	Indo-Pacific: N New Guinea: N Papuan: Tami: Skofro	Voorhoeve 1975a
Were (Sim)	SOV	NG	Indo-Pacific: Central New Guinea: SE New Guinea: Goilala	Ruhlen 1975
Wichita	SVO	WNA	Macro-Siouan: Caddoan	Steele 1975 Rood 1976
Wik-Munkan	SOV	A	Australian: Pama-Nyungan: Pama-Maric: Middle Pama	Ruhlen 1975 Sayers 1976
Witoto (Murui)	SOV	T	Ge-Pano-Carib: Macro-Carib: Witotoan	Ruhlen 1975 Minor & Loos 1963
Wiyot	SOV	CAL	Macro-Algonquian	Steele 1978
Wogeo	SOV	NG	Austronesian: Oceanic: NE New Guinea	Capell 1971a

254

Austronesian

Language	Order	Region	Classification	References
Wolio	VSO	SE	Austronesian: Malayo-Polynesian: Central and South Celebes: Muna-Butung	Ruhlen 1975 Hawkins 1983
Wolof (Dyolof)	SVO	EA	Niger-Kordofanian: Niger-Congo: W Atlantic: NW Atlantic:	Ruhlen 1975 Schwartz 1975
Wu (Changchow)	SVO	E	Sino-Tibetan: Chinese	Ruhlen 1975
Wu-Ming	SVO	E	Sino-Tibetan: Tibeto-Burman: Kam-Tai: N Tai	DeLancey (p.c.)
Xam (/xam, xamka!'e)	SVO	SA	Khoisan: S African Khoisan	Heine 1975a, 1975b
Xinalug	SOV	MC	Caucasian: N: NE: Lezghian	Ruhlen 1975 Hawkins 1983
Xinca	VSO	MA	Macro-Chibchan: Chibcha Proper	Ruhlen 1975 Hawkins 1983
Xu	SVO	SA	Khoisan: S African Khoisan: Central	Blansitt 1973 Heine 1975b
Xvarshi	SVO	MC	Caucasian: N: NE: Avaro-Andi-Dido: Dido	Ruhlen 1975 Hawkins 1983
Yaaku (Mogogodo)	SVO	EA	Afroasiatic: Cushitic: E Cushitic: Lowland E Cushitic	Heine 1975a, 1975b

LANGUAGE	ORDER	AREA	CLASSIFICATION	SOURCE
Yabem	SOV	NG	Austronesian: Oceanic: NE New Guinea Austronesian	Capell 1971a Renck 1977b
Yaghnobi (W)	SOV	MC	Indo-European: Indo-Iranian: Iranian: E Iranian	Ruhlen 1975
Yahang	SVO	NG	Indo-Pacific: N Guinea: Torricelli: Maimai	Keenan 1978
Yaka	SOV	CA	Niger-Kordofanian: Niger-Congo: Benue-Congo: Bantoid: Bantu: NW Bantu: Zone A: Kaka	Ruhlen 1975
Yakut	SOV	NNE	Altaic: Turkic: N Turkic	Ruhlen 1975 Steele 1978 Hawkins 1983
Yaminawa	SOV	AND	Ge-Pano-Carib: Macro-Panoan: Pano-Tacana: Pano	Loos 1970
Yanyula	SOV	A	Australian: Yanyulan	Ruhlen 1975
Yao	SVO	EA	Niger-Kordofanian: Niger-Congo: Benue-Congo: Bantoid: Bantu: SE Bantu: Zone P: Yao	Whiteley 1966
Yao (Hwei Kang Pa)	SVO	E	Sino-Tibetan: Miao-Yao: Yao	Ruhlen 1975 Mao and Chou 1972
Yapese	VSO	MIC	Austronesian: Oceanic: Micronesian	Ruhlen 1975 Dryer 1984

256

Language	Order	Region	Classification	References
Yaqui	SOV	WNA	Aztec-Tanoan: Uto-Aztecan: Sonoran	Jensen 1977
Yareba	SOV	NG	Indo-Pacific: Central New Guinea: SE New Guinea: Mailu: Yareba	Ruhlen 1975 Hawkins 1983 Lindenfeld 1973
Yavapai	SOV	WNA	Hokan: Yuman: Pai	Dryer 1984
Yay (Muong Hum)	SVO	SE	Sino-Tibetan: Tibeto-Burman: Kam-Tai: Tai: N	Redden 1976 Kendall 1976
Yaygir	SVO	A	Australian: Pama-Nyungan: Kumbainggaric	Ruhlen 1975
Yeletyne	SOV	NG	Indo-Pacific: Yele	Crowley 1979
Yenets	SOV	NNE	Uralic: Samoyedic	Henderson 1975 Whitehead 1982
Yenimu	SOV	NG	Indo-Pacific: C New Guinea: C & S New Guinea: Awyu	Ruhlen 1975
Yesan-Mayo	SOV	NG	Indo-Pacific: Central New Guinea: N New Guinea: Sepik: Upper Sepik: Tama	Voorhoeve 1975a
Yoruba	SVO	WA	Niger-Kordofanian: Niger-Congo: Kwa:	Mallinson & Blake 1981 Whitehead 1982
				Heine 1975b Ruhlen 1975

257

LANGUAGE	ORDER	AREA	CLASSIFICATION	SOURCE
				Sedlak 1975
Yuan	SVO	SE	Sino-Tibetan: Kam-Tai: SW	Hawkins 1983
Yuchi	SOV	ENA	Macro-Siouan	Dryer 1984
Yukaghir	SOV	NNE	Yukaghir (Paleosiberian)	Ruhlen 1975 Hawkins 1983
Yukulta	SVO	A	Australian: Pama-Nyungan: Tangkic	Dryer 1984
Yulu	SVO	CA	Nilo-Saharan: C Sudanic: Kara	Heine 1975b
Yungor	SOV	A	Australian: Daly: Mulluk: Daly	Tryon 1974
Yupik (Kuskokwim)	SVO	NNA	Eskimo-Aleut: Yupik	Ruhlen 1975
Yupna	SOV	NG	Indo-Pacific: Central New Guinea: Huon-Finisterre: Finisterre: E	Ruhlen 1975 Whitehead 1982
Yurak Samoyed	SOV	NNE	Uralic: Samoyedic	Ruhlen 1975 Steele 1978
Yurok	SOV	CAL	Macro-Algonquian	Steele 1978
Zahao	SOV	SE	Sino-Tibetan: Tibeto-Burman: Naga-Kuki-Chin: Chin: C Chin	DeLancey (p.c.)
Zaiwa	SOV	SE	Sino-Tibetan: Tibeto-Burman: Bodo-Naga-Chin:	DeLancey (p.c.)

Kachin

Language	Order	Area	Classification	References
Zan (Migrelian)	SOV	MC	Caucasian: S	Ruhlen 1975 Hawkins 1983
Zande	SVO	CA	Niger-Kordofanian: Niger-Congo: Adamawa-Eastern: III	Heine 1975b
Zaparo	SVO	AND	Andean-Equatorial: Andean: Zaparoan	Peeke 1962
Zapotec (Rincon)	VSO	MA	Oto-Manguean: Zapotecan	Ruhlen 1975 Sedlak 1975 Hawkins 1983
Zimakani	SOV	NG	Indo-Pacific: Central New Guinea: Central & S New Guinea: Marind	Voorhoeve 1975a
Zoque (Copainala)	SVO	MA	Penutian: Mixe-Zoque	Ruhlen 1975 Hawkins 1983
Zuni	SOV	WNA	Penutian: Zuni	Cook 1975 Ruhlen 1975

REFERENCES FOR APPENDIX A

Abrahamson, A. 1962. Cayapa: grammatical notes and texts.
Ecuadorian Indian Languages I. 217-247. ed. B.
Elson. Norman: Oklahoma: Summer Institute of
Linguistics

Adam, L. 1897. *Grammaire Compareé des Dialectes de la
Famille Kariri.* Paris: J. Maisonneuve. (Also
published in *Bibliotheque Linguistique Americaine* vol.
20)

Aginsky, E.G. 1935. *A Grammar of the Mende Language.*
Language Dissertations 20. Philadelphia: Linguistic
Society of America

Allen, N.J. 1975. Sketch of Thulung grammar. *East Asia
Papers 6.* Ithaca, New York: Cornell University

Anderson, L. and Wise, M. R. 1963. Contrastive features of
Candoshi clause-types. *Studies in Peruvian Indian
Languages: I.* 67-102. ed. B. Elson. Norman,
Oklahoma: Summer Institute of Linguistics

Applegate, R. 1972. *Ineseño Chumash Grammar.* Unpublished
dissertation. Department of Linguistics, University of
California, Berkeley

Appleyard, D.L. 1975. A descriptive outline of Kemant.
Bulletin of the School of Oriental and African Studies.
38: 316-350

Arms, D.G. 1974. *Transitivity in Standard Fijiian.*
Unpublished dissertation. Department of Linguistics,
University of Michigan

Awbery, G.M. 1976. *The Passive in Welsh.* Cambridge:
Cambridge University Press

260

Bandhu, C. 1973. Clause patterns in Nepali. *Clause, Sentence, and Discourse Patterns in Selected Languages of Nepal, 2.* 1-80. ed. A. Hale and D. Watters. Norman, Oklahoma: Summer Institute of Linguistics

Barnard, J.T.O. 1934. *A Handbook of the Rawang Dialect of the Nung Language.* Rangoon, Burma: Superintendent of Government Printing and Stationery

Baumann, J.J. 1979. An historical perspective on ergativity in Tibeto-Burman. *Ergativity: Towards a Theory of Grammatical Relations.* 419-434. ed. F. Plank. New York: Academic Press

Bee, D. 1973. Usarufa: a descriptive grammar. *The Languages of the Eastern Family of the East New Guinea Highland Stock.* 1: 225-324. ed. H. McKaughan. Seattle: University of Washington Press

Bender, B. W. 1971. Micronesian languages. *Current Trends in Linguistics. Vol 8: Linguistics in Oceania.* 426-465. ed. T. Sebeok. The Hague: Mouton

Benjamin, G. 1976. An outline of Temian grammar. *Austroasiatic Studies 1*: 129-188. ed. P. Jenner *et al.* Honolulu: The University of Hawaii Press

Benton, R.A. 1971. *Pangasinan Reference Grammar.* Honolulu: The University of Hawaii Press

Benzing, J. 1955. *Lamutische Grammatik.* Wiesbaden: Franz Steiner Verlag

Beuchat, H. and Rivet, P. 1909. La langue Jíbaro ou Šiwora. *Anthropos* 4: 805-822

Bhattacharya, S. 1975. *Studies in Comparative Munda Linguistics.* Simla: Indian Institute of Advanced Study

Bird, C.S. 1966. *Aspects of Bambara Syntax.* Unpublished dissertation. Department of Linguistics, UCLA

Birk, D.B.W. 1976. *The Malakmalak Language, Daly River (Western Arnhem Land).* Pacific Linguistics. Series B. 45. Canberra: The Australian National University

Blake, B. 1969. A brief description of the Kalkatungu language. *Australian Aboriginal Studies* 20. Linguistic Series 8. Canberra: Australian Institute of Aboriginal Studies

_____. 1979. Pitta-pitta. *Handbook of Australian Languages*. 183-244. ed. R.M.W. Dixon and B.J. Blake. Canberra: Australian National University Press

Blansitt, E. 1973. Bitransitive clauses. *Working Papers in Language Universals* 13: 1-68. Stanford, California: Language Universals Project, Stanford University

Boelaars, J.H.M.C. 1950. *The Linguistic Position of South-Western New Guinea*. Lerden: E.J. Brill

Bokamba, E.G. 1975. Observations on the immediate dominance constraint, topicalization and relativization. *Studies in African Linguistics* 6: 1-22

_____. 1976. On the syntax and semantics of Wh-questions in Kikongo and Kiswahili. *Studies in the Linguistics Sciences* 6.2. Champaign: University of Illinois

Bokamba, E. and Dramé, M. 1978. Where do relative clauses come from in Mandingo? *Papers from the Fourteenth Regional Meeting of the Chicago Linguistic Society*. 24-83. ed. Farkas *et al*. Chicago: Chicago Linguistic Society

Bonnerjea, B. 1935. Contribution to Garo linguistics and ethnology. *Anthropos* 30: 509-531, 837-850

Borgman, D.M. 1974. Deep and surface case in Sanuma. *Linguistics* 132: 5-18

Bradley, C. 1970. *A Linguistic Sketch of Jicaltepec Mixtec*. Norman, Oklahoma: Summer Institute of Linguistics

Brown, H.A. 1973. The Eleman language family. *The Linguistic Situation in the Gulf District and Adjacent Area, Papua New Guinea*. 280-376. ed. K. Franklin. Pacific Linguistics, Series C., no. 26. Canberra: Department of Linguistics, Australian National University

Bruens, A. 1942-45. The structure of Nkom and its relations to Bantu and Sudanic. *Anthropos* 37-40: 826-866

Buchanan, D. 1978. Djambarrpuynyu clauses. *Papers in Australian Linguistics, no. 11*. 143-199. ed. J.F. Kirton *et al*. Pacific Linguistics, Series A, no. 51. Canberra: Department of Linguistics, Australian National University

Buechel, E. 1939. *A Grammar of Lakota*. Rosebud, South
Dakota: Rosebud Educational Society

Bunn, G. 1974. Golin grammar. *Workpapers in Papua New
Guinea Linguistics 5*. Ukarumpa, Papua New Guinea:
Summer Institute of Linguistics

Burton, E. 1969. A brief sketch of Cua clause structure.
Mon-Kmer Studies III. Publication No. 4 of the
Linguistic Circle of Saigon. Saigon: Linguistic Circle
of Saigon and Summer Institute of Linguistics

Byarushengo, E.R. and Tenenbaum, S. 1976. Agreement and
word order: a case for pragmatics in Haya. *Papers from
the Berkeley Linguistics Society* 2: 89-99. Berkeley:
University of California

Callaghan, C.A. 1970. *Bodega Miwok Dictionary*. Berkeley:
University of California Press

Camp, E. and Liccardi, M. 1967. Itonama. *Bolivian Indian
Grammars: 2*. 257-352. ed. E. Matteson. Norman,
Oklahoma: Summer Institute of Linguistics

Capell, A. 1969. *Grammar and Vocabulary of the Language of
Sonsoral-Tobi*. Oceanic Linguistic Monograph no. 12.
Sydney: University of Sydney

_____. 1971a. The Austronesian languages of Australian
New Guinea. *Current Trends in Linguistics* 8: 240-340.
ed. T. A. Sebeok. The Hague: Mouton

_____. 1971b. *Arosi grammar*. Pacific Linguistics.
Series B. Canberra: The Australian National University

_____. 1976a. General picture of Austronesian
languages, New Guinea area. *New Guinea Area Languages
and Language Study 2. Austronesian Languages*. 5-52.
ed. S.A. Wurm. Canberra: The Australian National
University

_____. 1976b. Features of Austronesian languages in the
New Guinea area in contrast with other Austronesian
languages of Melanesia.

_____. 1976b. Features of Austronesian languages in the
New Guinea area in contrast with other Austronesian
languages of Melanesia. *New Guinea Area Languages and*

263

Language Study 2. Austronesian Languages. 235-282. ed. S.A. Wurm. Canberra: The Australian National University

_____. 1976c. Austronesian and Papuan "mixed" languages: general remarks. *New Guinea Area Languages and Language Study 2.* 527- 579. ed. S.A. Wurm. Pacific Linguistics. Series C. 39. Canberra: The Australian National University

Carlin, R. 1970. Tzutuzil (Mayan) clause nuclei. *Anthropological Linguistics* 12: 103-111

Carter, H. 1972. Morphotonology of Zambian Tonga: some developments of Meeussen's system - II. *African Language Studies* 13: 52-87

Chadwick, N. 1975. *A Descriptive Study of the Djingili Language.* Canberra: The Australian Institute of Aboriginal Studies

Chafe, W. 1976b. *The Caddoan, Iroquoian and Siouan Languages.* The Hague: Mouton

Chang, Y. and Kworay, C. 1972. A brief description of the Miao language. The Miao language team, Chinese Academy of Sciences. *Miao Linguistic Studies.* ed. H. C. Purnell, Jr. Data paper 88. Southeast Asia program. Ithaca: Cornell University, Department of Asian Studies

de Clerq, P. 1907. Grammaire de Kiyombe. *Anthropos* 2: 449-466, 761-794

Chowning, A. 1973. Milke's 'New Guinea cluster': the evidence from Northwest New Britain. *Oceanic Linguistics* 12.1 & 2:189-243

_____. 1978. Comparative grammars of five New Britain languages. *Second International Conference on Austronesian Linguis-tics: Proceedings. Fascicle 2: Eastern Austronesian.* 1129-1157. ed. S.A. Wurm and L. Carrington. Pacific Linguistics. Series C., no. 61. Canberra: Department of Linguistics, Australian National University

Chung, S. 1976. On the subject of two passives in Indonesian. *Subject and Topic.* 57-98. ed. C.N. Li. New York: Academic Press

_____. 1978. *Case Marking and Grammatical Relations in Polynesian.* Austin: University of Texas Press

Claassen, O.R. and McElhanon, K.A. 1970. Languages of the Finisterre range-New Guinea. *Papers in New Guinea Linguistics* 11. Pacific Linguistics. Series A., no. 23. Canberra: Australian National University

Clark, M. 1980. Source phrases in White Hmong (Laos). *Working Papers in Linguistics*. 12.2: 1-50. Honolulu: The University of Hawaii

Clarke, E. 1977. Missionary lingua franche: Wedau. *New Guinea Area Languages and Language Study 3. Language, Culture, Society and the Modern World, Fascicle 2*. 953-970. ed. S.A. Wurm. Canberra: Australian National University

Cole D.T. and Mokaila, D.M. 1962. *A Course in Tswana*. Washington, D.C.: Mokaila and Georgetown University

Cook, C.D. 1975. Nucleus and margin in Zuni clause types. *Linguistics* 152: 5-38

Cooreman, A. 1985. *Transitivity and Discourse Continuity in Chamorro*. Unpublished dissertation. Department of Linguistics University of Oregon

Cowan, M. 1969. *Tzotzil Grammar*. Norman, Oklahoma: Summer Institute of Linguistics

Craig, C. 1977. *The Structure of Jacaltec*. Austin: University of Texas Press

Crapo, R.H. 1976. *Big Smokey Valley Shoshoni*. Reno: Desert Research Institute Publications in the Social Sciences

Cromack, R.E. 1968. Language systems and discourse structure in Cashinawa. *Hartford Studies in Linguistics* 23. Hartford, Connecticut: Hartford Seminary Foundation

Crowley, T. 1978. *The Middle Clarence Dialects of Bandjalang*. Canberra: Australian Institute of Aboriginal Studies

Crowley, . 1979. Yaygir. *Handbook of Australian Languages*. 363-384. ed. R.M.W. Dixon and B.J. Blake. Canberra: Australian National University

Culicover, P. and Wexler, K. 1974. The invariance principle and universals of grammar. *Social Science Working Papers* 55. Irvine, California: University of California

References for Appendix A

Dakubu, M.E. 1970. The Adangme verb reconsidered. *Journal of African Languages* 9: 19-26

Dalgish, G.M. 1977. Personal pronouns, object markers and syntactic evidence in Dho-Lho. *Studies in African Linguistics* 8: 101-120

Das, A.S.K. 1973. *Structure of Malto*. Tamilnadu, India: Annamalai University

Davis, J.J. 1973. Notes on Nyaheun grammar. *Mon-Khmer Studies IV*. 69-76. ed. D. Thomas and Nguyen. Carbondale, Illinois: Summer Institute of Linguistics and Center for Vietnamese Studies

Davis, P. and Saunders, R. 1978. Bella Coola syntax. *Linguistics Studies of Native Canada*. 37-66. ed. E. Cook and J. Kaye. Vancouver: University of British Columbia Press

Day, A.C. 1966. *The Syntax of Tho; a Thai Language of Vietnam*. Unpublished dissertation. University of London

Day, C. 1973. *The Jacaltec Language*. The Hague: Mouton

Diebler Jr., E.W. 1973. *Gahuku Verb Structure*. Unpublished dissertation. Department of Linguistics, University of Michigan

Derbyshire, Desmond C. 1977. Word order universals and the existence of OVS languages. *Linguistic Inquiry* 8: 590-597

_____. 1980. A diachronic explanation for the origin of OVS in some Carib languages. Pre-publication draft

Derbyshire, . 1982 and Pullum, G. K. 1981. Object initial languages. *International Journal of American Linguistics* 47: 192-214

Dik, S.C. 1978. *Functional Grammar*. Amsterdam: North-Holland Publishing Company

)oke, C.M. 1922. *The Grammar of the Lamba Language*.
London: Kegan Paul, Trend, Trubner and Company

)ouglas, W. 1958. *An Introduction to the Western Desert
Language*. *Oceanic Linguistics Monographs 4*. Sydney:
University of Sydney

_____. 1976. *The Aboriginal Languages of the
South-West of Australia*. Canberra: The Australian
Institute of Aboriginal Studies

)owning, B.T. 1977. Typological regularities in postnominal
relative clauses. *Current Themes in Linguistics:
Bilingualism, Experimental Linguistics, and Language
Typology*. 163-194. ed. F.R. Eckman. New York: John
Wiley and Sons

_____. 1978. Some universals of relative clause
structure. *Universals of Human Language*. *Volume 4:
Syntax*. 375-418. ed. J. Greenberg. Stanford:
Stanford University Press

)ryer, M.S. 1979. *The Positional Tendencies of Sentential
Noun Phrases in Universal Grammar*. Unpublished
dissertation. Department of Linguistics, University of
Michigan

)ryer, 1984. A statistical study of word order universals.
Final report for Social Science and Humanities Research
Council of Canada

)utton, T.E. 1975. A Koita grammar sketch and vocabulary.
Studies in Languages of Central and Southeast Papua.
281-412. ed. T.E. Dutton. Pacific Linguistics.
Series C., no. 29. Canberra: Australian National
University

_____. 1976. Magori and similar languages of
Southeast Papua. *New Guinea Languages and Language
Study 2*. 581-636. ed. S.A. Wurm. Pacific
Linguistics. Series C., no. 39. Canberra: Australian
National University

:dgerton, F.E. 1963. The tagmemic analysis of sentence
structure in Western Apache. *Studies in the Athapascan
Language*. 102-154. ed. H. Hoijer. Berkeley: University
of California Press

:dwards, W.F. 1979. A comparison of selected linguistic
features in some Cariban and Arawakan languages in
Guyana. *Anthropological Linguistics 21*: 277-297

References for Appendix A

Ehrmann, M. 1972. *Contemporary Cambodian: Grammatical Sketch*. Washington, D.C.: Foreign Service Institute

Einaudi, P.F. 1976. *A Grammar of Biloxi*. Garland Studies in American Indian Linguistics. New York: Garland Publishing Company

Elbert, S. 1974. <u>Puluwat Grammar</u>. Pacific Linguistics. Series B., no. 29. Canberra: Department of Linguistics, Australian National University

Elbert, S. and Pukui, M.K. 1979. *Hawaiian Grammar*. Honolulu: University of Hawaii Press

Elliot, R. 1961. Ixil (Mayan) clause structure. *Mayan Studies I*. 129-158. ed. B. Elson. Norman, Oklahoma: Summer Institute of Linguistics

Endle, Rev. S. 1884. *Outline Grammar of the Kachári (Bara) Language*. Shillong: Assam Secretariat Press

Emeneau, M.B. 1955. *Kolami: a Dravidian Language*. University of California Publications in Linguistics 12. Berkeley: University of California

Epeé, R. 1975. The case for a focus position in Duala. *Proceedings of the Sixth Conference on African Linguistics. Working Papers in Linguistics* 20: 210-226. ed. R. Herbert. Columbus: Ohio State University

Filbeck, David. 1973. Rice in a grammar of T'in. *Journal of Linguistics* 9: 209-221

Firestone, H.L. 1965. *Description and Classification of Sirionó, a Tupi-Guarani Language*. The Hague: Mouton

Foster, M.L.C. 1971. Tarascan. *Studies in American Indian Languages* 65. 77-111. ed. J. Sawyer. Berkeley: University of California Publications in Linguistics

Franklin, K.J. 1967. Kewa sentence structure. *Papers in New Guinea Linguistics 7*. Pacific Linguistics. Series A., no. 13. Canberra: Australian National University

Furbee-Losee, L. 1976. *The Correct language, Tojolabal: A Grammar with Ethnographic Notes*. New York: Garland Publishing

Furby, E.S. and Furby, C.E. 1977. *A Preliminary Analysis of Garawa Phrases and Clauses*. Pacific Linguistics. Series B., no. 42. Canberra: Department of Linguistics, Australian National University

Garland, R. and Garland, S. 1975. A grammar sketch of Mountain Koiali. *Studies in Languages of Central and Southeast Papua*. 413-470. ed. T.E. Dutton. Pacific Linguistics. Series C., no. 29. Canberra: Australian National University

George, I. 1977. Rule typology in Nupe. *Language and Linguistic Problems in Africa*. 226-236. ed. P.F.A. Kotey and H. Der-Hous-sikian. Columbia, South Carolina: Hornbeam Press

Gerdts, D.B. 1980. Antipassives and causatives in Halkomelem. *Proceedings of the Sixth Annual Meeting of the Berkeley Linguistics Society*. 300-315. Berkeley, California: Berkeley Linguistics Society

Gill H. and Gleason, H. A., Jr. 1969. *A Reference Grammar of Panjabi*. Patiala, India: Punjabi University Press

Givón, T. 1975. Serial verbs and syntactic change. *Word Order and Word Order Change*. ed. C.N. Li. Austin: University of Texas Press

_____. 1976a. On the SOV reconstruction of Southern Nilotic: internal evidence from Topusa. *Studies in African Linguistics*. Supplement 6. 73-93. Los Angeles: University of California Department of Linguistics and the African Studies Center

_____. 1976b. Topic, pronoun and grammatical agreement. *Subject and Topic*. 149-188. ed. N. Li. New York: Academic Press

_____. 1979. Language typology in Africa: a critical review. *Journal of African Languages and Linguistics* 1: 199-224

Glock, N. 1972. Clause and sentence in Saramaccan. *Journal of African Languages* 11: 45-61

Glover, W. 1974. *Sememic and Grammatical Structure in Gurung*. Nepal: Summer Institute of Linguistics

Goddard, J. 1967. Agarabi narratives and commentary. *Papers in New Guinea Languages no. 7.* 1-27. ed. J. Goddard and K.J. Franklin. Pacific Linguistics. Series A, no. 13. Canberra: Australian National University

de Goeje, C. H. 1930. The inner structure of the Warau language of Guiana. *Journal de la Societe des Americanistes* 22: 23-72

Goschnick, H. 1977. Haroi clauses. *Papers in South East Asian Linguistics no. 14: Chamic Studies.* 105-124. ed. D. Thomas *et al.* Pacific Linguistics. Series A, no. 48. Canberra: Department of Linguistics, Australian National University

Gowda, G.K.S. 1975. *Ao Grammar.* Hyderabad: Central Institute of Indian Languages

Gragg, G. 1972. Cleft sentences in Tigrinya. *Journal of African Languages* 11: 74-89

de la Grasserie, M.R. 1904. Les Langues de Costa Rica. *Journal de la Societe des Americanistes* 1: 154-187

Greenberg, J. 1966 (1963). Some universals of grammar with particular reference to the order of meaningful elements. *Universals of Language.* 2nd edition pp 7 ed. J. Greenberg. Cambridge, Massachusetts

_____. 1978. Diachrony, synchrony, and language universals. *Universals of Human Language. Volume 1: Method and Theory.* 61-92. ed. J. Greenberg. Stanford, California: Stanford University Press

Gregerson, E.A. 1976. A note on the Manam language of Papua New Guinea. *Anthropological Linguistics* 18: 95-11

Grierson, George A. 1903. *Linguistic Survey of India, Volume III. Tibeto-Burman Family, Part 3.* Calcutta: Office of the Superintendent Government Printing

_____. 1966 (1903)a. *Linguistic Survey of India,* Volume III. *Tibeto-Burman Family,* Part 2. Delhi: Motilal Banarsidass

_____. 1966 (1904)b. *Linguistic Survey of India,* Volume II. *Mon-Khmer and Siamese-Chinese Families.* Second edition. Delhi: Motilal Banarsidass

_____. 1966 (1904). *Linguistic Survey of India*, Volume III. *Tibeto-Burman Family*, Part 3. Second edition. Delhi: Motilal Banarsidass

_____. 1967 (1904). *Linguistic Survey of India*, Volume III. *Tibeto-Burman Family*, Part 2. *Bodo, Naga and Kachin Groups*. Delhi: Motilal Banarsidass

Grisward, P.J. 1910. Notes grammaticales sur la langue des Telei, Bougainville, Iles, Salomones. *Anthropos* 5: 82-94, 381-406

Grüöner, K.H. 1978. *Arleng Alam die Sprache der Mikir: Grammatik und Texte*. Wiesbaden: Franz Steiner Verlag

Hamilton, R.C. 1900. *An Outline Grammar of the Dafla Language*. Shillong: Assam Secretariat Printing

Harries, L. 1950. *A Grammar of Mwera*. Johannesburg: Witwatersrand University Press

Harris, J.K. 1969. Preliminary grammar of Gunbalung. *Papers in Australian Linguistics* 4. Pacific Linguistics. Series A., no. 17. Canberra: Australian National University

Harrison, S. 1976. *Mokilese Reference Grammar*. Honolulu: The University of Hawaii Press

Haumonte, J.D.; Parisont, J.; and Adam, L. 1882. Grammaire et vocabulaire de la langue Taensa. *Bibliotheque Linguistique Americaine*, Volume 9. Nendeln, Liechtenstein: Kraus Reprint

Haviland, J. 1979. Guugu Yimidhirr. *Handbook of Australian Languages*. 27-182. ed. R.M.W. Dixon and B. Blake. Canberra: Australian National University

Hawkins, J. A. 1983. *Word Order Universals*. New York: Academic Press.

Healey, A.; Isoroembo, A.; and Chittleborogh, M. 1969. Preliminary notes on Orokaiva grammar. *Papers in New Guinea Linguistics 9*. 33-64. Pacific Linguistics. Series A., no. 18. Canberra: Australian National University

Healey, P.M. 1965. *Telefol Clause Structure*. *Papers in New Guinea Linguistics*. Series A, no. 5. Canberra: Australian National University

Heath, J. 1974. Some related transformations in Basque. *Papers from the Tenth Regional Meeting of the Chicago Linguistic Society.* 248-258. ed. M.W. LaGaly *et al.* Chicago: Chicago Linguistic Society

Heine, B. 1975a. Language typology and convergence areas in Africa. *Linguistics* 144: 5-26

—————. 1975b. The study of word order in African languages. *Proceedings of the Sixth Conference on African Linguistics.* ed. R.K. Herbert. Columbus: Ohio State University, Department of Linguistics

Henderson, J.E. 1975. Yeletnye, the language of Rossel Island. *Studies in Languages of Central and Southeast New Guinea.* 817-834. ed. T.E. Dutton. Pacific Linguistics. Series C., no. 29. Canberra: Australian National University

Henry, J. 1948. The Kaingang language. *International Journal of American Linguistics* 14: 194-204

Hertz, H.F. no date. *The Kachin or Chingpaw Language.* Title pages lost: University of Michigan library - PL 4001.K3 H58

Hess, H.H. 1968. *The Syntactic Structure of Mesquital Otomi.* The Hague: Mouton

Hewer, J. 1976. Interrogative sentences in Kasem. *Linguistics* 171: 5-18

Hobbin, H.I. 1928-30. Notes on a grammar of the language of Ontgong Java. *Bulletin of the London University School of Oriental and African Studies* 5: 823-854

Hodges, K.S. 1976. Object relations in Kimeru causatives. *Studies in the Linguistics Sciences* 6.2. Champaign: Department of Linguistics, University of Illinois

Hodgkinson, N. 1981. Bitransitive word order and ergativity. Unpublished paper. Department of Linguistics, University of Oregon

Hofer, E.D. 1974. *Topics in Sarcee Syntax.* Unpublished master's thesis. Calgary: Department of Linguistics, University of Calgary

Hoffman, C. 1953. *A Grammar of the Margi Language.* London: Oxford University Press

Hoftmann, H.   1971.   *The Structure of Lelemi Language*.
Leipzig: VEB Verlag Enzyklopadie

Hoijer, H.   1931.   *Tonkawa: An Indian Language of Texas*.
Chicago: University of Chicago Press

Horton, A.E.   1949.   *A Grammar of Luvale*.   Johannesburg:
Witwaterstrand Press

Householder, Jr., F.W.   1965.   *Basic Course in Azerbaijani*.
Uralic and Altaic Series 45.   Bloomington: Indiana
University Publications

Hoskison, J.T.   1975.   Focus and topic in Gude.   *Proceedings
of the Sixth Conference on African Linguistics*.   *Working
Papers in Linguistics* 20: 227-233.   ed.   R.   Herbert.
Columbus: Ohio State University

Hsieh, H.   1977.   Noun-modifier order as a consequence of VSO
order.   *Lingua* 42: 91-109

Huckett, J.   1974.   Notes on Iduna grammar.   *Three Studies in
Languages of Eastern Papua*.   *Workpapers in Papua New
Guinea Languages*.   3: 63-133.   Ukarumpa, Papua New
Guinea: Summer Institute of Linguistics

Hudson, R.A.   1974.   A structural sketch of Beja.   *African
Language Studies XV*.   111-142.   ed.   D.W.   Arnott.
London: School of Oriental and African Studies

Huestis, G.   1963.   Bororo clause structure.   *International
Journal of American Linguistics* 29: 230-238

Hulstaert, G.   1966.   *Grammaire du Lomóngo: Troisieme Partie,
Syntaxe*.   Annales 1.8.   Sciences Humaines 58.   Tervuren,
Belgique: Musée Royal de l'Afrique Centrale

Hunt, Rev. R.J.   *Mataco Grammar*.   1940. Tucuman: Instituto
de Antropologia, Universidad Nacional de Tucuman

Hutchinson, L.   1969.   *Pronouns and Agreement in Temne*.
Unpublished dissertation.   Department of Linguistics.
University of Indiana

Ingram, D.   1975.   A note on word order in proto-Salish.
International Journal of American Linguistics 41:
165-168

Innes, G.   1966.   *An Introduction to Grebo*.   London: School
of Oriental and African Studies

Ivans, W.G. 1911. Grammar of the language of Sa'a, Malaita, Solomon Islands. *Anthropos* 6: 755-773, 926-940

Jacobs, R. 1973. Syntactic compression and semantic change. *Papers from the Ninth Regional Meeting of the Chicago Linguistic Society.* 232-241. ed. C. Corum *et al.* Chicago: Chicago Linguistic Society

Janzen, H. 1976. Structure and function of clauses and phrases in Pale. *Austroasiatic Studies* 1. 669-691. ed. P. Jenner *et al.* Honolulu: The University of Hawaii Press

Jenness, D. and Ballantyne, A. Rev. 1928. *Language, Mythology, and Songs of Bwaidoga.* New Plymouth, New Zealand: Thomas Avery and Sons

Jensen, C. 1980. Word Order in Oiampi. Unpublished manuscript. Department of Linguistics, University of Oregon

Jensen, J.T. 1977. *Yapese Reference Grammar.* Honolulu: University of Hawaii Press

Jha, S. 1958. *The Formation of the Maithili Language.* London: Luzac and Company

Johnson, Jr., C. W. 1975. A more than passing look at passives: Swahili. *LACUS* (Linguistic Association of Canada and the United States) Forum 5: 311-319

Jones, Jr., R.B. 1961. *Karen Linguistic Studies.* University of California Publications in Linguistics 25. Berkeley: University of California Press

Josephs, L.S. 1975. *Palauan Reference Grammar.* Honolulu: The University of Hawaii Press

Judy, R.A. 1965. Pronoun introducers in Movima clauses. *Anthropological Linguistics* 7: 5-15

_____ and Judy, J.E. 1967. Movima. *Bolivian Indian Grammars: 2.* 353-408. ed. E. Matteson. Norman, Oklahoma: Summer Institute of Linguistics

Kálmán, B. 1965. *Vogul Chrestomathy.* Uralic and Altaic Series, 46. Bloomington: Indiana University Publications

Keenan E.L. 1978. Handouts from a course in typology and Universal Grammar. Unpublished course notes. LSA Summer Institute, Salzburg

_____ and Comrie, B. 1979. Data on the noun phrase accessibility hierarchy. *Language* 55: 333-351

_____ and Hull, R. 1973. The logical syntax of direct and indirect questions. *You Take the High Node and I'll Take the Low Node. The Comparative Syntax Festival. Papers from the Chicago Linguistic Society.* 348-371. ed. C. Corum *et al.* Chicago: Chicago Linguistic Society

Kemp, W. 1977. Noun phrase questions and the question of movement rules. *Papers from the Thirteenth Regional Meeting of the Chicago Linguistic Society.* 198-212. ed. W.E. Beach *et al.* Chicago: Chicago Linguistic Society

Kendall, M.B. 1971. Sonrai relative clauses. *African Language Review* 9: 34-50

Kendall, M. 1976. *Selected Problems in Yavapai Syntax: The Verde Valley Dialect.* New York: Garland Publishing Company

Kennard, E. 1936. Mandan grammar. *International Journal of American Linguistics* 9: 1-43

Kimenyi, A. 1976. Subjectivization rules in Kinyarwanda. *Papers from the Berkeley Linguistics Society 2*: 258-268. Berkeley: Berkeley Linguistics Society

Kok, P.P. 1921-22. Ensayo de gramatica Dagseje o Tokano. *Anthropos* 16-17:838-865

Kokora, P. 1970. Apercu grámmatical du Koyo. *Annales de l'Université d'Abidjan.* Series H-III-Fascicle I. 97-114

Kölver, B. 1969. *Tulu Texts.* Wiesbaden: Franz Steiner Verlag

Kooyers, O. 1975. Hierarchy of Washkuk (Kwoma) clauses. *Linguistics* 147: 5-14

Krishnamurti, Bh. 1969. *Konda or Kubi: A Dravidian Language.* Hyderabad: Tribal Cultural Research and Training Institute, Government of Andhra Pradesh

Kroskrity, P.V. 1978. On the lexical integrity of Arizona Tewa /-di/: a principled choice between homophony and polysemy. *International Journal of American Linguistics* 44: 24-30

Krueger, J.R. 1961. *Chuvash Manual*. Uralic and Altaic Series 7. Bloomington: Indiana University Press

Lang, A. 1975. *The Semantics of Classificatory Verbs in Enga (and Other Papua New Guinea Languages)*. Pacific Linguistics. Series B., no. 39. Canberra: Australian National University

Langdon, M. 1979. Some thoughts on Hokan. *The Languages of Native America*. 592-649. ed. L. Campbell and M. Mithun. Austin: University of Texas Press

Lanyon-Orgill, P.A. 1943-46. Grammar of the Pokai language, central division of Papua, New Guinea. *Bulletin of the London University School of African and Oriental Studies* 11: 641-668

Laughren, M. 1976. Serial verbs. *Bulletin de l'Institut Fondamental d'Afrique Noire* 38: 872-889

Lawton, R.S. 1977. Missionary lingua franche: Dobu. *New Guinea Area Languages and Language Study 3. Language, Culture, Society, and the Modern World, Fascicle 2*. 907-946. ed. S.A. Wurm. Canberra: Australian National University

Laycock, D. 1973. Sissano, Warapu and Melanesian pidginization. *Oceanic Linguistics* 12: 245-277

_____. 1978. A little Mor. *Second International Conference on Austronesian Linguistics: Proceedings. Fascicle 1, Western Austronesian*. 285-316. ed. S.A. Wurm and L. Carrington. Pacific Linguistics. Series C, no. 61. Canberra: Department of Linguistics, Australian National University

Laycock, D.C. and Z'graggren, J. 1975. The Sepik-Ramu phylum. *New Guinea Area languages and Language Study, 1*. 731-765. ed. S.A. Wurm. Pacific Linguistics. Series C., no. 38. Canberra: Australian National University

Lee, K.D. 1975. *Kusaiean Reference Grammar*. Honolulu: The University of Hawaii Press

Levinsohn, Stephen H. 1976. *The Inga Language*. The Hague: Mouton

Li, C.N. and Lang, R. 1979. The syntactic irrelevance of an ergative case in Enga and other Papuan languages. *Ergativity: Towards a Theory of Grammatical Relations*. ed. F. Plank. New York: Academic Press

Li, C.N. and Thompson, S.A. 1976a. Strategies for signalling grammatical relations in Wappo. *Papers from the Thirteenth Regional Meeting of the Chicago Linguistic Society*. 450-467. ed. W.E.Beach *et al*. Chicago: Chicago Linguistic Society

Li, F.K. 1946. Chipewyan. *Linguistic Structures of Native America*. 398-423. ed. C. Osgood. Viking Fund Publications in Anthropology 6. New York: Viking Fund, Inc

Li, P.J.K. 1978. The case-marking systems of the four less-known Formosan languages. *Second International Conference on Austronesian Linguistics: Proceedings*. Fascicle 1, Western Austronesian. 569-615. ed. S.A. Wurm and L. Carrington. Pacific Linguistics. Series C., no. 61. Canberra: Department of Linguistics, Australian National University

Lincoln, P.C. 1976. Banoni, Pava, and Papuanization. *Papers in New Guinea Linguistics 19*. 77-205. Pacific Linguistics. Series A., no. 45. Canberra: Australian National University

_____. 1978. Rai coast survey: first report. *Working Papers in Linguistics* 10: 141-144. Honolulu: Department of Linguistics, University of Hawaii

Lindenfeld, J. 1973. *Yaqui Syntax*. University of California Publications in Linguistics 76. Berkeley: University of California Press

Linthicum, Jr., L.A. 1973. Defoliating subordinate clauses in Vietnamese. *You Take the High Node and I'll Take the Low Node. The Comparative Syntax Festival. Papers from the Chicago Linguistic Society*. 104-120. ed. C. Corum et. al. Chicago: Chicago Linguistic Society

Loeweke, E. and May, J. 1966. Fasu grammar. *Anthropological Linguistics* 8: 17-33

Longacre, R. 1966. Trique clause and sentences: a study in contrast, variation and distribution. *International Journal of American Linguistics* 32: 242-254

Loos, B.E. 1970. Rasgos sintáctico-fonémicos en la historia lingüística de los idiomas de la familia Pano. *XXXIX Congreso Internacional de Americanistas* 5: 181-184. Lima: Actas y Memorias

Lorimer, D.L.R. 1939. *The Burushaski Language*. 3 volumes. Oslo: H. Aschehong and Company

—————————. 1958. *The Wakhi Language, Volume I: Introduction, Phonetics, Grammar, and Texts*. London: School of Oriental and African Studies, University of London

Loukotka, C. 1955. Les Indiens Botocudo et leur langue. *Lingua Posnaniensis* 5: 112-135

Loving, R. 1973. An outline of Awa grammatical structures. *The Languages of the Eastern Family of the East New Guinea Highland Stock*. 65-87. ed. H. McKaughan. Seattle: University of Washington Press

Lynch, J.D . 1974. Lenakel phonology. *Working Papers in Linguistics* 7.1. Honolulu: Department of Linguistics University of Hawaii.

Mainwaring, Col. G.B. 1876. *A Grammar of the Róng (Lepcha) Language*. Calcutta: Baptist Mission Press

Mallison, G. and Blake, B. 1981. *Language Typology*. Amsterdam: North Holland

Manley, T.M. 1972. *Outline of Sre Structure*. Oceanic Linguistics Special Publication 12. Honolulu: The University of Hawaii Press

Mao Tsung-wa and Chou Tsu-yao. 1972. A brief description of the Yao language. *Miao and Yao Linguistic Studies*. Translated by Chang Yu-hung and Chu Kwo-ray. ed. H.C. Purnell, Jr. Ithaca: Cornell University, Department of Asian Studies

Maria, P.A. 1914. Essai de grammaire Kaiapó. *Anthropos* 9: 233-241

Masica, C. 1976. *Defining a Linguistic Area: South Asia*. Chicago: University of Chicago Press

Matteson, E. 1965. *The Piro (Arawakan) Language*. University of California Publications in Linguistics 42. Berkeley: University of California Press

Matthews, G.H. 1965. <u>Hidatsa Syntax</u>. The Hague: Mouton

Maxwell, J. 1974. San Mateo Chuh: A VOS language that's paid the price. Unpublished manuscript

McCarthy, J. 1965. Clause chaining in Kanite. *Anthropological Linguistics* 7: 59-70

McElhanon, K.A. 1967. Preliminary observations on Huon Peninsula Languages. *Oceanic Linguistics* 6: 1-45

McLendon, S. 1975. *A Grammar of Eastern Pomo*. Berkeley: University of California Press

_____. 1978. Ergativity, case and transitivity in East Pomo. *International Journal of American Linguistics* 44: 1-19

Meerendonk, Maj. M. 1949. *Basic Gurkhali Grammar*. Kuala Lumpur: Caxton Press

Meyer-Bahlburg, H. 1972. *Studien zur Morphologie und Syntax der Musgu*. Hamburge Philologische Studien 24. Hamburg: Helmut Buske Verlag

Michailovsky, B. 1976. Typological sketch of Hayu. Unpublished manuscript

Miller, W. 1965. *Acoma Grammar and Texts*. Berkeley: University of California Press

Minor, E.E. and Loos, E.E. 1963. The structure and contexts of Witoto predicates in narrative speech. *Studies in Peruvian Indian Languages: I*. 37-66. ed. B. Elson. Norman, Oklahoma: Summer Institute of Linguistics

Mirikitani, L. 1972. *Kapampangan Syntax*. Oceanic Linguistics Special Publications 10. Honolulu: The University of Hawaii Press

Mochinsky, J. 1974. *A Grammar of Southeastern Pomo*. Berkeley: University of California Press

Morolong, M. and Hyman, L. 1977. Animacy, objects and clitics in Sesotho. *Studies in African Linguistics* 8: 199-218

Morris, H.F. and Kirwan, B.E.R. 1957. *A Runyankore Grammar.* Nairobi: The Eagle Press

Morse, R. 1965. Syntactic frames for the Rvwang (Rawang) verb. *Lingua* 14: 338-369

Murane, Elizabeth. 1974. *Daga Grammar.* Norman, Oklahoma: Summer Institute of Linguistics

Newman, B. 1976. Deep and surface structure of the Longuda clause. *Linguistics* 171: 35-68

Nguyen Dang Liem. 1972. Clause units in Southeast Asian languages. *Proceedings of the 11th International Congress of Linguistics.* 213-252. ed. L. Heilmann. Bologna: Società Editrice il Mulin

Nimrendajú, K. 1924. Zur sprache der Šipáia-Indianer. *Anthropos* 19: 836-837

Oakley, H. 1965. Chorti. *Languages of Guatemala.* 235-250. ed. M.K. Mayers. The Hague: Mouton

Oates, W. and Oates, L. 1968. *Kapau Pedagogical Grammar.* Pacific Linguistics. Series C., no. 10. Canberra: Australian National University

Osborne, C.R. 1974. *The Tiwi Language. Australian Aboriginal Studies 55.* Linguistics Series 21. Canberra: Australian Institute of Aboriginal Studies

Ott, W.G. and Ott, R.H. 1967. Ignaciano. *Bolivian Indian Grammars: I.* 85-138. ed. E. Matteson. Norman, Oklahoma: Summer Institute of Linguistics

Ottaviano, J.C. and Ottaviano, I. 1967. Tacana. *Bolivian Indian Grammars: I.* 139-208. ed. E. Matteson. Norman, Oklahoma: Summer Institute of Linguistics

Pai, P. (Karapurkar). 1976. *Kokborok Grammar.* Mysore: Central Institute of Indian Languages

Pawley, A. 1978. The New Guinea Oceanic hypothesis. *Working Papers in Linguistics* 10: 9-48. Honolulu: University of Hawaii, Department of Linguistics

Peeke, C . 1962. Structural summary of Zaparo. *Studies in Ecuadorian Indian Languages: I.* 125-216. ed. B. Elson. Norman, Oklahoma: Summer Institute of Linguistics

Pike, K. L. 1966. *Tagmemic and Matrix Linguistics Applied to Selected African Languages.* Ann Arbor: The University of Michigan Center for Research on Language and Language Behavior

Pinkerton, S. 1976. *Studies in K'ekchi. Texas Linguistics Forum* 3. Austin, Texas: University of Texas, Department of Linguistics

Polomé, E.C. 1967. *Swahili Language Handbook.* Arlington, Virginia: Center for Applied Linguistics

Poppe, N. 1961. *Tatar Manual.* Uralic and Altaic Series, 25. Bloomington: Indiana University Press

Porterie-Gutierrez, L. 1976. Tipología de la oración simple en Aymara. *Actes de 17th Congres International des Americanistes.* 527-534

Prabodhachandran, V.R. 1973. *Malayalam: A Linguistic Description.* Via Tricandrum, India: The National Research Publishing Company

Prentice, D.J. 1971. *The Murut Languages of Sabah. Pacific Linguistics.* Series C., no. 18. Canberra: Australian National University

Press, M.L. 1979. *Chemehuevi: A Grammar and Lexicon.* Berkeley: University of California Press

Preuss, K.T. 1932. Grammatik der Cora-Sprache. *International Journal of American Linguistics* 7: 1-84

Pride, K. 1963. Chatino syntax. *Summer Institute of Linguistics Publications in Linguistics and Related Fields 12.* Norman, Oklahoma: Summer Institute of Linguistics

Prost, G. 1967. Chacobo. *Bolivian Indian Grammars: I.* 210-284. ed. E. Matteson. Norman, Oklahoma: Summer Institute of Linguistics

Prost, R.P.A. 1968. La langue Bisa; grammaire et dictionnaire. *Etudes Voltaiques Memoire* 1. Centre Ifan. Farnborough Hants, England: Gregg Press

Pullum, G. 1981. Languages with object before subject: a comment and a catalogue. Pre-publication draft

Quizar, S. O. 1979. *Comparative Word Order in Mayan*. Department of Linguistics University of Colorado unpublished dissertation

Ramstedt, G.J. 1939. *A Korean Grammar*. Helsinki: Suomalais- Ugrilainen Seura

Ransom, J.E. 1945. Notes on Duwamish phonology and morphology. *International Journal of American Linguistics* 11: 193-203

Redden, J.E. 1976. Walapai syntax: a preliminary statement. *Hokan Studies: Papers from the First Conference on Hokan Languages*. 103-111. ed. M. Langdon and S. Silver. The Hague: Mouton

Reece, L. 1970. *Grammar of the Wailbri Language of Central Australia*. Sydney: University of Sydney

Reineke, B. 1972. *The Structure of the Nkonya Language*. Leipzig: VEB Verlag Enzyklopädie

Reinhard, J. and Toba, T. 1970. *A Preliminary Linguistic Analysis and a Vocabulary of the Kusunda Language*. Nepal: Tribhuvan University, Summer Institute of Linguistics

Renck, G.L. 1977a. Missionary lingua franche: Kâte. *New Guinea Area Languages and Language Study 3. Language, Culture, Society and the Modern World, Fascicle 2*. 847-854. ed. S.A. Wurm. Canberra: Australian National University

_____. 1977b. Missionary lingua franche: Yabêm. *New Guinea Area Languages and Language Study 3. Language, Culture, Society and the Modern World, Fascicle 2*. 847-854. ed. S.A. Wurm. Canberra: Australian National University

Rigsby, B. 1975. Nass-Gitksan: an analytic ergative syntax. *International Journal of American Linguistics* 41: 346-354

Roberts, J.L. 1977. *Ergative Switching in Mabuyag*. Unpublished Master's thesis. University of Calgary

Robins, R.H. 1968. Basic sentence structure in Sundanese. *Lingua* 21: 351-358

Rood, D.S. 1973. Aspects of subordination in Lakhota and
    Wichita. *You Take the High Node and I'll Take the Low
    Node. Papers from the Comparative Syntax Festival.*
    71-88. ed. C. Corum *et al.* Chicago: Chicago
    Linguistic Society

_____. 1976. *Wichita Grammar.* Garland Studies in
    American Indian Linguistics. New York: Garland
    Publishing

Rosbottom, H. 1967. Guarani. *Bolivian Indian Grammars: 2.*
    99-193. ed. E. Matteson. Norman, Oklahoma: Summer
    Institute of Linguistics

Roup, D.H. 1971. *A Grammar of the Lisu Language.*
    Unpublished dissertation. Yale University

Rowlands, E.C. 1959. *A Grammar of Gambian Mandinka.* London:
    University of London, School of Oriental and African
    Studies

Ruhlen, M. 1975. *A Guide to the Languages of the World.*
    Stanford: Language Universals Project, Stanford
    University

Rule, W.M. 1977. *A Comparative Study of the Foe, Huli and
    Pole Languages of Papua New Guinea. Oceanic Linguistics
    Monographs 20.* Sydney: University of Sydney Press

Salisbury, R.F. 1956. The Siane language of the Eastern
    Highlands of New Guinea. *Anthropos* 51: 447-480

Samarin, W.J. 1963. *A Grammar of Sango.* Hartford,
    Connecticut: Hartford Seminary Foundation

Santandrea, S.S. 1957. An elementary study of the Golo
    language. *Anthropos* 52: 899-536

Sayers, B.J. 1976. *The Sentence in Wik-Munkan: a
    Description of Propositional Relationships.* Pacific
    Linguistics. Series B. no. 44. Canberra: Australian
    National University

Schebesta, P.P. 1926-28. Grammatical sketch of the Jahai
    dialect. *Bulletin of the London University School of
    Oriental and African Studies* 4: 803-826

Schuller, R. 1933. The language of the Tacana Indians
    (Bolivia). *Anthropos* 28: 99-116, 463-484

Schwartz, A. 1975. Wolof: a language with no direct object. *Journal of West African Languages* 10: 219-267

Sebeok, T. and Ingemann, F.J. 1961. *An Eastern Cheremis Manual: Phonology, Grammar, Texts, and Glossary.* Bloomington: Indiana University Publications

Sedlak, P.A.S. 1975. Direct/indirect object word order: a cross-linguistic analysis. *Working Papers in Language Universals* 18: 117-164. Stanford: Language Universals Project, Stanford University

Seidenadel, C.W. 1909. *The First Grammar of the Language Spoken by the Bontoc Igorot, with a Vocabulary and Texts.* Chicago: Open Court Publishing Company

Seiter, W.J. 1980. Instrumental advancement Niuean. *Linguistic Inquiry* 10: 595-622

Shaw, K. 1973. Grammatical notes on Samo. A tentative classification of the languages of the Mt. Bosavi region. Appendix B. 204-213. *The Linguistic Situation in the Gulf District and Adjacent Areas, Papua New Guinea.* ed. K. Franklin. Pacific Linguistics. Series C., no. 26. Canberra: Australian National University

Shell, O. 1952. Grammatical outline of Kraho (Ge family). *International Journal of American Linguistics* 18: 115-129

Sindapati, A.K. 1970. *Local Dialect Variations in Komering.* Unpublished thesis. Institut Keguruan dan Ilmu Pendidikan Malang

Sinha, N.K. 1975. *Mundari Grammar.* Mysore: Central Institute of Indian Languages

Sjoberg, A.F. 1963. *Uzbek Structural Grammar.* Uralic and Altaic Series, 18. The Hague: Mouton

Smith, Edwin W. 1907. *A Handbook of the Ila Language.* Oxford: Oxford University Press

Smith, N.V. 1970. Repetition of the verb in Nupe. *African Language Studies* 11: 319-339

Smythe, W.E. 1948-49. Elementary grammar of the Gumbaingar language (North coast, N.S.W.). *Oceania* 19: 130-191

_____. 1978. Bandjalang Grammar. *The Middle Clarence Dialects of Bandjalang*. Appendix: 247-395. Terry Crowley. Canberra: Australian Institute of Aboriginal Studies

Sneddon, J.N. 1970. The languages of Minahasa, North Celebes. *Oceanic Linguistics* 9: 11-36

Snell, B.A. and Wise, M.R. 1963. Noncontingent declarative clauses in Machiguenga (Arawak). *Studies in Peruvian Indian Languages: 1*. 103-144. ed. B.F. Elson. Norman, Oklahoma: Summer Institute of Linguistics

Spears, R. 1967. Tone in Mende. *Journal of African Linguistics* 6: 231-244

Spenset, H.; Spenset, I.J.; Wrisley, B.H.; and Sherman, G.E. 1967. Quechua. *Bolivian Indian Grammars: 2*. 27-97. ed. E. Matteson. Norman, Oklahoma: Summer Institute of Linguistics

Stanhope, J.M. 1972. The language of the Kire people, Bogia, Mandang District, New Guinea. *Anthropos* 67: 49-71

Starosta, S. 1973. Causative verbs in Formosan languages. *Working Papers in Linguistics 5.9*. Honolulu: Department of Linguistics, University of Hawaii

Steele, S. 1975. On some factors that affect and effect word order. *Word Order and Word Order Change*. 197-268. ed. C.N. Li. Austin: University of Texas Press

_____. 1978. Word order variation: a typological study. *Universals of Human Languages* 4. 585-624. ed. J.H. Greenberg. Stanford: Stanford University Press

Stennes, L. 1967. *A Reference Grammar of Adamawa Fulani*. East Lansing: African Studies Center, Michigan State University

Strange, G.N. 1965. Nominal elements in Upper Asaro. *Anthropological Linguistics* 7: 71-79

Subrahmanyam, P.S. 1968. *A Descriptive Grammar of Gondi*. Annamalainagar, India. Annamala University

Swadesh, M. 1946a. South Greenlandic (Eskimo). *Linguistic Structures of Native America*. 30-54. ed. C. Osgood. Viking Fund Publications in Anthropology 6. New York: The Viking Fund, Inc

285

_____. 1946b. Chitimacha. *Linguistic Structures of Native America*. 312-336. ed. C. Osgood. Viking Fund Publications in Anthropology 6. New York: Viking Fund, Inc

Swanton, J.R. 1911. Haida. *Handbook of American Indian Languages*. Bureau of American Ethnology Bulletin No. 40. 205-282. ed. F. Boas. Washington: Government Printing Office

Taylor, D. 1958. Island Carib IV: syntactic notes, texts. *International Journal of American Linguistics* 24: 36-60

Teeter, K.V. 1971. The main features of Malecite-Passamaquoddy grammar. *Studies in American Indian Languages*. 191-249. ed. J. Sawyer. Berkeley: University of California Publications in Linguistics

Tessmann, G. 1929. Die Tschama-Sprache. *Anthropos* 24: 241-271.

Thayer, J. E. 1978. *The Deep Structure of the Sentence in Sara-Ngambay Dialogues*. Norman, Oklahoma: Summer Institute of Linguistics

Thomas, D.D. 1971. *Chrau Grammar*. Oceanic Linguistics Special Publication 7. Honolulu: The University of Hawaii Press

Thomas, J.M.C. 1963. *Le Parler Ngbaka de Bokanga*. La Hague: Mouton

Thomson, N.P. 1975. Magi phonology and grammar - fifty years afterward. *Studies in Languages of Central and Southeast Papua*. Pacific Linguistics. Series C., no. 29: 599-666. ed. T.E. Dutton. Canberra: Australian National University

Todd, E. 1975. The Solomon language family. *New Guinea Area Languages and Language Study, 1*. Pacific Linguistics. Series C., no. 38: 806-846. ed. S.A. Wurm. Canberra: Australian National University

_____. 1978a. Roviana syntax. *Second International Conference on Austronesian Linguistics: Proceedings. Fascicle 2: Eastern Austronesian*. 1035-1042. ed. S.A. Wurm and L. Carrington. Pacific Linguistics. Series C., no. 61. Canberra: Department of Linguistics, Australian National University

_____. 1978b. A sketch of Nissan (Nehan) grammar. *Second International Conference on Austronesian Linguistics: Proceedings. Fascicle 2: Eastern Austronesian.* 1181-1239. ed. S.A. Wurm and L. Carrington. Pacific Linguistics. Series C, no. 61. Canberra: Department of Linguistics, Australian National University

Todd, T.L. 1975. Clause versus sentence in Choctaw. *Linguistics* 161: 39-68

Topping, D. 1973. *Chamorro Reference Grammar.* Honolulu: The University of Hawaii Press

Townsend, W.C. 1960 (reprint of 1926, unpublished ms.). Cakchiquel grammar. *Mayan Studies I.* 7-79. ed. B. Elson. Norman, Oklahoma: Summer Institute of Linguistics

Tracy, F. V. 1974. An introduction to Wapishana verb morphology. *International Journal of American Linguistics* 40: 12-125

Trask, R.L. 1979. On the origins of ergativity. *Ergativity: Towards a Theory of Grammatical Relations.* 385-406. ed. F. Plank. New York: Academic Press

Trefty, L. 1975. Relational grammar and Chicewa subjectivization rules. *Papers from the Eleventh Regional Meeting of the Chicago Linguistic Society.* 615-624. ed. R.E. Grossman *et al.* Chicago: Chicago Linguistic Society

Troike, R.C. 1967. A structural comparison of Tonkawa and Coahuilteco. *Studies in Southwestern Ethnolinguistics.* 321-332. ed. D.H. Hymes and W.E. Bittle. The Hague: Mouton

Tryon, D.T. 1967. *Nengone Grammar.* Linguistic Circle of Canberra Publications. Series B., no. 6. Canberra: Australian National University

_____. 1968a. *Dehu Grammar.* Pacific Linguistics. Series B., no. 7. Canberra: Australian National University

_____. 1968b. *Iai Grammar.* Pacific Linguistics. Series B., no. 8. Canberra: Australian National University

_____. 1972. *An Introduction to Maranungku (Northern Australia)*. Pacific Linguistics. Series B., no. 15. Canberra: Australian National University

_____. 1974. *Daly Family Languages, Australia*. Pacific Linguistics. Series C., no. 32. Canberra: Department of Linguistics, Australian National University

Tucker, A.N. and Bryan, M.A. 1966. *Linguistic Analyses. The Non-Bantu Languages of North-Eastern Africa. Handbook of African Languages Part III*. Oxford: Oxford University Press

Turner, P. 1968. Highland Chontal clause syntagmemes. *Linguistics* 38: 77-83

Tyler, S.A. 1969. *Koya: An Outline Grammar*. Berkeley: University of California Press

Ullrich, H.E. 1968. *Clause Structure of Northern Havyaka Kannada (Dravidian): A Tagmemic Analysis*. Unpublished dissertation. Department of Linguistics, University of Michigan

Ultan, R. 1969. Some general characteristics of interrogative systems. *Working Papers on Language Universals* 1: 41-63. Stanford: Language Universals Project, Stanford University

Van Hove, P.F. 1911. Equisse de la langue des Wankutšu. *Anthropos* 6: 385-410

Vanoverbergh, M. 1931. Iloko substantives and adjectives. *Anthropos* 26: 469-488

Varin, A. 1979. VSO and SVO order in Breton. *Archivum Linguisticum* 10: 83-101

Verstaelen, Eugene. 1968-69. Some elementary data of the Manobo language. *Anthropos* 63/64: 808-817

Vogt, Hans. 1940. *The Kalispel language: An Outline of the Grammar with Texts, Translations, and Dictionary*. Oslo: Det Norske Videnskaps-Akademi i Oslo

Voorhoeve, C.L. 1971. Miscellaneous notes on languages in West Irian, New Guinea. *Papers in New Guinea Linguistics, no 14*. 47-115. ed. T. Dutton *et al*. Pacific Linguistics. Series A., no. 28. Canberra: Australian National University

_____. 1975a. Central and Western trans-New Guinea phylum languages. *New Guinea Area Languages and Language Study 1.* Pacific Linguistics. Series C., no. 38:345-459. ed. S.A. Wurm. Canberra: Australian National University

_____. 1975b. West Papuan phylum languages on the mainland of New guinea: Bird's Head (Vogelkopf) Peninsula. *New Guinea Area Languages and Language Study 1.* Pacific Linguistics. Series C., no. 38: 717-728. ed. S.A. Wurm. Canberra: Australian National University

_____. 1975c. East Bird's Head, Geelvink Bay phyla. *New Guinea Area Languages and Language Study, 1.* Pacific Linguistics. Series C., no. 38: 867-868. ed. S.A. Wurm. Canberra: Australian National University

Watson, R. 1966. Clause to sentence gradations in Pacoh. *Lingua* 16: 166-189

Wells, M.A. 1979. *Siroi Grammar.* Pacific Linguistics. Series B., No. 51. Canberra: Australian National University

Welmers, W.E. 1946. *A Descriptive Grammar of Fanti.* dissertation. Baltimore: Waverly Press

_____. 1968. *Efik.* Institute of African Studies Occasional Publication 11. Nigeria: University of Ibadan

Westermann, D. and Bryan, M.A. 1952. *The Languages of West Africa, Part ii. Handbook of African Languages.* Oxford: Oxford University Press

_____. 1970. *The Languages of West Africa.* Folkestone and London: Dawsons of Pall Mall

Whitehead, C. R. 1982. Subject, object, and indirect object: towards a typology of Papuan languages. *Language and Linguistics in Melanesia* 13: 32-63

Whitehead, J. 1964 (1899). *Grammar and Dictionary of the Bobangi Language.* New Jersey: Gregg Press, Inc.

Whitely, W.H. 1966. *A Study of Yao Sentences.* Oxford: Clarendon Press

Williams, A.F. and Longacre, R. 1967. Popoloca clause types. *Acta Linguistica Hafniensa* 10: 161-186

Willis, G. and Ott, R. H. 1967. Ignaciano. *Bolivian Indian Grammar: I*. 85-138. ed. E. Matteson. Norman, Oklahoma: Summer Institute of Linguistics

Wilson, W.A.A. 1963. Relative constructions in Dagban. *Journal of African Languages* 2: 139-144

Wolfenden, E. 1971. *Hilagaynon Reference Grammar*. Honolulu: The University of Hawaii Press

Wurm, S. 1951. The Karakalpak language. *Anthropos* 46: 487-610

——————. 1977. Missionary lingua franche: Kiwai. *New Guinea Area Languages and Language Study, 3. Language, Culture, Society and the Modern World, Fascicle 2.* 893-906. ed. S. A. Wurm. Canberra: Australian National University

Yallop, C. 1977. *Alyawarra: An Aboriginal Language of Central Australia*. Canberra: Australian Institute of Aboriginal Studies

Yillah, M.S. 1975. Temne complementation. *Proceedings of the Conference on African Linguistics. Working Papers in Linguistics* 20: 194-201. Columbus: Ohio State University

Young, R.A. 1971. *The Verb in Bena-Bena: Its Form and Function*. Pacific Linguistics. Series B., no. 18. Canberra: Australian National University

Ziervogel, D. *A Grammar of Swazi*. Johannesburg: Witwatersrand University Press

Appendix B

THE GENETIC FRAME

This appendix presents the genetic frame used to conduct the
statistical study in Chapter 2. The classification levels
used as cells in the genetic frame are highlighted in
boldface. The frame follows closely the genetic
classifications of languages found in Voegelin and Voegelin
(1977), with several small exceptions. First, pidgins and
creoles were treated as a separate group rather than
subclassified under Germanic or Romance. Second, a number of
very small families, for example Yeniseian with four
languages, were collapsed into a single group. Third,
isolates were collapsed into a single group. The effect of
this upon the sampling procedure used in this volume is
discussed in Chapter 2.

In addition to the classification information, this
appendix provides some statistical information about each
group. For each level of classification four sets of figures
are provided. Under the column W can be found two figures.
The top figure, an integer, represents the total number of
languages in the world which fall under a given
classification. Directly beneath this number can be found a
decimal figure representing the fraction of the world's
languages represented by this group. So, for example, the
Hokan family contains 36 languages or .74% of the estimated
total of the world's languages.

Under the column D can also be found two figures. The
top figure represents the total number of such languages
contained in this database. The bottom figure represents the
percentage of such languages in the database. Thus, Hokan is
represented by 17 languages or 1.6% of the database.

Under the column S can be found two figures. The top
figure represents the number of languages with the given
classification found in the final sample of 402. The bottom
figure represents the percentage of such languages in the
final sample. Ideally, this number should be the same as the

291

world percentage. **Hokan** is represented by three languages in the database or .75% of the final sample, which equals its world estimate (.74%).

The final column I contains a single integer, which represents the number of languages in the given classification which a sample of 402 languages should have had. With this one can see where the sample was over- or under-represented. **Hokan** with three languages meets the sample ideal.

APPENDIX B: THE GENETIC FRAME

Caucasian	33	32	5	3
	00.67	03.01	01.24	
Austroasiatic	109	24	12	9
	02.23	02.26	02.99	
Munda-Nicobarese	17	7	3	1
	00.35	00.66	00.75	
Munda	11	6	2	1
	00.22	00.56	00.50	
Nicobarese	6	1	1	0
	00.12	00.09	00.25	
Malacca	10	2	1	1
	00.20	00.19	00.25	
Mon-Khmer	82	15	8	7
	01.68	01.41	01.99	
Macro-Chibchan	60	18	6	6
	00.23	01.69	01.49	
Chibcha Proper	30	14	3	3
	00.61	01.32	00.75	
Paezan	30	4	3	3
	00.61	00.38	00.75	
Hokan	36	17	3	3
	00.74	01.60	00.75	
Salish	23	9	3	2
	00.47	00.87	00.75	
Oto-Manguean	25	10	2	2
	00.51	00.94	00.50	

293

Appendix B: The Genetic Frame

Classification	W	D	S	I
Macro-Algonquian	30	13	2	2
	00.61	01.22	00.50	
Algonquian	17	6	1	1
	00.35	00.56	00.25	
Muskogean+Ungrouped	13	7	1	1
	00.27	00.66	00.25	
Muskogean	6	1	0	0
	00.12	00.09	00.00	
Ungrouped Macro-Algon.	7	6	1	1
	00.14	00.56	00.25	
Macro-Siouan	26	10	3	3
	00.53	00.94	00.75	
Siouan	10	5	1	1
	00.20	00.47	00.25	
Iroquoian	9	2	1	1
	00.18	00.19	00.25	
Caddoan+Ungrouped	7	3	1	1
	00.14	00.28	00.25	
Caddoan	4	2	1	0
	00.08	00.19	00.25	
Ungrouped Macro-Siouan	3	1	0	0
	00.06	00.09	00.00	
Andean-Equatorial	249	32	15	25
	05.09	03.01	03.73	
Andean+Jivaroan	29	7	3	2
	00.59	00.66	00.75	
Andean	24	5		
	00.49	00.47		
Jivaroan	5	2		
	00.10	00.19		
Macro-Tucanoan	37	1	1	3
	00.77	00.09	00.25	
Equatorial	183	24	11	14
	05.32	02.26	02.74	
Tupi	39	8	3	3
	00.80	00.75	00.75	
Ungrouped	25	2	1	2
	00.51	00.19	00.25	
Arawakan	119	14	7	9
	02.43	01.31	01.75	
Maipuran	90	11	7	7
	01.84	01.03	01.74	
Other Arawakan	29	3	0	2
	00.59	00.28	00.00	

Appendix B: The Genetic Frame

Classification	W	D	S	I
Ge-Pano-Carib	272	25	17	23
	05.56	02.35	04.23	
Macro-Carib	98	10	3	8
	02.00	00.94	02.00	
Carib	82	8	7	7
	01.68	00.75	01.74	
Other Macro-Carib	16	2	1	1
	00.33	00.19	00.25	
Macro-Ge-Bororo	94	5	4	8
	01.92	00.47	01.00	
Ge	49	3	2	4
	01.00	00.28	00.50	
Bororo	9	1	1	1
	00.18	00.09	00.25	
Other Macro-Ge	36	1	1	3
	00.74	00.09	00.25	
Macro-Panoan	71	10	5	6
	01.45	00.94	01.24	
Pano-Tacana	52	9	4	4
	01.06	00.85	01.00	
Other Macro-Panoan	19	1	1	2
	00.39	00.09	00.25	
Other Ge-Pano-Carib	9	0	0	1
	00.18	00.00	00.00	
Penutian	78	41	8	8
	01.60	03.86	01.99	
Mayan	25	23	3	2
	00.51	02.16	00.75	
Mixe-Zoque	9	3	1	1
	00.18	00.33	00.25	
Miwok-Costanoan	10	4	1	1
	00.20	00.38	00.25	
Other Penutian	34	11	3	3
	00.70	01.03	00.75	
Aztec-Tanoan	30	14	4	2
	00.61	01.31	01.00	
Na-Dene	32	7	3	3
	00.65	00.66	00.75	
Austronesian	792	132	57	64
	16.20	12.42	14.18	
S Halmahera Austronesian	23	1	1	2
	00.47	00.09	00.25	

Appendix B: The Genetic Frame

Classification	W	D	S	I
Oceanic	391	90	30	31
	08.00	08.47	07.46	
East Oceanic	116	24	8	9
	02.37	02.26	01.99	
Polynesian	27	15	3	2
	00.55	01.41	00.75	
Other E Oceanic	89	9	5	7
	01.82	00.85	01.24	
NW & Central Solomons	26	11	4	2
	00.53	01.03	01.00	
New Caledonia	23	2	1	2
	00.47	00.19	00.25	
Micronesia	9	8	1	1
	00.18	00.75	00.25	
Papua Austronesian	52	9	5	4
	01.06	00.85	01.24	
Bismarck Archipelago	34	4	3	3
	00.70	00.38	00.75	
Admiralty-West. Islands	24	0	0	2
	00.49	00.00	00.00	
NW New Hebrides	26	1	0	2
	00.53	00.09	00.00	
NW New Guinea	64	26	6	5
	01.31	02.45	01.49	
Other Oceanic	17	5	2	1
	00.35	00.47	00.50	
Malayo-Polynesian	378	41	26	30
	07.73	03.86	06.47	
Hesperonesian	218	28	18	18
	04.46	02.63	04.48	
West Indonesian	60	9	6	5
	01.23	00.85	01.49	
Philippine	106	12	10	9
	02.17	01.13	02.49	
Other Hesperonesian	52	7	2	4
	01.06	00.66	00.50	
North Celebes	15	6	3	1
	00.31	00.56	00.75	
Formosan	20	5	3	2
	00.41	00.47	00.75	
East Indonesian	101	1	1	8
	02.07	00.09	00.25	
Moluccan	24	1	1	2
	00.49	00.09	00.25	
Australian	258	55	24	22
	05.28	05.17	05.97	
Pama-Nyungan	176	29	4	4
	03.60	02.73	01.00	

Classification	W	D	S	I
SW Pama-Nyungan	47	4	4	4
	00.96	00.38	01.00	
Pama-Maric	36	7	3	3
	00.74	00.66	00.75	
Other Pama-Nyungan	93	18	8	8
	01.90	01.69	01.99	
Other Australian	82	26	9	7
	01.68	02.45	02.24	
Indo-Pacific	747	131	59	60
	15.28	12.32	14.68	
Central New Guinea	608	114	47	49
	12.43	10.72	11.69	
Southeast New Guinea	103	17	9	8
	02.11	01.60	02.24	
Northern New Guinea	258	19	3	21
	05.28	01.79	03.23	
Central/South New Guinea	124	39	1	10
	02.54	03.67	03.23	
Huon-Finisterre	62	8	5	5
	01.27	00.75	01.24	
E New Guinea Highlands	50	25	5	4
	01.02	02.35	01.24	
W New Guinea Highlands	11	6	2	1
	00.22	00.56	00.50	
Other Indo-Pacific	139	17	12	11
	02.85	01.60	02.99	
Khoisan	48	12	3	4
	00.98	01.13	00.75	
Nilo-Saharan	122	60	16	10
	02.49	05.64	03.98	
Eastern Sudanic	67	31	8	5
	01.37	02.92	01.99	
Central Sudanic	34	16	4	3
	00.70	01.51	01.00	
Other Nilo-Saharan	21	13	4	2
	00.43	01.22	01.00	
Niger-Kordofanian	1046	134	82	86
	21.39	12.61	20.40	
Kordofanian	29	11	2	2
	00.59	01.03	00.50	
Niger-Congo	1017	123	80	84
	20.80	11.57	19.90	

Appendix B: The Genetic Frame

Classification	W	D	S	I
Kwa	84	24	9	7
	01.72	02.26	02.23	
Adamawa-Eastern	87	16	10	7
	01.78	01.74	02.49	
West Atlantic	47	7	5	4
	00.96	00.66	01.24	
Gur	76	12	8	6
	01.55	01.13	01.99	
Mande	23	7	3	2
	00.47	00.66	00.75	
Benue-Congo	700	51	45	55
	14.31	04.78	11.19	
Plateau	84	6	4	7
	01.72	00.56	81.00	
Cross-River	47	1	1	4
	00.96	00.09	00.25	
Jukunoid	10	0	0	1
	00.20	00.00	00.00	
Bantoid	559	44	40	46
	11.43	04.13	09.95	
Bantu	559	35	33	36
	08.98	03.29	08.21	
Other Bantu	120	9	7	10
	02.45	00.85	01.74	
Afroasiatic	209	44	19	17
	04.27	04.14	04.73	
Berber	24	3	2	2
	00.49	00.28	00.50	
Cushitic	29	17	3	2
	00.59	01.60	00.75	
Omotic	23	3	2	2
	00.47	00.28	00.50	
Semitic	24	12	3	2
	00.49	01.13	00.75	
Chadic+Egyptian Coptic	109	9	9	9
	02.22	00.85	02.24	
Uralic	28	16	2	2
	00.57	01.51	00.50	
Altaic	61	38	4	5
	01.25	03.57	01.00	
Tungus	17	7	1	1
	00.35	00.66	00.25	
Turkic	30	21	2	2
	00.61	01.98	00.50	

Classification	W	D	S	I
Mongolian+Japanese+Korean	14	10	1	1
	00.29	00.94	00.25	
Japanese	4	2	0	0
	00.08	00.19	00.00	
Mongol	9	7	1	1
	00.18	00.66	00.25	
Korean	1	1	0	0
	00.02	00.09	00.00	
Indo-European	154	60	13	13
	03.15	05.64	03.23	
Indo-Iranian	71	25	6	6
	01.45	02.35	01.49	
Indic	37	14	3	3
	00.76	01.32	00.75	
Iranian+Nuristani	34	9	2	2
	00.70	00.85	00.50	
Italic	34	9	2	2
	00.70	00.85	00.50	
Romance	13	8	1	1
	00.27	00.75	00.25	
Ungrouped Italic	21	1	1	1
	00.43	00.09	00.25	
Celtic	8	4	1	1
	00.16	00.38	00.25	
Slavic+Baltic	21	10	2	2
	00.43	00.98	00.50	
Germanic	7	6	1	1
	00.14	00.56	00.25	
Other Indo-European	13	6	1	1
	00.27	00.56	00.25	
Sino-Tibetan	289	87	27	23
	05.91	08.18	06.22	
Tibeto-Burman	217	67	21	18
	04.44	06.30	05.22	
Bodo-Naga-Kachin	21	11	2	2
	00.43	00.10	00.50	
Burmese-Lolo	51	6	4	4
	01.04	00.56	01.00	
Gyarung-Mishmi	47	19	4	4
	00.96	01.79	01.00	
Naga-Kuki-Chin	88	24	9	7
	01.80	02.26	02.24	
Other Tibeto-Burman	10	7	2	1
	00.20	00.06	00.50	
Chinese+Dzorgaish	14	6	2	1
	00.27	00.56	00.50	

Appendix B: The Genetic Frame

Classification	W	D	S	I
Kam-Tai	54 01.10	14 01.32	4 01.00	4
Pidgins and Creoles	33 00.67	5 00.47	3 00.75	3
Dravidian	22 00.45	16 01.51	2 00.50	2
Isolates	47 00.96	9 00.85	4 01.00	4
Small Families	31 00.63	17 01.60	3 00.75	3

Appendix C

THE AREAL FRAME

Each line represents a separate cell in the areal frame.

NWNA	Northwest North America	EUR	Europe
NNA	Northern North America	NNE	North & Northeastern Asia
CAL	California	MC	Mid Central Asia
WNA	Western North America	I	Southern Asia
ENA	Eastern North America	E	Eastern Asia
MA	Mesoamerica	SE	Southeastern Asia
CC	Circumcaribbean	NG	New Guinea
AND	Andean South America	A	Australia
T	Tropical South America	MEL	Melanesia
SS	Southern South America	MIC	Micronesia
NA	Northern Africa	POL	Polynesia
WA	Western Africa	EA	Eastern Africa
CA	Central Africa	SA	Southern Africa

Kru 83-4
Krupa 8-9
Kuno 133
Kusaiean 68, 70

Lahu 87
Lake Miwok 97
Lang 93-5
Langacker 134
Lango 97
language divergence 6
language isolates 6
Lasnik 55
Lawrence 95
Lee 68, 70, 96
left-dislocation 55, 58-9,
    60, 64-5
Lehmann 81-3
Li 3, 13, 59, 62, 80,
    112-4
liaison 98-9
Liebelt 133
Lithuanian 61
Loftus 133
Lord 84
Lunda 87
Luvale 59, 92
Lyons 107

Mackworth 133
Macro-Ge 29
macroproposition 40
MacWhinney 3
Malagasy 2, 81, 83, 131, 136
Malay 91
Mallinson 2, 7-8, 20, 137
Mamvu 33
Mandarin 86-87
Manguean 28
Maninka 99
Marascuilo 26
Marathi 87
Mardirussian 79-80
Masai 67
Mathesius 1
Mayan 112
Mazatec 131
McCawley 90
McSweeney 26
Melanesia 19
Melpa 94

memory 4, 8, 39, 133
mental models 4
Merlan 78, 81
Mid Central Asia 29
Mixtecan 28
modal placement 87
Moerman 64
Mohawk 81
Mojave 81, 87
Mokilese 50, 71, 79
Morgan 55
Morolong 114
Mould 59
movement rules 4, 9, 53-4,
    61-3, 88-9, 131
Munro 81
Murdock 20, 28-9
mutual intelligibility 35

Nahuatl 80
Nass-Gitksan 81
Natural Topic Hierarchy 5,
    109
Navajo 87, 109, 115-6
Nebak 93
Netherlandic-German 35
Netsilik 35
New Guinea 19
Newman 99
Ngarinjn 70
Nguna 87
Nguyen 90-1
Niger-Congo 20
Niger-Kordofanian 20
Nilo-Saharan 20, 33
non-terms 9, 11, 117-8
North American 20
North and Northeastern Asia
    29
Norwegian 66

Oates 76
object 2, 4-6, 9-11, 13-4,
    16-7, 21, 32, 35, 56-9,
    75-7, 69-70, 73-4, 76-93,
    97-8, 100-1, 113-8, 121,
    123, 126-7, 132, 135, 139
object motion 134
Ochs 134
Oiampi 131
Ojibwa 42, 71, 81, 130-1